The Doctrines of Election

and Justification

The Doctrines of Election
and Justification

A.W. Pink

BAKER BOOK HOUSE
Grand Rapids, Michigan

Contents

PART ONE
THE DOCTRINE OF ELECTION

PART TWO
THE DOCTRINE OF JUSTIFICATION

PART ONE

The Doctrine of Election

1 Introduction

Election is a *foundational* doctrine. In the past, many of the ablest teachers were accustomed to commence their systematic theology with a presentation of the attributes of God, and then a contemplation of His eternal decrees; and it is our studied conviction, after perusing the writings of many of our moderns, that the method followed by their predecessors cannot be improved upon. God existed before man, and His eternal purpose long antedated His works in time. "Known unto God are all his works from the beginning of the world" (Acts 15:18). The divine councils went before creation. As a builder draws his plans before he begins to build, so the great Architect predestinated everything before a single creature was called into existence. Nor has God kept this a secret locked in His own bosom; it has pleased Him to make known in His Word the everlasting counsels of His grace, His design in the same, and the grand end He has in view.

When a building is in course of construction onlookers are often at a loss to perceive the reason for many of the details. As yet, they discern no order or design; everything appears to be in confusion. But if they could carefully scan the builder's "plan" and visualize the finished production, much that had puzzled would become clear to them. It is the same with the outworking of God's eternal purpose. Unless we are acquainted with His eternal decrees, history remains an insoluable enigma. God is not working at random: the gospel has been sent forth on no uncertain mission: the final outcome in the conflict between good and evil has not been left indeterminate; how many are to be saved or lost depends not on the will of the creature. Everything was infallibly determined and immutably fixed by God from the beginning, and all that happens in time is but the accomplishment of what was ordained in eternity.

The grand truth of election, then, takes us back to the beginning of all things. It antedated the entrance of sin into the universe, the fall of man, the advent of Christ, and the proclamation of the gospel. A right understanding of it, especially in its relation to the everlasting covenant, is absolutely essential if we are to be preserved from fundamental error. If the foundation itself be faulty, then the building erected on it cannot be sound; and if we err in our conceptions of this basic truth, then just in proportion as we do so will our grasp of all other truth be inaccurate. God's dealings with Jew and Gentile, His object in sending His Son into this world, His design by the gospel, yea, the whole of His providential dealings, cannot be seen in their proper perspective till they are viewed in the light of His eternal election. This will become the more evident as we proceed.

It is a *difficult* doctrine, and this in three respects. First, in the *understanding* of it. Unless we are privileged to sit under the ministry of some Spirit-taught servant of God, who presents the truth to us systematically, great pains and diligence are called for in the searching of the Scriptures, so that we may collect and tabulate their scattered statements on this subject. It has not pleased the Holy Spirit to give us one complete and orderly setting forth of the doctrine of election, but instead "here a little, there a little"—in typical history, in psalm and prophecy, in the great prayer of Christ (John 17), in the epistles of the apostles. Second, in the *acceptation* of it. This presents a much greater difficulty, for when the mind perceives what the Scriptures reveal thereon, the heart is loath to receive such an humbling and flesh-withering truth. How earnestly we need to pray for God to subdue our enmity against Him and our prejudice against His truth. Third, in the *proclamation* of it. No novice is competent to present this subject in its scriptural perspective and proportions.

But notwithstanding, these difficulties should not discourage, still less deter us, from an honest and serious effort to understand and heartily receive all that God has been pleased to reveal thereon. Difficulties are designed to humble us, to exercise us, to make us feel our need of wisdom from on high. It is not easy to arrive at a clear and adequate grasp of any of the great doctrines of Holy Writ, and God never intended it should be so. Truth has to be "bought" (Prov. 23:23): alas that so few are willing to pay the price—devote to the prayerful study of the Word the time wasted on newspapers or idle recreations. These difficulties are not insurmountable, for the Spirit has been given to God's people to guide them into all truth. Equally so for the minister of the Word: an humble waiting upon God, coupled with a diligent effort to be a workman that needeth not to be ashamed, will in due time fit him to expound this truth to the glory of God and the blessing of his hearers.

It is an *important* doctrine, as is evident from various considerations. Perhaps we can express most impressively the momentousness of this truth by pointing out that apart from eternal election there had never been any Jesus Christ, and therefore, no divine gospel; for if God had never chosen a people unto salvation, He had never sent His Son; and if He had sent no Saviour, none had ever been saved. Thus, the gospel itself originated in this vital matter of election. "But we are bound to give thanks always to God for you, brethren beloved of the Lord, because God hath from the beginning chosen you to salvation" (II Thess. 2:13). And *why* are we "bound to give thanks"? Because election is the root of all blessings, the spring of every mercy that the soul receives. If election be taken away, everything is taken away, for those who have *any* spiritual blessing are they who have *all* spiritual blessings *"according as* he hath chosen us in him before the foundation of the world" (Eph. 1:3, 4).

It was well said by Calvin, "We shall never be clearly convinced, as we ought to be, that our salvation flows from the fountain of God's free mercy, till we are acquainted with His eternal election, which illustrates the grace of God by this comparison; that He adopts not all promiscuously to the hope of salvation, but He gives to some what He refuses to others. Ignorance of this principle evidently detracts from the divine glory, and diminishes real humility—If, then, we need to be recalled to the origin of election, to prove that we obtain salvation from no other source than the mere good pleasure of God, then they who desire to extinguish this principle, do all they can to obscure what ought to be magnificently and loudly celebrated."

It is a *blessed* doctrine, for election is the spring of all blessings. This is made unmistakably clear by Ephesians 1:3, 4. First, the Holy Spirit declares that the saints have been blessed with all spiritual blessings in the heavenlies in Christ. Then He proceeds to show *why* and *how* they were so blessed: it is *according as* God hath chosen us in Christ before the foundation of the world. Election in Christ, therefore, precedes being blessed with all spiritual blessings, for we are blessed with them only as being in Him, and we are only in Him as *chosen* in Him. We see, then, what a grand and glorious truth this is, for all our hopes and prospects belong to it. Election, though distinct and personal, is not, as is sometimes carelessly stated, a mere abstract choice of persons unto eternal salvation, irrespective of union with their Covenant-Head, but a choice of them *in Christ.* It therefore implies every other blessing, and all other blessings are given only through it and in accordance with it.

Rightly understood there is nothing so calculated to impart comfort and courage, strength and security, as a heart-apprehension of this truth. To be assured that I am one of the high favorites of Heaven imparts the confidence that God most certainly will supply my every need and make all things work together for my good. The knowledge that God has predestinated me unto eternal glory supplies an absolute guarantee that no efforts of Satan can possibly bring about my destruction, for if the great God be *for* me, who can be against me! It brings great peace to the preacher, for he now discovers that God has not sent him forth to draw a bow at a venture, but that His Word *shall* accomplish that which He pleases, and shall prosper whereto He sends it (Isa. 55:11). And what encouragement it should afford the awakened sinner. As he learns that election is solely a matter of divine *grace*, hope is kindled in his heart: as he discovers, that election singled out some of the vilest of the vile to be the monuments of divine mercy, why should *he* despair!

It is a *distasteful* doctrine. One had naturally thought that a truth so God-honoring, Christ-exalting, and so blessed, had been cordially espoused by all professing Christians who had had it clearly presented to them. In view of the fact that the terms "predestinated," "elect," and "chosen," occur so frequently in the Word, one would surely conclude that all who claim to accept the Scriptures as divinely inspired would receive with implicit faith this grand truth, referring the act itself—as becometh sinful and ignorant creatures so to do— unto the sovereign good pleasure of God. But such is far, very far from being the actual case. No doctrine is so detested by proud human nature as this one, which make nothing of the creature and everything of the Creator; yea, at no other point is the enmity of the carnal mind so blatantly and hotly evident.

We commenced our addresses in Australia by saying, "I am going to speak to-night on one of the most hated doctrines of the Bible, namely, that of God's sovereign election." Since then we have encircled this globe, and come into more or less close contact with thousands of people belonging to many denominations, and thousands more of professing Christians attached to none, and to-day the only change we would make in that statement is, that while the truth of eternal punishment is the one most objectionable to nonprofessors, that of God's sovereign election is the truth most loathed and reviled by the majority of those claiming to be believers. Let it be plainly announced that salvation originated not in the will of man, but in the will of God (see John 1:13; Rom. 9:16), that were it not so none would or could be saved—for as the result of the fall man has lost all desire and will unto that which is good (John 5:40; Rom. 3:11)—and that even the elect themselves have to be *made* willing (Ps. 110:3), and loud will be the cries of indignation raised against such teaching.

It is at *this* point the issue is drawn. Merit-mongers will not allow the supremacy of the divine will and the impotency-unto-good of the human will, consequently they who are the most bitter in denouncing election by the sovereign pleasure of God, are the warmest in crying up the free-will of fallen man. In the decrees of the council of Trent—wherein the Papacy definitely defined her position on the leading points raised by the Reformers, and which Rome has never rescinded—occurs the following: "If any one should affirm that since the fall of Adam man's free will is lost, let him be accursed." It was for their faithful adherence to the truth of *election,* with all that it involves, that Bradford and hundreds of others were burned at the stake by the agents of the pope. Unspeakably sad is it to see so many professing Protestants agree with the mother of harlots in this fundamental error.

But whatever aversion men may now have to this blessed truth, they will be compelled to hear it in the last day, hear it as the voice of final, unalterable, and eternal decision. When death and hades, the sea and dry land, shall give up the dead, then shall the Book of Life—the register in which was recorded from before the foundation of the world the whole election of grace—be opened in the presence of angels and demons, in the presence of the saved and of the lost, and that voice shall sound to the highest arches of Heaven, to the lowest depths of hell, to the uttermost bound of the universe: "And whosoever was not found written in the Book of Life was cast into the lake of fire" (Rev. 20:15). Thus, this truth which is hated by the non-elect above all others, is the one that shall ring in the ears of the lost as they enter their eternal doom! Ah, my reader, the reason why people do not receive and duly prize the truth of election, is because they do not feel their due need of it.

It is a *separating* doctrine. The preaching of the sovereignty of God, as exercised by Him in foreordaining the eternal destiny of each of His creatures, serves as an effectual flail to divide the chaff from the wheat. "He that is of God heareth God's words" (John 8:47): yes, no matter how contrary they may be to *his* ideas. It is one of the marks of the regenerate that they set to their seal that God is true. Nor do they pick and choose, as will religious hypocrites: once they perceive a truth is clearly taught in the Word, even though it be utterly opposed to their own reason and inclinations, they humbly bow to it and implicitly receive it, and would do so though not another person in whole world believed it. But it is far otherwise with the unregenerate. As the apostle declares, "They are of the world: therefore speak they of the world, and the world heareth them. We are of God: he that knoweth God heareth us; he that is not of God heareth not us. Hereby know we the spirit of truth, and the spirit of error" (I John 4:5, 6).

We know of nothing so devisive between the sheep and the goats as a faithful exposition of this doctrine. If a servant of God accepts some new charge, and he wishes to ascertain which of his people desire the pure milk of the Word, and which prefer the Devil's substitutes, let him deliver a series of sermons on this subject, and it will quickly be the means of "taking forth the precious from the vile" (Jer. 15:19). It was thus in the experience of the Divine Preacher: when Christ announced "no man can come unto me, except it were given unto him of my Father," we are told, "from that time many of his disciples went back, and walked no more with him" (John 6:65, 66)! True it is that by no means all who intellectually receive "Calvinism" as a philosophy or theology, give evidence (in their daily lives) of regeneration; yet equally true is it that those who continue to cavil against and steadfastly refuse any part of the truth, are not entitled to be regarded as Christians.

It is a *neglected* doctrine. Though occupying so prominent a place in the Word of God, it is to-day but little preached, and still less understood. Of course, it is not to be expected that the "higher critics" and their blinded dupes should preach that which makes nothing of man; but even among those who wish to be looked up to as "orthodox" and "evangelical," there are scarcely any who give this grand truth a real place in either their pulpit ministrations or their writings. In some cases this is due to ignorance: not having been taught it in the seminary, and certainly not in the "Bible Institutes," they have never perceived its great importance and value. But in too many cases it is a desire to be popular with their hearers which muzzles their mouths. Nevertheless, neither ignorance, prejudice, nor enmity can do away with the doctrine itself, or lessen its vital momentousness.

In bringing to a close these introductory remarks, let it be pointed out that this blessed doctrine needs to be handled *reverently*. It is not a subject to be reasoned about and speculated upon, but approached in a spirit of holy awe and devotion. It is to be handled *soberly,* "When thou art in disputation, engaged upon a just quarrel to vindicate the truth of God from heresy and distortion, look into *thy* heart, set a watch on thy lips, beware of wild fire in thy zeal" (E. Reynolds, 1648). Nevertheless, this truth is to be dealt with *uncompromisingly,* and plainly, irrespective of the fear or favor of man, confidently leaving all "results" in the hand of God. May it be graciously granted *us* to write in a manner pleasing to God, and *you* to receive whatever is from Himself.

2 Its Source

Accurately speaking, election is a branch of predestination, the latter being a more comprehensive term than the former. Predestination relates to *all* creatures, things, and events; but election is restricted to rational beings—angels and humans. As the word *predestinate* signifies, God from all eternity sovereignly ordained and immutably determined the history and destiny of each and all of His creatures. But in this study we shall confine ourselves to predestination as it relates to or concerns rational creatures. And here too a further distinction must be noticed. There cannot be an election without a rejection, a taking without a passing by, a choice without a refusal. As Psalm 78 expresses it, "He *refused* the tabernacle of Joseph, and chose not the tribe of Ephraim; but *chose* the tribe of Judah" (vv. 67, 68). Thus predestination includes both reprobation (the preterition or passing by of the non-elect, and then the foreordaining of them to condemnation—Jude 4—because of their sins) and election unto eternal life, the former of which we shall not now discuss.

The doctrine of election means, then, that God singled out certain ones in His mind both from among angels (I Tim. 5:21) and from among men, and ordained them unto eternal life and blessedness; that before He created them, He decided their destiny, just as a builder draws his plans and determines every part of the building before any of the materials are assembled for the carrying out of his design. Election may thus be defined: it is that part of the counsel of God whereby He did from all eternity purpose in Himself to display His grace upon certain of His creatures. This was made effectual by a definite decree concerning them. Now in every decree of God three things must be considered: the beginning, the matter or substance, the end or design. Let us offer a few remarks upon each.

The *beginning* of the decree is the *will of God*. It originates solely in His own sovereign determination. Whilst determining the estate of His creatures God's own will is the alone and absolute cause thereof. As there is nothing above God to rule Him, so there is nothing outside of Himself which can be in any wise an impulsive cause unto Him; to say otherwise is to make the will of God no will at all. Herein He is infinitely exalted above us, for not only are we subject to One above us, but *our* wills are being constantly moved and disposed by external causes. The will of God could have no cause outside of itself, or otherwise there would be something prior to itself (for a cause ever precedes the effect) and something more excellent (for the cause is ever superior to the effect), and thus God would not be the independent Being which He is.

The *matter* or substance of a divine decree is God's purpose *to manifest* one or more of His attributes or perfections. This is true of all the divine decrees, but as there is variety in God's attributes so there is in the things He decrees to bring into existence. The two principal attributes He exercises upon His rational creatures are His grace and His justice. In the case of the elect God determined to exemplify the riches of His amazing grace, but in the case of the non-elect He saw fit to demonstrate His justice and severity—withholding His grace from them because it was His good pleasure so to do. Yet it must not be allowed for a moment that this latter was a point of cruelty in God, for His nature is not grace alone, nor justice alone, but both together; and therefore in determining to display *both* of them there could not be a point of injustice.

The *end* or design of every divine decree is God's own *glory*, for nothing less than this could be worthy of Himself. As God swears by Himself because He can swear by none greater, so because a greater and grander end cannot be proposed than His own glory, God has set up that as the supreme end of all His decrees and works. "The Lord hath made all things *for himself*" (Prov. 16:4)—for His own glory. As all things are from Him as the first cause, so all things are *to* Him (Rom. 11:36) as the final end. The good of His creatures is but the secondary end; His own glory is the supreme end, and everything else is subordinate thereto. In the case of the elect it is God's amazing grace which will be magnified; in the case of the reprobate His pure justice will be glorified. What follows in this chapter will largely be an amplification of these three points.

The source of election, then, is *the will of God*. It should be scarcely necessary to point out that by "God" we mean, Father, Son, and Holy Spirit. Though there are three persons in the Godhead, there is but one undivided nature common to Them all, and so but one will.

They are one, and They agree in one: "He is in *one* mind, and who can turn him?" (Job 23:13). Let it also be pointed out that the will of God is not a thing apart from God, nor is it to be considered only as a part of God: the will of God is God Himself willing: it is, if we may so speak, His very nature in activity, for His will is His very essence. Nor is God's will subject to any fluctuation or change: when we affirm that God's will is immutable, we are only saying that God Himself is, "without variableness or shadow or turning" (James 1:17). Therefore the will of God is *eternal*, for since God Himself had no beginning, and since His will is His very nature, then His will must be from everlasting.

To proceed one step further. The will of God is absolutely *free*, uninfluenced and uncontrolled by anything outside of itself. This appears from the making of the world—as well as of everything in it. The world is not eternal, but was *made* by God, yet whether it should be or should not be created, was determined by Himself alone. The time when it was made—whether sooner or later; the size of it—whether smaller or larger; the duration of it—whether for a season or forever; the condition of it—whether it should remain "very good" or be defiled by sin; was all settled by the sovereign decree of the Most High. Had He so pleased, God could have brought this world into existence millions of ages earlier than He did. Had He so pleased, He could have made it and all things in it in a moment of time, instead of in six days and nights. Had He so pleased, He could have limited the human family to a few thousands or hundreds, or have made it a thousand times larger than it is. No other reason can be assigned why God created it when and as it is than His own imperial will.

God's will was absolutely *free* in connection with *election*. In choosing a people unto eternal life and glory, there was nothing outside Himself which moved God to form such a purpose. As He expressly declares, "I will have mercy on whom *I will* have mercy, and I will have compassion on whom *I will* have compassion" (Rom. 9:15)—language could not state more definitely the absoluteness of divine sovereignty in this matter. "Having predestinated us unto the adoption of children by Jesus Christ to himself, according to the good pleasure of his will' (Eph. 1:5): here again all is resolved into the mere pleasure of God. He bestows His favors or withholds them as pleaseth Himself. Nor does He stand in any need of *our* vindicating His procedure. The Almighty is not to be brought down to the bar of human reason: instead of seeking to *justify* God's high sovereignty, we are only required to *believe it,* on the authority of His own Word. "I thank thee, O Father, Lord of heaven and earth, because thou hast hid these things from the wise and prudent, and hast revealed them unto babes: even so, Father; for *so* it seemed good in thy sight" (Matt. 11:25, 26)—the Lord Jesus was content to rest there, and so must we be.

Some of the ablest expositors of this profound truth have affirmed that the *love* of God is the moving cause of our election, citing "In love having predestinated us" (Eph. 1:5); yet *in* so doing, we think they are chargeable with a slight inaccuracy or departure from the rule of faith. While fully agreeing that the last two words of Ephesians 1:4 (as they stand in the A.V.) belong properly to the beginning of verse 5, yet it should be carefully noted that verse 5 is *not* speaking of our original election, but of our being predestinated *unto* the adoption of children: the two things are quite distinct, separate acts on the part of God, the second following upon the first. There is *an order* in the divine counsels, as there is in God's works of creation, and it is as important to heed what is said of the former as it is to attend unto the divine procedure in the six days' work of Genesis 1.

An object must exist or subsist *before* it can be loved. Election was the first act in the mind of God, whereby He chose the persons of the elect to be holy and without blame (v. 4). Predestination was God's second act, whereby He ratified by decree the *state* of those to whom His election had given a real subsistence before Him. Having chosen them in His dear Son unto a perfection of holiness and righteousness, God's love went forth to them, and bestowed upon them the chiefest and highest blessing His love could confer: to make them His children by adoption. God is love, and all His love is exercised upon Christ and those in Him. Having made the elect His own by the sovereign choice of His will, God's heart was set upon them as His special treasure.

Others have attributed our election to the *grace* of God, quoting "There is a remnant according to the election of grace" (Rom. 11:5). But here again we must distinguish between things that differ, namely, between the *beginning* of a divine decree and its *matter* or substance. It is true, blessedly true, that the elect are the objects upon which the grace of God is specially exercised, but that is quite another thing from saying that their election   *originated* in God's grace. The order we are here insisting upon is clearly expressed in Ephesians 1. First, "He [God] hath chosen us in him [Christ] before the foundation of the world: that we should be holy and without blame [righteous] before him" (v. 4): that was the *initial* act in the divine mind. Second, "in love having predestinated us unto the adoption of children by Jesus Christ to himself," and that "according to the good pleasure of his will" (v. 5): that was God *enriching* those upon whom He had set His heart. Third, "to the praise of the glory of his grace, wherein he hath made us accepted in the beloved" (v. 6): that was both the

subject and *design* of God's decree—the manifestation and magnifica-
tion of His grace.

"The election of grace" (Rom. 11:5), then, is *not* to be understood
as the genitive of *origin,* but of object or character, as in "the Rose *of*
Sharon," "the tree *of* life," "the children *of* disobedience." The
election of the church, as of all His acts and works, is to be traced
right back to the uncontrolled and uncontrollable will of God. Nowhere else in Scripture is the *order* of the divine counsels so definitely
revealed as in Ephesians 1, and nowhere else is emphasis placed so
strongly upon God's will. He predestinated unto the adoption of
children "according to the good pleasure of his *will*" (v. 5). He has
made known to us "the mystery of his *will*" (not "grace") and that
"according to his good pleasure which he hath *purposed* in himself"
(v. 9). And then, as though that was not sufficiently explicit, the
passage closes with "being predestinated according to the purpose of
him who worketh *all* things after the counsel of his own *will,* that we
should be to the praise of his glory" (vv. 11, 12).

Let us dwell for a moment longer upon that remarkable expression
"who worketh all things after *the counsel of* his own will" (v. 11). Note
well it is not "the counsel of his own *heart,*" nor even "the counsel of
his own *mind,*" but WILL: not "the will of his own counsel," but "the
counsel of his own will." Herein God differs radically from us. Our
wills are influenced by the thoughts of our minds and moved by the
affections of our hearts; but not so God's. "He doeth according to his
will in the army of heaven, and among the inhabitants of the earth"
(Dan. 4:35). God's will is supreme, determining the *exercise of* all His
perfections. He is infinite in wisdom, yet His will regulates the operations of it. He is full of mercy, but His will determines when and to
whom He shows it. He is inflexibly just, yet His will decides whether
or not justice shall be put forth: observe carefully *not* "Who *can* by no
means clear the guilty" (as is so generally misquoted), but "Who *will*
by no means clear the guilty" (Exod. 34:7). God first wills or
determines that a thing *shall* be, and then His wisdom contrives the
execution of it.

Let us now point out what has been *disproved.* From all that has
been said above it is clear, first, that our *good works* are not the thing
which induced God to elect us, for that act passed in the divine mind
in eternity—long before we had any actual existence. See how this
very point is set aside in, "For the children being not yet born, neither
having done any good or evil, that the purpose of God according to
election might stand, not for works, but of him that calleth" (Rom.
9:11). Again we read, "For we are his workmanship, created in Christ
Jesus *unto* good works, which God hath before ordained that we should
walk in them" (Eph. 2:10). Since, then, we were elected prior to our

creation, then good works could not be the moving cause of it: no, they are the fruits and effects of it.

Second, the *holiness* of men, whether in principle or in practice, or both, is not the moving cause of election, for as Ephesians 1:4 so plainly declares "He hath chosen us in him before the foundation of the world, that we should be holy and without blame before him"—not because we *were* holy, but so that we *might* be. That we "*should be holy*" was something future, which follows upon it, and is the means to a further end, namely, our salvation, to which men are chosen. "God hath from the beginning chosen you to salvation, through sanctification of the Spirit" (II Thess. 2:13). Since, then, the sanctification of God's people was the design of His election, it could not be the cause of it. "This is the will of God, even your sanctification" (I Thess. 4:3): not merely the approving will of God, as being agreeable to His nature; nor merely His preceptive will, as required by the Law; but His *decretive* will, His determinate counsel.

Third, nor is *faith* the cause of our election. How could it be? Throughout their unregeneracy all men are in a state of unbelief, living in this world without God and without hope. And when we had faith, it was not of ourselves—either of our goodness, power, or will. No, it was a gift from God (Eph. 2:9), and the operation of the Spirit (Col. 2:12), flowing from His grace. "As many as were ordained to eternal life believed" (Acts 13:48), and *not* "as many as believed, were ordained to eternal life." Since, then, faith flows from divine grace, it cannot be the cause of our election. The reason why other men do not believe, is because they are not of Christ's sheep (John 10:26); the reason why *any* believe is because God gives them faith, and therefore it is called "the faith of God's elect" (Titus 1:1).

Fourth, it is not God's *foreview* of these things in men which moved Him to choose them. God's foreknowledge of the future is founded upon the determination of His *will* concerning it. The divine decree, the divine foreknowledge, and the divine predestination is the *order* set forth in the Scriptures. First, "Who are the called according to his purpose"; second, "for whom he did foreknow"; third, "he also did predestinate" (Rom. 8:28, 29). The decree of God as *preceding* His foreknowledge is also stated in, "Him, being delivered by the determinate counsel and foreknowledge of God" (Acts 2:23). God foreknows everything that *will* be, because He has ordained everything that *shall* be; then it is to put the cart before the horse when we make foreknowledge the cause of God's election.

In conclusion let it be said that the *end* of God in His decree of election is the manifestation of His own glory, but before entering into detail upon this point we will quote several passages which state the broad fact itself. "But know that the Lord hath set apart him that is godly *for himself*" (Ps. 4:3). "Set apart" here signifies chosen or severed from the rest; "him that is godly" refers to David himself (Ps. 89:19, 20); "for himself," and not merely for the throne and kingdom of Israel. "For the Lord hath chosen Jacob *unto himself*, and Israel for his peculiar treasure" (Ps. 135:4). "To give drink to my people, my chosen. This people have I formed *for myself;* they shall show forth my praise" (Isa. 43:20, 21), which is parallel with Ephesians 1:5, 6. So in the New Testament: when Christ was pleased to give to Ananias an account of the conversion of His beloved Paul, He said, "he is a chosen vessel *unto me*" (Acts 9:15). Again, "I have reserved *to myself* seven thousand men, who have not bowed the knee to Baal" (Rom. 11:4 ASV), which is explained in the next verse as "a remnant according to the election of grace."

3 Its Grand Original

The decrees of God, His eternal purpose, the inscrutable counsels of His will, are indeed a great deep; yet this we know, that from first to last they have *a definite relation to Christ,* for He is the Alpha and the Omega in all covenant transactions. Beautifully did Spurgeon express it: "Search for the celestial fountain, from which the divine streams of grace flow to us, and you will find Jesus Christ the well-spring in covenant love. If your eyes shall ever see the covenant roll, if you shall ever be permitted in a future state to see the whole plan of redemption as it was mapped out in the chambers of eternity, you shall see the blood-red line of atoning sacrifice running across the margin of every page, and you shall see that from the beginning to the end one object was always in view--the glory of the Son of God." It therefore seems strange that many who see that election is the foundation of salvation, yet overlook the glorious *Head of election,* in whom the elect were chosen and from whom they receive all blessings.

"Blessed be the God and Father of our Lord Jesus Christ, who hath blessed us with all spiritual blessings in the heavenlies in Christ: according as he hath chosen us in him before the foundation of the world" (Eph. 1:3, 4). Since we were chosen *in* Christ, it is evident that we were chosen *out of* ourselves; and since we were chosen in *Christ,* it necessarily follows that He was chosen before we were. This is clearly implied in the preceding verse, wherein the Father is expressly designated "the God and Father of our Lord Jesus Christ." Now according to the analogy of Scripture (i.e., when He is said to be "the God" of any one) God was "the God" of Christ first, because He chose Him to that grace and union. Christ as man was predestinated as truly as we were, and so has God to be His *God* by predestination and free grace. Second, because the Father made a covenant with Him (Isa. 42:6). In view of the covenant made with them, He became known as "the God of Abraham, of Isaac and of Jacob;" so in view of the covenant He made with Christ, He became His "God." Third, because God is the author of all Christ's blessedness (Ps. 45:2, 7).

"According as He [God] hath chosen us in him" means, then, that in election Christ was made *the Head* of the elect. "In the womb of election He, the Head, came out first [adumbrated in every normal birth, A.W.P.], and then we, the members" (Thos. Goodwin). In all things Christ must have the "pre-eminence," and therefore is He "the Firstborn" in election (Rom. 8:29). In the order of *nature* Christ was chosen first, but in the order of *time* we were elected with Him. We were not chosen for ourselves apart, but *in Christ,* which denotes three things. First, we were chosen in Christ as the members of His body. Second, we were chosen in Him as the pattern which we should be conformed unto. Third, we were chosen in Him as the final end, i.e., it was for Christ's glory, to be His "fulness" (Eph. 1:23).

"Behold my servant, whom I uphold: *mine elect,* in whom my soul delighteth" (Isa. 42:1): that this passage refers to none other than the Lord Jesus Christ is unmistakably plain from the Spirit's citation of it in Matthew 12:15-21. Here, then, is the grand original of election: in its first and highest instance election is spoken of and applied to the Lord Jesus! It was the will of the eternal three to elect and predestinate the second person into creature being and existence, so that as God-man, "the firstborn of every creature" (Col. 1:15), He was the subject of the divine decrees and the immediate and principal object of the love of the co-essential three. And as the Father hath life in Himself, so hath He given to the Son—considered as God-man—to have life in Himself (John 5:26), to be a fountain of life, of grace and glory, unto His beloved Spouse, who received her being and wellbeing from Jehovah's free grace and everlasting love.

When God determined *to create,* among all the myriad creatures, both angelic and human, which rose up in the divine mind, to be brought into being by Him, the man Christ Jesus was singled out of them, and appointed to union with the second person in the blessed trinity, and was accordingly sanctified and set up. This original and highest act of election was one of pure sovereignty and amazing grace. The celestial hosts were passed by, and the seed of the woman was determined upon. Out of the innumerable seeds which were to be created in Adam, the line of Abraham was selected, then of Isaac, and then of Jacob. Of the twelve tribes which were to issue from Jacob, that of Judah was chosen, God elected not an angel to the high union with His Son, but "one *chosen* out of the people" (Ps. 89:19). What shall those say who so much dislike the truth that the heirs of heaven are elected, when

they learn that Jesus Christ Himself is the subject of eternal election!
"Jehovah is the first cause and the last end of all things. His essence
and existence are of and from Himself. He is Jehovah, the self-existing
essence: the fountain of life, and essential blessedness—'The King
eternal, immortal, invisible, the only wise God, who alone hath immortality, dwelling in that light to which no mortal eye can approach.'
And throughout a vast eternity the eternal three enjoyed boundless
and incomprehensible blessedness in the contemplation of those essential perfections which belong to the Father. Son, and Spirit, the
everlasting Jehovah: who is His own eternity, and cannot receive any
addition to His essential happiness or glory by any or all of His
creatures. He is exalted above all blessing and praise. The whole
creation before Him, and as viewed by Him, is less than nothing and
vanity. If any should curiously inquire, what was God engaged in
before He stretched out the heavens and laid the foundations of the
earth? The answer is: the blessed, co-equal, and co-essential three,
Father, Son, and Spirit, had a mutual inbeing and society together,
and were essentially blessed in that divine eternal life, in the mutual
interests or propriety they have in each other, in mutual love and
delight—as also in the possession of one common glory.

"But as it is the nature of goodness to be *communicative of itself,*
so it pleased the eternal trinity to purpose to go forth into *creature
acts.* The ever blessed three, to whom nothing can be added or
diminished, the spring and fountain of whose essential blessedness
arises from the immense perfections in the infinite nature in which
they exist—in the mutual love they have to each other—and their
mutual converse together—were pleased to delight in creature fellowship and society. The eternal Father predestinated His coessential Son
into creature being and existence, and from everlasting He wore the
form and bore the personage of God-man. The creation of all things is
attributed in Scripture to divine sovereignty: 'Thou hast created all
things, and for thy pleasure they are and were created' (Rev. 4:11).
Nothing out of God can move Him: or be a motive to Him; His *will* is
His rule, His *glory* His ultimate end. 'For of Him (as the first cause),
and through Him (as the preserving cause), and to Him (as the final
cause), are all things' (Rom. 11:36).

"God in His actual creation of all, is the end of all. 'The Lord hath
made all things for himself' (Prov. 16:4), and the sovereignty of God
naturally ariseth from the relation of all things to Himself as their
Creator, and their natural and inseparable dependence upon Him, in
regard of their being and well-being. He had the being of all things in
His own will and power, and it was at His own pleasure whether He
would impart it or not. 'Known unto God are all his works from the
beginning of the world' (Acts 15:18). He comprehends and grasps all

things in His infinite understanding. As He hath an incomprehensible essence, to which ours is but as the drop in a bucket, so He hath an incomprehensible knowledge, to which ours is but as a grain of dust. His primitive decree and view, in the creation of heaven and earth, angels and men, being His own glory, and that which gave foundation to it and was the basis to support it, was Jehovah's design to exalt His Son as God-man, to be the foundation and corner-stone of the whole creation of God. God had never gone forth into creature acts, had not the second person condescended by the assumption of our nature to become a creature. Though this took place after the fall, yet the decree concerning it was before the fall. Jesus Christ, the fellow of the Lord of hosts, was the first of all the ways of God" (S. E. Pierce).

Nowhere does the sovereignty of God shine forth so conspicuously as in His acts of election and reprobation, which took place in eternity past, and which nothing in the creature was the cause of. God's act of choosing His people in Christ was before the foundation of the world, without the consideration of the fall, nor was it upon the foresight and footing of works, but was wholly, *of grace,* and all to the praise and glory of it. In nothing else is Jehovah's sovereignty so manifest: indeed the highest instance of it was in predestinating the second person in the Trinity to be the God-man. That this came under *the decree* of God is clear, again, from the words of the apostle: "Who verily [says he in speaking of Christ] was *foreordained* before the foundation of the world" (I Peter 1:20) and who is said to be laid "in Sion a chief cornerstone, *elect,* precious" (I Peter 2:6). This grand original of election, so little known to-day, is of such transcendent importance that we dwell upon it a little longer, to point out some of the reasons why God was pleased to predestinate the man Christ Jesus unto personal union with His Son.

Christ was predestinated for higher ends than the saving of His people from the effects of their fall in Adam. First, He was chosen for God Himself to delight in, far more so and infinitely above all other creatures. Being united to the second person, the man Christ Jesus was exalted to a closer union and communion with God. The Lord of hosts speaks of Him as "the man that is *my fellow*" (Zech. 13:7), "mine elect, in whom my soul delighteth" (Isa. 42:1). Second, Christ was chosen that God might behold the image of Himself and all His perfections in a creature, so that His excellences are seen in Christ as in no other: "Who being the brightness of his glory and the express image of his person" (Heb. 1:3), which is spoken of the person of Christ as God-man. Third, by the union of the man Christ Jesus with the everlasting Son of God, the whole fulness of the Godhead was to dwell personally in Him, He being "the Image of the invisible God" (Col. 1:15, 19).

The Man Christ Jesus, then, was chosen unto the highest union and communion with God Himself. In Him the love and grace of Jehovah shine forth in their superlative glory. The Son of God gave subsistence and personality to His human nature, so that the Son of God and His human nature are not merely one *flesh* as man and wife (which is the closest union with us), nor one *spirit* only (as is the case between Christ and the Church: I Cor. 6:17), but one *person*, and hence this creature nature is advanced to a fellowship in the society of the blessed Trinity, and therefore to Him God communicates Himself without measure (John 3:34). Descending now to a lower plane, the Man Christ Jesus was also chosen to be an Head to an elect seed, who were chosen in Him, given a super-creation subsistence, and blessed in Him with all spiritual blessings.

If God will love, He must have an object for His love, and the object must have an existence before Him to exercise His love upon, for He cannot love a non-enity. It must therefore be that the God-man, and the elect in Him existed in the divine mind as objects of God's everlasting love, before all time. In Christ the Church was chosen from everlasting: the one the Head, the other His body; the one being the bridegroom, the other His bride: the one being chosen and appointed for the other. They were chosen together, yet Christ first in the order of the divine decrees. As, then, Christ and the Church had existed in the will, thoughts, and purpose of the Father from the beginning, He could love them and rejoice in them. As the God-man declares "Thou hast sent me, and hast loved them, as thou hast loved me . . . for thou lovest me before the foundation of the world" (John 17:23, 24).

The Son of God being, before all time, predestinated to be God-man, He was secretly anointed or set up as such, and His human nature had a covenant subsistence before God. In consequence of this, He was the Son of man in heaven before He became the Son of man on earth; He was the Son of man secretly before God before He became the Son of man openly and manifestly in this world. Therefore did the Psalmist exclaim, "Let thy hand be upon the man of thy right hand, upon the son of man whom thou madest strong for Thyself" (80:17); and therefore did Christ Himself declare, "What and if ye shall see the Son of *man* ascend up *where he was before?*" (John 6:62). "God, out of His eternal and infinite goodness of love, and purposing Christ to become a creature, and communicate with His creatures, ordained in His eternal counsel that person in the Godhead should be united to our nature and to one particular of His creatures, that so in the person of the Mediator the true ladder of salvation might be fixed, whereby God might descend to His creatures and His creatures ascend unto Him" (Sir Francis Bacon).

"Christ was first elected as Head and Mediator, and as the Corner-stone to bear up the whole building; for the act of the Father's election in Christ supposeth Him first chosen to this mediatory work and to be the Head of the elect part of the world. After this election of Christ, others were predestinated 'to be conformed unto His image' (Rom 8:29) i.e., to Christ as Mediator, and taking human nature; not to Christ barely considered as God. This conformity being specially intended *in election,* Christ was in the purpose of the Father the first exemplar and copy of it. One foot of the compass of grace stood in Christ as the centre, while the other walked about the circumference, pointing one here and another there, to draw a line, as it were, between every one of those points and Christ. The Father, then, being the prime cause of the election of some out of the mass of mankind, was the prime cause of the election of Christ to bring them to the enjoyment of that to which they were elected. Is it likely that God, in founding an everlasting kingdom, should consult about the members before He did about the Head? Christ was registered at the top of the book of election, and His members after Him. It is called, therefore, 'the book of the Lamb' " (S. Charnock).

That passage of Scripture which enters most fully into what we are here contemplating is Proverbs 8, at which we will now glance. There are many passages in that book wherein the "wisdom" spoken of signifies far more than a moral excellency, and something even more blessed than the personification of one of the divine attributes. In not a few passages (1:20, 21, for example) the reference is *to Christ,* one of whose titles is "the wisdom of God" (I Cor. 1:24). It is as such He is to be regarded here in chapter 8. That it is a *person* which is there in view is clear from verse 17, and that it is a *divine* person appears from verse 15; yet not a divine person considered abstractedly, but as the God-man. This is evident from what is there predicated of Him.

"The Lord possessed me in the beginning of his way, before his works of old" (v. 22). The speaker is Christ Himself, the alone Mediator between the Creator and His creatures. The words "The Lord possessed me *in* the beginning of his way" tend to hide what is there affirmed. There is no prefix in the original Hebrew, nothing there to warrant the interposed "in," while the word rendered "be-ginning" signifies the first or chief. Thus it should be translated "the Lord possessed me: the beginning (or Chief) of his way, before his works of old." Christ was the firstborn of all God's thoughts and designs, delighted in by Him long before the universe was brought into existence.

"I was set up from everlasting, from the beginning, or ever the earth was" (v. 23). "Our Redeemer came forth of the womb of a decree from eternity, before He came out of the womb of the virgin in time; He was hid in the will of God before He was made manifest in the flesh of a Redeemer; He was a lamb slain in decree before He was slain upon the cross; He was possessed by God in the beginning, or the beginning of His way, the Head of His works, and set up from everlasting to have His delights among the sons of men" (Prov. 8:22, 23, 31), (S. Charnock).

"When there were no depths, I was brought forth; when there were no fountains abounding with water. Before the mountains were settled, before the hills was I brought forth" (vv. 24, 25). Christ is here referring to His being "brought forth" in God's mind, being predestinated into creature existence before the world was made. The first of all God's intentions respected the union of the Man Christ Jesus unto His Son. The Mediator became the foundation of all the divine counsels: see Ephesians 3:11 and 1:9, 10. As such the triune Jehovah "possessed" Him as a treasury in which were laid up all His designs. He was then "set up" or "anointed" (v. 23) in His official character as Mediator and Head of the Church. As the God-man He had a virtual influence and was the Executor of all the works and will of God.

"Then I was by him, as one brought up with him: and I was daily his delight, rejoicing always before him" (v. 30). It is not the complacency of the Father in the Son considered absolutely as the second Person, but His satisfaction and joy in the Mediator as He viewed Him in the glass of His decrees. It was as incarnate that the Father said, "This is my beloved Son in whom I am well pleased" (Matt. 3:17), and it was with the foreordained God-man, who had a real subsistence before the divine mind, that He was delighted in by Jehovah before the world was. In His eternal thoughts and primitive views, the man that was His fellow became the Object of God's ineffable love and complacency. It was far more than that Jehovah simply *purposed* that the Son should become incarnate; His decree gave Christ a real subsistence before Him, and as such afforded infinite satisfaction to His heart.

So little understood is this blessed aspect of our subject, and so important do we deem it, that some further remarks thereon seem called for. That Christ is the firstborn or head of the election of grace was prefigured at the beginning of God's works, in fact the creation of this world and the formation of the first man were on purpose to make *Christ known*. As we are told in Romans 5:14 "which is the figure of Him that was to come." In his creation, formation, and constitution as the federal head of our race, Adam was a remarkable type of Christ as God's Elect. In amplifying this statement it will be necessary to go over some of the same ground that we covered in *Spiritual Union and Communion,* but we trust the reader will bear with us if we here repeat a number of the things.

There is a certain class of people—despising all doctrine, and particularly disliking the doctrine of God's absolute sovereignty—who often exhort us to "preach Christ," but we have long observed that *they* never preach Christ in His *highest* official character, as the Covenant-Head of God's people, that they never say one word about Him as God's "Elect, in whom my soul delighteth!" Preaching Christ is a far more comprehensive task than many suppose, nor can it be done intelligently by any man until he begins at the beginning and shows that the man Christ Jesus was eternally *predestinated* unto union with the second person of the Godhead. "I have exalted one chosen out of the people" (Ps. 89:19): that exaltation commenced with the elevation of Christ's humanity to personal union with the eternal Word—unique honor!

The very words "chosen in Christ" necessarily imply that He was chosen *first,* as the soil in which we were set. When God chose Christ it was not as a single or private person, but as a public person, as Head of His body, we being chosen in Him as the members thereof. Thus, inasmuch as we were then given a representative subsistence before God, God could make a covenant with Christ on our behalf. That He *did* so enter into an eternal compact with Christ in this character as Head of the election of grace is clear from, "I have made a covenant with *my chosen,* I have sworn unto David my servant" (Ps. 89:3)—adumbrated in the covenant He made in time with him who was typically "the man after his own heart," for David was as truly shadowing forth Christ when God made a covenant with him as Joseph was when he supplied food to his needy brethren, or as Moses was when he led forth the Hebrews out of the house of bondage.

Let those, then, who desire to preach Christ, see to it that they give Him the pre-eminence in *all* things—election not excepted! Let them learn to give unto Jesus of Nazareth His full honor, that which the Father Himself hath given to Him It is a superlative honor that Christ is the channel through which all the grace and glory we have, or shall have, flows to us, and was set up as such from the beginning. As Romans 8:29 so plainly teaches, it was in connection with *election* that God appointed His own beloved Son to be "the firstborn among many brethren." Christ being appointed as the masterpiece of divine wisdom, the grand prototype, and we ordained to be so many little copies and models of Him. Christ is the first and last of all God's thoughts, counsels, and ways.

The universe is but the theatre and this world the principal stage on which the Lord God thinks fit to act out some of His deepest designs. His creating of Adam was a shadow to point to a better Adam, who was to have an universal headship over all the creatures of God, and whose glories were to shine forth visibly in and through every part of the creation. When the world was created and furnished, man was brought forth. But before his formation we read of that renowned consultation of the eternal three: "And God said, Let *us* make man in our image" (Gen. 1:26). This respected *Christ,* the God-man, who was from all eternity the object and subject of all the counsels of the Trinity. Adam, created and made after God's Image, which consisted of righteousness and true holiness, was the type, for Christ is par excellent *"the image* of the invisible God" (Col. 1:15).

The formation of Adam's body, by God's immediate hand, out of the dust of the ground, was a figure or shadow of the assumption of human nature by the Son of God, whose humanity was formed immediately by the Holy Spirit: as Adam's body was produced from the virgin earth, so Christ's human nature was produced from the virgin's womb. Again; that union of soul and body in Adam was a type to express that most profound and greatest of all mysteries, the hypostatical union of our nature in the person of Christ: as it is justly expressed in what is commonly called the Athanasian Creed, "As the reasonable soul and flesh is one man, so God and man is one Christ." Again; as Adam's person comprised the perfections of all creatures, and was suited to take in all the comforts and pleasures they could afford and impart, so the glory of Christ's humanity excels all creatures, even the angels themselves. The more attentively we consider the person and position of the first Adam the better may we discern how fully and fittingly he was a figure of the last Adam.

As Adam, placed in paradise, had all the creatures of the earth brought before him and was made to have dominion over them all (Gen. 1:28), thus being crowned with mundane glory and honor, so in this too he accurately foreshadowed Christ, who hath universal empire and dominion over all worlds, beings, and things, as may be seen from Psalm 8, which is applied to the Saviour in Hebrews 2:9, where sovereignty over all creatures is ascribed to Him, the earth and the heavens, sun, moon and stars magnifying Him. For though He was for a little while abased beneath the angels in His humiliation, yet now in His exaltation, He is crowned King of kings and Lord of lords. Moreover, though the God-man, the "fellow of the Lord of hosts," went through a season of degradation before His exaltation, nevertheless His glorification was foreordained before the world began: "I appoint unto you a kingdom, as my Father hath *appointed* unto me" (Luke 22:29); "It is he which was *ordained* of God to be the Judge of quick and dead" (Acts 10:42).

That Christ had both a precedency and presidency in election was also shadowed forth in this primo-primitive type, for we read, "And Adam gave names to all cattle, and to the fowl of the air, and to every beast of the field; but for Adam there was not found a help meet for him" (Gen. 2:20). Yet mark the perfect accuracy of the type: when God created Adam, He created Eve *in* him (and in blessing Adam— Gen. 1:28—He blessed all mankind in him); so when God elected Christ, His people were *chosen in* Him (Eph. 1:4), and therefore they had a virtual being and subsistence in Him from all eternity, and consequently He was styled "the everlasting *Father*" (Isa. 9:6 and cf. Heb. 2:13); and consequently in blessing Christ, God blessed all the elect in Him and together with Him (Eph. 1:3; 2:5).

Though Adam came forth "very good" from the hands of his Maker and was given dominion over all the creatures of the earth, yet we read "but for Adam there was not found a help meet for him." Consequently, He provided a suitable partner for him, which being taken out of his side was then "builded" (Gen. 2:22 margin), brought to, and welcomed by him. In like manner, though Christ was the beginning of God's way, set up from everlasting, and delighted in by the Father (Prov. 8:22, 23, 30), yet God did not think it good for him to be alone, and therefore He decreed a spouse for Him, who should share His communicable graces, honors, riches, and glories; a spouse which, in due time, was the fruit of His pierced side, and brought to Him by the gracious operations of the Holy Spirit.

When Eve was formed by the Lord God and brought to Adam so as to effect a marriage union, there was shadowed forth that highest mystery of grace, of God the Father presenting His elect and giving them to Christ: "Thine they were, and thou gavest them me" (John 17:6). Foreviewing them in the glass of the divine decrees, the Mediator loved and delighted in them (Prov. 8:31), betrothed them unto Himself, taking the Church as thus presented by God unto Him in a deed of marriage settlement and covenant contract as the gift of the Father. As Adam *owned* the relation between Eve and himself saying, "This is now bone of my bones, and flesh of my flesh" (Gen. 2:23), so Christ became an everlasting husband unto the Church. And as Adam and Eve were united *before* the fall, so Christ and the Church were one in the mind of God *prior* to any foreviews of sin.

If, then, we are to "preach Christ" in His *highest* official glory, it must be plainly shown that He was not ordained in God's eternal purpose for the Church, but the Church was ordained *for Him*. Notice how the Holy Spirit has emphasized this particular point in the type. "For a man indeed ought not to cover his head, forasmuch as he is the image and glory of God: but the woman is *the glory of the man*. For the man is not of the woman; but the woman of the man. Neither was the man created for the woman; but the woman for the man" (I Cor. 11:7-9). Yet as Adam was not complete without Eve, so neither is Christ without the Church: she is His "fulness" or "complement" (Eph. 1:23), yea, she is His crown of glory and royal diadem (Isa. 62:3)—the Church may be said to be necessary for Christ as an empty vessel for Him to supply with grace and glory. All His delights are in her, and He will be glorified in her and by her through all eternity, putting His glory upon her (John 17:22). "Come hither, I will show thee the Bride, the Lamb's wife . . . descending out of heaven from God, *having the glory of God"* (Rev. 21:9-11)

In His character as God's "Elect" Christ was shadowed forth by others than Adam. Indeed it is striking to see what a number of those who were prominent types of Christ were made the subjects of a *real election* of God, by which they were designated to some special office. Concerning Moses we read "Therefore he said that he would destroy them, had not Moses his *chosen* stood before him in the breach, to turn away his wrath" (Ps. 106:23). Of Aaron it is said, "No man taketh this honor unto himself, but he that is *called* of God, as was Aaron" (Heb. 5:4). Of the priests of Israel it is recorded, "The sons of Levi shall come near; for them the Lord thy God hath *chosen* to minister unto him; and to bless in the name of the Lord" (Deut. 21:5). Regarding David and the tribe from which he came, it is written, "He *refused* the tabernacle of Joseph, and chose not the tribe of Ephraim; but *chose* the tribe of Judah, the mount Zion which he loved. . . . He *chose* David also his servant, and took him from the sheepfolds" (Ps. 78:67, 68, 70). Each of these cases adumbrated the grand truth that the Man Christ Jesus was chosen by God to the highest degree of glory and blessedness of all His creatures.

"And there shall in no wise enter into it any thing that defileth, neither whatsoever worketh abomination, or maketh a lie: but they which are written in the Lamb's book of life" (Rev. 21:27). This expression "The Book of Life" is doubtless a figurative one, for the Holy Spirit delights to represent spiritual, heavenly, and eternal things—as well as the blessing and benefits of them—under a variety of images and metaphors, that our minds may the more readily understand and our hearts feel the reality of them, and thus we be made more capable of receiving them. Yet this we are to know: the similitude thus made use of to represent them to our spiritual view are but shadows, yet what is shadowed forth by them has *real* being and substance.

The sun in the firmament is an instituted emblem in the nature of Christ—He being that to the spiritual world which the former is to the natural—yet the former is but the shadow, and Christ is the real substance, hence He is styled "the Sun of righteousness." So when Christ is compared to the light, He is the *"true* Light" (John 1:9), when compared to a vine, He is the *"true* Vine" (John 15:1), when to bread, He is "the true Bread," the Bread of life, that Bread of God which came down from heaven (John 6). Let this principle, then, be duly kept in mind by us as we come across the many metaphors which are applied to the Redeemer in the Scriptures. So here in Revelation 21:27 while allowing that "the Book of Life" is a figurative expression, we are far from granting that there is not in heaven that which is figured by it, nay, the very reality itself.

This expression "the Book of Life" has its roots in Isaiah 4:3, wherein God refers to His chosen remnant as "every one that is written among the living in Jerusalem," and it is this which explains the meaning of all the later references thereto. God's eternal act *of election* is spoken of as writing the names of His chosen ones in the Book of Life, and the following things are suggested by this figure. First, the exact knowledge which God has of all the elect, His particular remembrance of them, His love for and delight in them. Second, that His eternal election is one of particular persons whose *names* are definitely recorded by Him. Third, to show they are absolutely safe and secure, for *God* having written their names in the Book of Life, they shall never be blotted out (Rev. 3:5). When the seventy returned from their missionary journey, elated because the very demons were subject to them, Christ said, "But rather rejoice, because your names are *written in heaven*" (Luke 10:20 and cf. Phil. 4:3; Heb. 12:23), which shows that God's election to eternal life is of particular persons—by name—and therefore is sure and immutable.

Let us now particularly observe that this election-register is designated "the *Lamb's* Book of Life," and this for at least two reasons. First, because the Lamb's name heads it, His being the *first* one written therein, for He must have the pre-eminence; after which follows the enrollment of the particular names of all His people—note how *His* name is the first one recorded in the New Testament: Matthew 1:1! Second, because Christ, is the root and His elect are branches, so that they receive their *life from Him* as they are in Him and supported by Him. It is written "When Christ, who is *our life,* shall appear, then shall ye also appear with Him in glory" (Col. 3:4). Christ is our life because He is the very "Prince of life" (Acts 3:15). Thus, the divine register of election in which are enrolled all the names of Christ's members, is aptly termed "the Lamb's Book of Life," for they are entirely dependent upon Him for life.

But it is in connection with the first reason that we would offer a further remark. It is called the Lamb's Book of Life because His is the first name in it. This is no arbitrary assertion of ours, but one that is clearly warranted by the Bible, "Lo, I come (in the volume of the book it is written of Me)" (Heb. 10:7). The speaker here is the Lord Jesus and, as is so often the case (such is the fulness of His words), there is a *double* reference in it: first to the archives of God's eternal counsels, the scroll of His decress; second, to the Holy Scriptures, which are a partial transcript of them. In keeping with this twofold reference is the *double* meaning of the word "volume." In Psalm 40:7 "volume" is unquestionably the signification of the Hebrew word there used; but in Hebrews 10:7 the Greek word most certainly ought to be rendered "head"—*kephale* occurs seventy-six times in the New Testament, and it is *always* rendered "head" except here. Thus, properly translated, Hebrews 10:7 reads "*at the head* of the book it is written of me."

Here, then is the proof of our assertion. The Book of Life—the Divine register of election—is termed the Lamb's Book of Life" because *His* name is the first one written therein, and He who had Himself scanned that roll said, as He entered this world, "at the *head of* the book it is written of me." A further reference to this Book was made by Christ in "In thy book all my members were written" (Ps. 139:16). The Psalmist was referring to his natural body, first as formed in the womb (v. 15), and then as being the subject of the divine decrees (v. 16). But the deeper reference is to Christ, speaking, as the antitypical David, of the members of His mystical body. "The substance of the Church, whereof it was to be formed, was under the eyes of God, as proposed in the decree of election" (John Owen).

Should an exercised reader be asking, How may I now be assured that *my* name is written in the Lamb's Book of Life? We answer, very briefly. First, by God's having taught you to see and brought you to feel your inward corruption, your personal vileness, your awful guilt, your dire *need* of the sacrifice of the Lamb. Second, by causing you to make Christ of first importance in your thoughts and estimation, perceiving that He alone can save you. Third, by bringing you to believe in Him, rest your whole soul upon Him, desiring to be found in Him, not having your own righteousness, but His. Fourth, by making Him infinitely precious to you, so that He is all your desire. Fifth, by working in you a determination to please and glorify Him.

4 Its Verity

Before proceeding further with an orderly opening up of this profound but precious doctrine, it may be better (especially for the benefit of those less familiar with the subject) if we now demonstrate *its Scripturalness*. We must not take anything for granted, and as numbers of our readers have never received any systematic instruction upon the subject—yea, some of them know next to nothing about it—and as others have heard and read only perversions and caricatures of this doctrine, it seems essential that we should pause and establish its verity. In other words, our present object is to furnish proof that what we are now writing upon is not some theological invention of Calvin's or any other man's, but is clearly revealed in Holy Writ, namely, that God, before the foundation of the world, made a difference between His creatures, singling out certain ones to be the special objects of His favor.

We shall deal with the subject in a more or less general way—occupying ourselves with *the fact itself;* reserving the more detailed analysis and the drawing of distinctions for later chapters. Let us begin by asking, Has God an elect people? Now this question must be propounded to God Himself, for He alone is competent to answer it. It is, therefore, to His holy Word we have to turn, if we would learn *His* answer thereto. But ere doing so, we need to earnestly beg God to grant us a teachable spirit, that we may humbly receive the divine testimony. The things of God can no man know, till God Himself declares them; but when He *has* declared them, it is not only crass folly, but wicked presumption, for any one to contend or disbelieve. The Holy Scriptures are the rule of faith, as well as the rule of conduct. To the law and the testimony, then, we now turn.

Concerning the nation of Israel we read, "The Lord thy God hath *chosen* thee to be a special people unto Himself, above all people that are upon the face of the earth" (Deut. 7:6); "For the Lord hath *chosen* Jacob unto himself, and Israel for his peculiar treasure" (Ps. 135:4); "But thou, Israel, art my servant, Jacob whom I have *chosen,* the seed of Abraham my friend. Thou whom I have taken from the ends of the earth, and called thee from the chief men thereof, and said unto thee, thou art my servant; I have *chosen* thee, and not cast thee away" (Isa. 41:8, 9). These testimonies make it unmistakably plain that ancient Israel were the favored, elect people of God. We do not here take up the question as to *why* God chose them, or as to *what* they were chosen unto; but notice only the bare fact itself. In Old Testament times God had an elect nation.

Next, it is to be observed that even in favored Israel God made a distinction: there was an election within an election; or, in other words, God had a special people of His own from among the nation itself. "For they are *not all Israel,* which are of Israel: neither, because they are the seed of Abraham, are they all *children:* but, in Isaac shall thy seed by called" (Rom. 9:6-8). "God hath not cast away his people which he foreknew. . . . I have reserved to myself seven thousand men who have not bowed the knee to the image of Baal: even so that at this present time also there is a remnant according to the *election* of grace. . . . Israel hath not obtained that which he seeketh for; but the *election* hath obtained it" (Rom. 11:2-7). Thus we see that even in visible Israel, the nation chosen to outward privileges, God had an election—a *spiritual* Israel, the objects of His love.

The same principle of Divine selection appears plainly and conspicuously in the teaching of the New Testament. There too it is revealed that God has a peculiar people, the subjects of His special favor, His own dear children. The Saviour and His apostles describe this people in various ways, and often designate them by the term of which we here treat. "For the *elect's* sake those days shall be shortened . . . insomuch that, if it were possible, they shall deceive the very *elect* . . . and they shall gather together *His elect* from the four winds" (Matt. 24:22, 24, 31). "Shall not God avenge His own *elect,* which cry day and night unto Him?" (Luke 18:7). "Who shall lay any thing to the charge of *God's elect?*" (Rom. 8:33). "That the purpose of God according to election might stand" (Rom. 9:11). "I endure all things for *the elect's* sake" (II Tim. 2:10), "The faith of *God's elect*" (Titus 1:1). Many other passages might be quoted, but these are sufficient to clearly demonstrate that God has an elect people. God Himself says He has, who will dare say He has not!

The word "elected" in one of its forms, or its synonym "chosen" in one of its forms, occurs upon the sacred page considerably over one hundred times. The term, then, belongs to the divine vocabulary. It must mean something; it must convey some definite idea. What, then, is its significance? The humble inquirer will not force a construction upon the word, or seek to read into it his own preconceptions, but will prayerfully endeavor to ascertain the mind of the Spirit. Nor should this be difficult, for there is no word in human language which has a more specific meaning. The concept universally expressed by it is that one is taken and another left, for if all were taken there would be *no* "choice." Moreover, *the right of choice* always belongs to him who chooses: the act is his, the motive is his. Therein "choice" differs from compulsion, the paying of a debt, discharging an obligation, or responding to the requirements of justice. Choice is a free and sovereign act.

Let there be no uncertainty about the meaning of our term. God has made a choice, for election signifies selection and appointment. God has exercised His own sovereign will and singled out from the mass of His creatures those upon whom He determined to bestow His special favors. There cannot be an election without a singling out, and there cannot be a singling out without a passing by. The doctrine of election means that from all eternity God made a choice of those who were to be His special treasure, His dear children, the co-heirs of Christ. The doctrine of election means that before His Son became incarnate God marked out the ones who should be saved by Him. The doctrine of election means that God has left nothing to chance: the accomplishment of His purpose, the success of Christ's undertaking, the peopling of heaven, is not contingent upon the fickle caprice of the creature. God's will, and not man's will, fixes destiny.

Let us now call attention to a most remarkable and little known example of divine election. "I charge thee before God, and the Lord Jesus Christ, and *the elect angels*" (I Tim. 5:21). If then, there are "elect angels" there must necessarily be non-elect, for there cannot be the one without the other. God, then, in the past made a selection among the hosts of heaven, choosing some to be vessels of honor and others to be vessels of dishonor. Those whom He chose unto His favor, stood steadfast, remained in subjection to His will. The rest fell when Satan revolted, for upon his apostasy he dragged down with himself one third of the angels (Rev. 12:4). Concerning them we read, "God spared not the angels that sinned, but cast them down to hell, and delivered them into chains of darkness" (II Peter 2:4). But those of them who belong to the election of grace are "the holy angels": holy as the consequence of their election, and not elected because they were holy, for election antedated their creation. The supreme example of election is seen in Christ; the next highest in that God made choice among the celestial hierarchies.

Let us next observe and admire the marvel and singularity of God's choice among men. He has selected a portion of Adam's race to be the high favorites of heaven. "Now this is a wonder of wonders, when we come to consider that the heaven, even the heaven of heavens, is the Lord's. If God must have a chosen race, why did He not select one from the majestic order of angels, or from the flashing cherubim and seraphim who stand around His throne? Why was not Gabriel fixed upon? Why was he not so constituted that from his loins there might spring a mighty race of angels, and why were not those chosen of God from before the foundation of the world? What could there be in *man*, a creature lower than the angels, that God should select him rather than the angelic spirits? Why were not the cherubim and seraphim given to Christ? Why did He not assume the nature of angels, and take *them* into union with Himself? An angelic body might be more in keeping with the person of Deity than a body of weak and suffering flesh and blood. There was something congruous if He had said unto the angels, 'Ye shall be My Sons.' But no! though all these were His own; He passes them by and stoops to man" (C. H. Spurgeon).

Some may suggest that the reason why God made choice of Adam's descendants in preference to the angels, was that the human race fell in Adam and thus afforded a more suitable case for God to display His rich mercy upon. But such a supposition is entirely fallacious, for, as we have seen, one third of the angels themselves fell from their high estate, yet so far from God showing them mercy, He "hath reserved in everlasting chains under darkness unto the judgment of the great day" (Jude 6). No Saviour was provided for them, no gospel has ever been preached to them. How striking and how solemn is this: the fallen angels passed by; the fallen sons of Adam made the recipients of the overtures of divine mercy.

Here is a truly marvelous thing. God determined to have a people who should be His peculiar treasure, nearer and dearer to Himself than any other creatures; a people who should be conformed to the very image of His Son. And that people was chosen from the descendants of Adam. Why? Why not have reserved that supreme honor for the celestial hosts? They are a higher order of beings; they were created before us. They were heavenly creatures, yet God passed them by; we are earthly, yet the Lord set His heart upon us. Again we ask, why? Ah, let those who hate the truth of God's high sovereignty and contend against the doctrine of unconditional election, carefully ponder this striking example of it. Let those who so blatantly insist that it would be unjust for God to show partiality between man and man, tell us why did He show partiality between race and race, bestowing favors upon men which He never has upon angels? Only one answer is possible: *because it so pleased Him.*

Election is a divine secret, an act in the will of God in eternity past.

But it does not forever remain such. No, in due time, God is pleased to make openly manifest His everlasting counsels. This He has done in varying degrees, since the beginning of human history. In Genesis 3:15 He made known the fact that there would be two distinct lines: the woman's "seed," which denoted Christ and His people, and the Serpent's "seed," which signified Satan and those who are conformed to his likeness; God placing an irreconcilable "enmity" between them. These two "seeds" comprehend the elect and the non-elect. Abel belonged to the election of grace: evidence of this being furnished in his "faith" (Heb. 11:4), for only those "ordained to eternal life" (Acts 13:48) savingly "believe." Cain belonged to the non-elect: evidence of this is found in the statement "Cain, who was of that Wicked one" (I John 3:12). Thus at the beginning of history, in the two sons of Adam and Eve, God "took" the one into His favor, and "left" the other to suffer the due reward of his iniquities.

Next, we behold election running in the line of Seth, for it was of his descendants (and not those of Cain's) we read, "Then began men to call upon the name of the Lord" (Gen. 4:26). But in the course of time they too were corrupted, until the entire human race became so evil that God sent the flood and swept them all away. Yet even then the principle of divine election was exemplified: not only in Enoch, but that "Noah found grace in the eyes of the Lord" (Gen. 6:8). It was the same after the flood, for a marked discrimination was made between the sons of Noah: "Blessed be the Lord God of Shem" (Gen. 9:26), which imports that God had chosen and blessed him. On the other hand, "Cursed be Canaan: a servant of servants shall he be unto his brethren" (Gen. 9:25), which is expressive of preterition and all that is involved in God's rejection. Thus, even of those who emerged from the ark, God made one to differ from another.

From the sons of Noah sprang the nations which have peopled the world. "By these [i.e., Noah's three sons] were the nations divided in the earth after the flood" (Gen. 10:32). From those seventy nations God chose the one in which the great current of His election would run. In Genesis 10:25 we read that this dividing of the nations was made in the time of Eber, the grandson of Shem. Why are we told this? To intimate that God then began to separate the Jewish nation unto Himself in Eber, for Eber was their father; hence it is also that at the beginning of Shem's genealogy we are told, "Shem also (the elected and blessed of God), the father of all the children of Eber" (10:21). This is very striking, for Shem had other and older children (whose line of descendants is also recorded), as Asshur and Elim, the fathers of the Assyrians and the Persians.

The seemingly dry and uninteresting detail in Genesis 10 to which we have just alluded, marked a most important step forward in the outworking of the divine counsels, for it was then that God began to separate unto Himself the Israelites in Eber, whom He had appointed to be their father. Till then the Hebrews had lain promiscuously mingled with the other nations, but now God "divided" them from the rest, as the other nations were divided from one another. Accordingly, we find Eber's posterity, even when very few in number, were designated "Hebrews" as their *national* denomination ("Israel" being their *religious name*) in distinction from those among whom they lived: "Abraham the *Hebrew*" (Gen. 14:13), "Joseph the *Hebrew*" (Gen. 39:14). Hence, when they became a nation in numbers, and while living in the midst of the Egyptians, they are again styled "Hebrews" (Exod. 1:15), while in Numbers 24:24 they are distinctly called "*Eber*"!

What we have sought to explain above is definitely confirmed by "Remember the days of old, consider the years of many generations: ask thy father, and he will show thee; thy elders, and they will tell thee. When the most High *divided* to the nations their inheritance, when he separated the sons of Adam, he set the bounds of the people according to the number of the children of Israel. *For* the Lord's portion is his people; Jacob is the lot of his inheritance" (Deut. 32:7-9). Notice, first, the Lord here bade Israel cast their minds back to ancient times, the traditions of which had been handed down by their fathers. Second, the particular event alluded to was when God "divided" to the nations their inheritance, the reference being to that famous division of Genesis 10. Third, those nations are spoken of *not* "as the sons of Noah" (who was in the elect line), but as "the sons of *Adam*"—another plain hint that *he* headed the line of the reprobate. Fourth, that when God allotted to the non-elect nations their earthly portion, even then the eye of grace and favor was upon the children of Israel. Fifth, "according to the *number* of the children of Israel," which was seventy when they first settled in Egypt (Gen. 46:27)—the exact number of the nations mentioned in Genesis 10!

The chief link of connection between Eber and the nation of Israel was, of course, Abraham, and in his case the principle of divine election shines forth with sunlight clearness. The divine call which he received marked another important stage in the development of God's eternal purpose. At the tower of Babel God gave over the nations to walk in their own evil ways, afterward taking up Abraham to be the founder of the favored nation. "Thou art the Lord the God, who didst *choose* Abraham, and broughtest him forth out of Ur" (Neh. 9:7). It was not Abraham who chose God, but God who chose Abraham. "The God of glory appeared unto our father Abraham, when he was in

Mesopotamia" (Acts 7:2): this title "the God of glory" is employed here to emphasize the signal favor which was shown to Abraham, the glory of His grace in electing him, for there was nothing in him by nature that lifted him above his fellows and entitled him to the divine notice. It was unmerited kindness, sovereign mercy, which was shown him.

This is made very evident by what is told us in Joshua 24 of his condition *before* Jehovah appeared to him: "Thus saith the God of Israel, your fathers dwelt on the other side of the flood in old time, even Terah, the father of Abraham, and the father of Nachor: and they served *other gods*" (v. 2). Abraham was living in the heathen city of Ur, and belonged to an idolatrous family! At a later date God pressed this very fact upon his descendants, reminding them of the lowly and corrupt state of their original, and giving them to know it was for no good in him that he had been chosen: "Hearken to me, ye that follow after righteousness, ye that seek the Lord: look unto the rock whence ye are hewn, and to the hole of the pit whence ye are digged. Look unto Abraham your father, and unto Sarah that bare you; for I called him alone, and blessed him" (Isa. 51:1, 2). What a flesh-withering word is that: the great Abraham is here likened (by God) to "the hole of the pit"—such was his condition when the Lord first appeared unto him.

But there is more in the above passage. Observe carefully the words "I called him *alone*." Remember that this was while he dwelt in Ur, and as modern excavations have shown, that was a city of vast extent: out of all its huge number of inhabitants God revealed himself to *one only!* The Lord here emphasized that very fact and calls upon us to mark the singularity of His election by this word "alone." See here, then, the absolute sovereignty of God, exercising His own imperial will, choosing whom He pleases. He had mercy upon Abraham simply because He was pleased to do so, and He left the remainder of his countrymen in heathen darkness simply because it so seemed good in His sight. There was nothing more in Abraham than in any of his fellows why God should have selected *him:* whatever goodness was found in him later was what God Himself put there, and therefore it was the consequence and not the cause of His choice.

Striking as is the case of Abraham's own election, yet God's dealings with his offspring is equally if not more noteworthy. Therein God furnished an epitome of what has largely characterized the history of all His elect, for it is a very rare thing to find a whole family which (not simply makes a profession, but) gives evidence of enjoying His special favor. The common rule is that one is taken and other is left, for those who are given to really believe this precious but solemn truth, are made to experimentally realize its force in connection with their own kin. Thus Abraham's own family furnished in his next and immediate successors, a prototype of the future experience of the elect. In his family we behold the most striking instances of both election and preterition, first in his sons, and then in his grandsons.

That Isaac was a child of pure electing grace (which was the cause and not the consequence of his faith and holiness), and that as such he was placed in Abraham's family as a precious gift, while Ishmael was excluded from that pre-eminent favor, is quite evident from the history of Genesis. Before he was born, yea, before he was conceived in the womb, God declared unto Abraham that Isaac was heir of the same salvation with him, and had irrevocably estated the covenant of grace upon him thereby distinguishing him from Ishmael; who, though blessed with temporal mercies, was not in the covenant of grace, but rather was under the covenant of works (see Gen. 17:19-21 and compare the Spirit's comments thereon in Gal. 4:22-26).

Later, while Isaac was yet young, and lay bound as a sacrifice upon the altar, God ratified the promises of blessing which He had made before his birth, confirming them with a solemn oath: "By myself have I sworn, saith the Lord, for because thou hast done this thing, hast not withheld thy son, thine only son: that in blessing I will bless thee, and in mutiplying I will multiply thy seed as the stars of the heaven" (Gen. 22:16, 17). That oath respected the *spiritual* seed, the heirs of promise, such as Isaac was, the declared son of promise. To that the apostle referred when he said, "wherein God, willing more abundantly to show unto the heirs of promise the immutability of his counsel, confirmed it by an oath" (Heb. 6:17). And what was His "immutable counsel" but His eternal decree, His purpose of election? God's counsels are His decrees within Himself from everlasting (Eph. 1:4, 9, 10). And what is a promise with an oath but God's immutable counsel or election put into promissory form. And who are the "heirs of promise" but the elect, such as Isaac was.

An objector would argue that the choosing of Isaac in preference to Ishmael was not an act of pure sovereignty, seeing that the former was the son of Sarah, while the latter was the child of Hagar, the Egyptian bondwoman—thus supposing that God's gifts are regulated by something in the creature. But the next instance precludes even that sophistry and entirely shuts us up to the uncaused and uninfluenced will of the Most High. Jacob and Esau were by the *same* father and mother, twins. Concerning them we read, "(For the children being not yet born, neither having done any good or evil, that the purpose of God according to *election* might stand, not of works, but of him that calleth;) It was said unto her, The elder shall serve the younger. As it is written, Jacob have I loved, but Esau have I hated" (Rom. 9:11-13). Let us bow in awed silence before such a passage.

The nation which sprang from Abraham, Isaac, and Jacob, was God's chosen and favored people, singled out and separated from all other nations, to be the recipients of the rich blessings of God. It was that very fact which added so greatly to the enormity of their sins, for increased privileges entail increased responsibility, and increased responsibility not discharged involves increased guilt. "Hear this word that the Lord hath spoken against you, O children of Israel. . . . *You only* have I *known* of all the families of the earth: therefore I will punish you for all your iniquities" (Amos 3:1, 2). From the days of Moses until the time of Christ, a period of fifteen hundred years, God suffered all the heathen nations to walk in their own ways, leaving them to the corruptions and darkness of their own evil hearts. No other nation had God's Word, no other nation had a divinely appointed priesthood. Israel alone was favored with a written revelation from heaven.

And why *did* the Lord choose Israel to be His special favorites? The Chaldeans were more ancient, the Egyptians were far wiser, the Canaanites were more numerous; yet they were passed by. What, then, was the reason why the Lord singled out Israel? Certainly it was not because of any excellency in them, as the whole of their history shows. From Moses till Malachi they were a stiff-necked and hard-hearted people, unappreciative of divine favors, unresponsive to the divine will. It could not have been because of any goodness in them: it was a clear case of the divine sovereignty: "The Lord thy God hath chosen thee to be a special people unto himself, above all people that are upon the face of the earth. The Lord did not set his love upon you, nor choose you because ye were more in number than any people; for ye were the fewest of all people; but because the Lord loved you, and because He would keep the oath which He had sworn unto your fathers" (Deut. 7:6-8). The explanation of all God's acts and works was to be found in Himself—in the sovereignty of His will, and not anything in the creature.

The same principle of divine selection is as plainly and prominently revealed in the New Testament as in the Old. It was strikingly exemplified in connection with the birth of Christ. First, in the place where He was born. How startlingly the sovereignty of God was displayed in that momentous event. Jerusalem was not the Saviour's birthplace, nor was it one of the prominent towns of Palestine; instead, it was in a small village! The Holy Spirit has called particular attention to this point in one of the leading Messianic prophecies: "But thou, Bethlehem Ephratah, though thou be *little* among the thousands of Judah, *yet* out of *thee* shall he come forth unto me that is to be ruler in Israel" (Mic. 5:2). How different are God's thoughts and ways from man's! How He despises what we most esteem, and honors that which we look down upon. One of the most insignificant of all places was chosen by God to be the scene of the most stupendous of all events.

Again; the high sovereignty of God and the principle of His singular election appeared in those to whom He first communicated these glad tidings. To whom was it God sent the angels to announce the blessed fact of the Saviour's birth? Suppose Scripture had been silent upon the point: how differently would we have conceived of the matter. Would we not have naturally thought that the first ones to be informed of this glorious event had been the ecclesiastical and religious leaders in Israel? Surely the angels would deliver the message in the *temple*. But no, it was neither to the chief priests nor to the rulers they were sent, but unto the lowly shepherds keeping watch over their flocks in the fields. And again we say, how entirely different are God's thoughts and ways from man's. And what thus took place at the beginning of this Christian era was indicative of God's way throughout its entire course (see I Cor. 1:26-29).

Let us next observe that this same grand truth was emphasized by Christ Himself in His public ministry. Look at His first message in the Nazareth synagogue. "And there was delivered unto him the book of the prophet Esaias. And when he had opened the book, he found the place where it was written, the Spirit of the Lord is upon me, because he hath anointed me to preach the gospel to the poor [i.e., the poor in spirit, and not to wealthy Laodiceans]; he hath sent me to heal the broken-hearted [not the stout-hearted, but those sorrowing before God over their sins], to preach deliverance to the captives [and not to those who prate about their "free will"], and recovering of sight to the blind [not those who think they *can* see], and to set at liberty them that are bruised [not those who deem themselves whole], To preach the acceptable year of the Lord" (Luke 4:17-19).

The immediate sequel is indeed solemn: "And He began to say unto them, This day is this Scripture fulfilled in your ears. And all bear him witness, and wondered at the gracious words which proceeded out of his mouth" (vv. 21, 22). So far so good: they were pleased at His "gracious words"; yes, but would they tolerate the preaching of *sovereign grace?* "But I tell you of a truth, many widows were in Israel in the days of Elias, when the heaven was shut up three years and six months, when great famine was throughout the land; but unto *none of them* was Elias sent, save unto Sarepta, a city of Sidon, unto a woman that was a widow. And many lepers were in Israel in the time of Eliseus the prophet; and *none of them* was cleansed, saving Naaman the Syrian" (vv. 25-27). Here Christ pressed upon them the truth of God's high sovereignty, and *that* they could not endure: "And all they in the synagogue, when they heard these things, were filled with wrath; and rose up, and thrust Him out of the city" (vv. 28, 29) and mark it well that it was the respectable worshippers of the synagogue who thus gave vent to their hatred of this precious truth! Then let not the servant to-day be surprised if he meet with the same treatment as his Master.

His sermon at Nazareth was by no means the only time when the Lord Jesus proclaimed the doctrine of election. In Matthew 11 we hear Him saying, "I thank Thee, O Father, Lord of heaven and earth, because thou hast *hid* these things from the wise and prudent, and hast *revealed* them unto babes. Even so, Father: for so it seemed good in thy sight" (vv. 25, 26). To the seventy He said, "Notwithstanding, in this rejoice not, that the spirits are subject unto you; but rather rejoice, because your names are *written in heaven*" (Luke 10:20). In John 6 it will be found that Christ, in the hearing of the multitude, hesitated not to speak openly of a company whom the Father had "given to him" (vv. 37, 39). To the apostles He said, "Ye have not chosen me, but I have chosen you, and ordained you, that ye should go and bring forth fruit" (John 15:16): how shocked would the great majority of church-goers be today if they heard the Lord say such words unto His own! In John 17:9 we find Him saying, "I pray not for the world, but for them which thou hast given me."

As an interesting and instructive illustration of *the emphasis* which the Holy Spirit has placed upon this truth we would call attention to the fact that in the New Testament God's people are termed "believers" but twice, "Christians" only three times, whereas the designation *elect,* is found fourteen times and *saints* or separated ones sixty-two times! We would also point out that various other terms and phrases are used in the Scriptures to express election: "And the Lord said unto Moses, I will do this thing also that thou hast spoken: for thou hast found grace in my sight, and *I know thee* by name" (Exod. 33:17); "Before I formed thee in the belly *I knew thee,* and before thou camest forth out of the womb I sanctified thee" (Jer. 1:5; cf. Amos 3:2). "I speak not of you all: I know whom I have *chosen*" (John 13:18; cf. Matt. 20:16). "As many as were *ordained to* eternal life believed" (Acts 13:48). "God at the first did visit the Geniles, to *take out of them* a people for his name" (Acts 15:14). "Church of the firstborn, which are *written in heaven*" (Heb. 12:23).

This basic truth of election undergirds the whole scheme of salvation: that is why we are told "the *foundation of God* standeth sure, having this seal, the Lord *knoweth them that are his*" (II Tim. 2:19). Election is necessarily and clearly implied by some of the most important terms used in Scripture concerning various aspects of our salvation, yea, they are unintelligible without it. For example, every passage which makes mention of "redemption" presupposes eternal election. How so? Because "redemption" implies a previous possession: it is Christ *buying back* and delivering those who were God's at the beginning. Again; the words *"re*-generation" and *"re*-newing" necessarily signify a *previous* spiritual life—lost when we fell in Adam (I Cor. 15:22). So again the term *"re*-conciliation:" this not only denotes a state of alienation before the reconciliation, but a condition of harmony and amity, before the alienation. But enough: the truth of election has now been abundantly demonstrated from the Scriptures. If these many and indubitable proofs are not sufficient, it would be a waste of time to further multiply them.

Let it now be pointed out that this grand truth was definitely held and owned by our forefathers. First, a brief quotation from the ancient Creed of the Waldenses (eleventh century)—those renowned confessors of the Christian Faith in the dark ages, in the midst of the most terrible persecutions from the Papacy: "That God saves from corruption and damnation those whom He has chosen from the foundation of the world, not for any disposition, faith, or holiness that He foresaw in them, but of His mere mercy in Christ Jesus His Son; passing by all the rest, according to the irreprehensible reason of His own free will and justice." Here is one of the Thirty-nine Articles of the Church of England: "Predestination to life is the everlasting purpose of God whereby, before the foundations of the world were laid, He hath constantly decreed by His secret counsel to us to deliver from curse and condemnation those whom He had chosen in Christ out of mankind, and to bring by Christ to everlasting salvation as vessels made to honor."

This is from the Westminster Confession of Faith, subscribed to by all Presbyterian ministers, "By the decree of God, for the manifestation of His glory, some men and angels are predestinated unto everlasting life, and others foreordained to everlasting death. These angels and men, thus predestinated and foreordained, are particularly and unchangeably designed; and their number is so certain and definite, that it cannot be either increased or diminished." And here is the third article from the old Baptist (English) Confession: "By the decree of God, for the manifestation of His glory, some men and angels are predestinated or foreordained to eternal life through Jesus Christ, to the praise of His glorious grace; others being left to act in their sin to their just condemnation, to the praise of His glorious justice."

Let it not be thought that we have quoted from these human standards in order to bolster up our cause. Not so: the present writer, by divine grace, would believe and teach this grand truth if none before him had ever held it, and if every one in Christendom now repudiated it. But what has just been adduced is good evidence that we are here advancing no heretical novelty, but a doctrine proclaimed in the past in each section of the orthodox Church upon earth. We have also made the above quotations for the purpose of showing how far the present generation of professing Christians have *departed from the Faith* of those to whom under God, they owe their present religious liberties. Just as the modern denials of the divine inspiration and authority of the Scriptures (by the higher critics), the denial of immediate creation (by evolutionists), the denial of the deity of Christ (by unitarians), so the present denial of God's sovereign election and of man's spiritual impotency, are equally departures from the Faith of our forefathers, which was based upon the inerrant Word of God.

The truth of divine election has been most conspicuously exemplified in the history of Christendom. If it be true that during the last two thousand years of the Old Testament dispensation the spiritual blessings of God were largely confined to a single people, it is equally true that for the last five hundred years one section of the human race has been more signally favored by heaven than all the other sections put together. God's dealings with the Anglo-Saxons have been as singular and sovereign as His dealings with the Hebrews of old. Here is a fact which cannot be gainsaid, staring us all in the face, exposing the madness of those who deny this doctrine: for centuries past the vast majority of God's saints have been gathered out of the Anglo-Saxons! Thus, the very testimony of modern history unmistakably rebukes the folly of those who repudiate the teachings of God's Word on this subject, rendering their unbelief without excuse.

Tell us, ye who murmur against the divine sovereignty, why is it that the Anglo-Saxon race has been singled out for the enjoyment of far the greater part of God's spiritual blessings? Were there no other races equally needy? The Chinese practiced a nobler system of morality and were far more numerous: why, then, were they left for so long is gospel darkness? Why was the whole African continent left for many centuries before the Sun of Righteousness shone there again with healing in His wings? Why is America today a thousand times more favored than India, which has thrice the population? To all of these questions we are compelled to fall back upon the answer of our blessed Lord: "Even so, Father: for so it seemed good in thy sight." And just as with Israel of old there was an election within an election, so in Germany, in Great Britain, and in the U.S.A., certain particular places have been favored with one faithful minister after another, while other places have been cursed with false prophets. "I caused it to rain upon one city, and caused it not to rain upon another city" (Amos 4:7)—true now in a spiritual way.

Finally, the veracity of election is clearly evidenced by the fierce opposition of Satan against it. The Devil fights *truth,* not error. He vented His hatred against it when Christ proclaimed it (Luke 4:28, 29); he did so when Paul preached it (as Rom. 9:14, 19 more than hints); he did so when the Waldenses, the Reformers, and the Puritans heralded it—using the Papists as his tools to torment and murder thousands of them who confessed it. He still opposes it. Today he does so in his guise as an angel of light. He pretends to be very jealous of the honor of God's character, and declares that election makes Him out to be a monster of injustice. He uses the weapon of ridicule: if election be true, why preach the gospel? He seeks to intimidate: even if the doctrine of election be Scriptural, it is not wise to preach it. Thus, the teaching of Scripture, the testimony of history, and the opposition of Satan, all witness to the veracity of this doctrine.

5 Its Justice

Somewhat against our inclinations we have decided to depart again from the logical method of exposition, and instead of now proceeding with an orderly unfolding of this doctrine, we pause to deal with the principal objection which is made against the same. No sooner is the truth set forth of God's singling out certain of His creatures to be subjects of His special favors, than a general cry of protest is heard. No matter how much Scripture is quoted to the point nor how many plain passages be adduced in illustration and demonstration of it, the majority of those who profess to be Christians loudly object, alleging that such teaching slanders the divine character, making God guilty of gross injustice. It seems, then, that this difficulty should be met, that reply should be made to such a criticism of the doctrine, ere we proceed any further with our attempt to give a systematic setting forth of it.

In such an age as ours, when the principles of democracy, socialism and communism are so widely and warmly espoused, in a day when human authority and dominion are being more and more despised, when it is the common custom to "speak evil of dignities" (Jude 8), it is scarcely surprising that so many who make no pretension of bowing to the authority of Holy Writ should rebel against the concept of God's being partial. But it is unspeakably dreadful to find the great majority of those who profess to receive the Scriptures as divinely inspired, gnashing their teeth against its author when informed that He has sovereignly elected a people to be His peculiar treasure, and to hear them charging Him with being a hateful tyrant, a monster of cruelty. Yet such blasphemies only go to show that "the carnal mind *is* enmity against God."

It is not because we have any hope of converting such rebels from

the error of their ways that we feel constrained to take up the present
aspect of our subject—though it may please God in His infinite grace
to use these feeble lines to the enlightening and convicting of a few of
them. No, rather is it that some of God's dear people are disturbed by
these ravings of His enemies, and know not how to answer in their
own minds this objection, that if God makes a sovereign selection
from among His creatures and predestinates them to blessings which
He withholds from countless millions of their fellows, then such
partiality makes Him guilty of treating the latter unjustly. And yet the
fact stares them in the face on every hand, both in creation and
providence, that God distributes His mercies most *unevenly*. There is
no equality in His bestowments either in physical health and strength,
mental capacities, social status, or the comforts of this life. Why, then,
should we be staggered when we learn that His *spiritual* blessings are
distributed unevenly?

Before proceeding further it should be pointed out that the design
of every false scheme and system of religion is to depict the character
of God in such a way that it is agreeable to the tastes of the *carnal*
heart, acceptable to depraved human nature. And *that* can only be
done by a species of misrepresentation: the ignoring of those of His
prerogatives and perfections which are objectionable, and the dispro-
portionate emphasizing of those of His attributes which appeal to
their selfishness—such as His love, mercy, and long-sufferance. But let
the character of God be faithfully presented as it is actually portrayed
in the Scriptures—in the *Old Testament* as well as the New—and nine
out of every ten of church-goers will frankly state that they find it
"impossible to love Him." The plain fact is, dear reader, that to the
present generation the Most High of Holy Writ is "the unknown God."

It is just because people today are so ignorant of the divine
character and so lacking in godly fear, that they are quite in the dark
as to the nature and glory of divine justice, presuming to arraign it.
This is an age of blatant irreverence, wherein lumps of animate clay
dare to prescribe what the Almighty ought and ought not to do. Our
forefathers sowed the wind, and today their children are reaping the
whirlwind. The "divine rights of kings" was scoffed at and tabooed by
the sires, and now their offspring repudiate the "divine rights of the
King of kings." Unless the supposed "rights" of the creature are
"respected," then our moderns have no respect for the Creator, and if
His high sovereignty and absolute dominion over all be insisted upon,
they hesitate not to vomit forth their condemnation of Him. And,
"evil communications corrupt good manners" (I Cor. 15:33)! God's
own people are in danger of being infected by the poisonous gas which
now fills the air of the religious world.

Not only is the miasmic atmosphere obtaining in most of the "churches" a serious menace to the Christian, but there is in each of us a serious tendency to humanize God: viewing His perfections through our own intellectual lenses instead of through the glass of Scripture, interpreting His attributes by human qualities. It was of this very thing that God complained of old when He said, "Thou thoughtest that I was altogether such an one as thyself" (Ps. 50:21), which is a solemn warning for us to take to heart. What we mean is this: when we read of God's mercy or righteousness we are very apt to think of them according to the qualities of *man's* mercy and justice. But this is a serious mistake. The Almighty is not to be measured by any human standard: He is so infinitely above us that any comparison is utterly impossible, and therefore it is the height of madness for any finite creature to sit in judgment upon the ways of Jehovah.

Again; we need to be much on our guard against the folly of making invidious distinctions between the divine perfections. For example, it is quite wrong for us to suppose that God is more glorious in His grace and mercy than He is in His power and majesty. But this mistake is often made. How many are more thankful unto God for blessing them with health than they are for His bestowing the gospel upon them: but does it therefore follow that God's goodness in giving material things is greater than His goodness in bestowing spiritual blessings? Certainly not. Scripture often speaks of God's wisdom and power being manifested in creation, but where are we told of His grace and mercy in making the world? Inasmuch as men commonly fail to glorify God for His wisdom and power, does it thence follow that He is not to be so much adored for them? Beware of extolling one of the divine perfections above another.

What is justice? It is treating each person equitably and fairly, giving to him his due. Divine justice is simply doing that which is right. But this raises the question, *What* is due unto the creature? what is it that God *ought* to bestow upon him? Ah, my friend, every sober-minded person will at once object to the introduction of the word "ought" in such a connection. And rightly so. The Creator is under no obligation whatever unto the works of His own hands. He alone has the right to decide whether such and such a creature should exist at all. He alone has the prerogative to determine the nature, status, and destiny of that creature; whether it shall be an animal, a man, or an angel; whether it shall be endowed with a soul and subsist forever, or be without a soul and endure only for a brief time; whether it shall be a vessel unto honor and taken into communion with Himself, or a vessel unto dishonor which is rejected by Him.

As the great Creator possessed perfect freedom to create or not

create, to bring into existence whatever creatures He pleased (and a
visit to the zoo will show He has created some which strike the
beholder as exceedingly queer ones); and therefore He has the unques-
tionable right to decree concerning them as He pleases. The justice of
God in election and preterition, then, is grounded upon His high
sovereignty. The dependence of all creatures upon Him is entire. His
proprietorship of all creatures is indisputable. His dominion over all
creatures is absolute. Let these facts be established from Scripture—
and their complete demonstration therefrom is a very simple matter—
and where is the creature who can with the slightest propriety say
unto the Lord most high "What doest *Thou*?" Instead of the Creator
being under any obligation to His creature, it is the creature who is
under binding obligations to the One who gave it existence and now
sustains its very life.

God has the absolute right to do as He pleases with the creatures of
His own hand: "Hath not the potter power over the clay; of the same
lump to make one vessel unto honor and another unto dishonor?"
(Rom. 9:21) is His own assertion. Therefore He may give to one and
withhold from another, bestow five talents on one and only a single
talent on another, without any imputation of injustice. If He may *give*
grace and glory to whom He will without such a charge, then He may
also *decree to do so* without any such charge. Are men chargeable
with injustice when they choose their own favorites, friends, companions, and confidents? Then obviously there is no injustice in *God's*
choosing whom He will to bestow His special favors upon, to indulge
with communion with Himself now and to dwell with Him for all
eternity. Is a man free to make selection of the woman which he
desires for his wife? and does he in anywise *wrong* the other women
whom he passes by? Then is the great God *less free* to make selection
of those who constitute the spouse of His Son? Shame, shame, upon
those who would ascribe less freedom to the Creator than to the
creature.

Upon a little reflection it should be evident to all right-minded
people that there is no parity between human and divine justice:
human justice requires that we should give each of our fellows his due,
wheras no creature is due *anything* from God, not even what He is
pleased to sovereignly give him. In his most reverent discussion of the
nature of God's attributes W. Twisse (moderator of the Westminister
Assembly) pointed out that if human justice be of the same nature with
divine justice then it necessarily follows: first, that which is just in
man is just with God. Second, that it must be after the same manner
just: as human justice consists in subjection and obedience to God's
law, so God Himself must be under obligation to His own Law. Third,

as a man is *under obligation* to be just, so God is under obligation to be just, and therefore as Saul sinned and acted unjustly in slaying the priests, so had God been unjust in doing the like.

Unless the perversity of their hearts blinded their judgment men would readily perceive that divine *justice* must necessarily be of quite another order and character than human, yea, as different from and superior to it as divine *love* is from human. All are agreed that a man acts unjustly, that he sins, if he suffers his brother to transgress when it lies in his power to keep him from so doing. Then if divine justice were the same in kind, though superior in degree, it would necessarily follow that God sins every time He allows one of His creatures to transgress, for most certainly He has the power to prevent it; yea, and can exercise that power without destroying the liberty of the creature: "I also *withheld thee from* sinning against Me; therefore suffered I thee not to touch her" (Gen. 20:6). Cease, then, ye rebels from arraigning the Most High, and attempting to measure *His* justice by your petty tape-lines—as well seek to fathom His wisdom or define His power, as comprehend His inscrutable justice. "Clouds and darkness are round about him," and this be it noted, is expressly said in connection with: "righteousness [justice] and judgment are the habitation of His *throne*" (Ps. 97:2).

Lest some of our readers demur at our quoting from such a high Calvinist as Mr. Twisse, we append the following from the milder James Ussher. "What is the divine justice? It is an essential property of God, whereby He is infinitely just in himself, of himself, for, from, and by Himself, and none other: 'For the righteous Lord loveth righteousness' (Ps. 11:7). What is the *rule* of His justice? Answer: His own *free will,* and nothing else: for whatsoever He willeth is just, and because He willeth it therefore it *is* just; not because it is just, therefore He willeth it (Eph. 1:11; Ps. 115:3)." Such men as these were conscious of their ignorance, and therefore they cried unto Heaven for instruction, and God was pleased to grant them clear vision. But the pride-inflated pharisees of our day think they can *already* see, and therefore feel no need of Divine illumination: consequently they remain blind (John 9:40, 41).

So again that justly renowned teacher W. Perkins: "We must not think that God doeth a thing because it is good and right, but rather is the thing good and right because *God* willeth and worketh it. Examples hereof we have in the Word. God commanded Abimelech to deliver Sarah to Abraham, or else He would destroy him and all his household (Gen. 20:7). To man's reason that might seem unjust, for why should Abimelech's servants be punished for their master's fault? So again Achan sinned, and all the house of Israel were penalized for it

(Josh. 7). David numbered the people, and the whole nation was smitten by a plague (II Sam. 24). All these to *man's reason* may seem unequal; yet being the works of *God* we must with all reverence judge them most just and holy." Alas, how little of this humility and reverence is manifested in the churches to-day! How ready is the present generation to criticize and condemn whatever of God's ways and works suit them not!

So far from the truth are most of those who are now looked up to as "the champions of orthodoxy," that even they are often guilty of turning things upside down, or putting the cart in front of the horse. It is commonly assumed by them that God Himself is under law, that He is under a moral constraint to do what he does, so that He cannot do otherwise. Others wrap this up in more sophisticated terms, insisting that it is His own *nature* which regulates all His actions. But this is merely an artful subterfuge. Is it by a necessity of His nature or by the free exercise of His sovereignty that He bestows favor upon His creatures? Let Scripture answer: "Therefore hath he mercy on whom he *will* have mercy, and whom he *will* he hardeneth" (Rom. 9:18). Why, my reader, if God's nature obliged Him to show saving mercy to *any*, then by parity of reason it would oblige Him to show mercy to *all*, and thus bring every fallen creature to repentance, faith, and obedience. But enough of this nonsense.

Let us now approach this aspect of our subject from an entirely different angle. How could there possibly be any injustice in God's electing those whom He did, when had He *not* done so *all* had inevitably perished, angels and men alike? This is neither an invention nor an inference of ours, for Scripture itself expressly declares "*Except* the Lord of Sabbaoth had left us a seed, *we* had been as Sodom" (Rom. 9:29). Not one of God's rational creatures, either celestial or earthly, had ever been eternally and effectually saved apart from the grave of divine *election*. Though both angels and men were created in a state of perfect holiness, yet they were mutable creatures, liable to change and fall. Yea, inasmuch as their continuance in holiness was dependent upon the exercise of their own wills, unless God was pleased to supernaturally preserve them, their fall was certain.

"Behold, he put no trust in his servants; and his *angels* he charged with *folly*" (Job 4:18). The angels were perfectly holy, yet if God gave them no other assistance than that with which He had capacitated them at their creation, then no "trust" or reliance was to be placed in them, or their standing. If they were holy to-day, they were liable to sin to-morrow. If God but sent them on an errand to this world, they might fall before they returned to Heaven. The "folly" which God imputes to them in the above passage is their creature *mutability:* for them to maintain their holiness unchangeably to eternity, without the danger of losing the same, was utterly beyond their *creature* endowment. Therefore, for them to be immutably preserved is a grace which issues from another and higher spring than the covenant of works or creation endowment, namely, that of election grace, super-creation grace.

It was meet that God should, from the beginning, make manifest the infinite gulf which divides the creature from the Creator. God alone is *immutable,* without variableness or shadow of turning. Fitting was it, then, that God should *withdraw* His preserving hand from those whom He had created upright, so that it might appear that the highest creature of all (Satan, "the anointed cherub" Ezek. 28:14) *was mutable,* and would inevitably fall into sin when left to the exercise of his own free will. Of God alone can it be predicated that He "cannot be tempted with evil" (James 1:13). The creature, though holy, may be tempted to sin, fall, and be irretrievably lost. The fall of Satan, then, made way for evidencing the more plainly the absolute *necessity* of electing grace—the imparting to the creature the image of God's own immutable holiness.

Because of the mutability of the creature-state God foresaw that if all His creatures were left to the conduct of their own wills, they were in a continual hazard of falling. He, therefore, made an election of grace to remove all hazard from the case of His chosen ones. This we know from what is revealed of their history. Jude tells us of "the angels which kept not their first estate, but left their own habitation" (v. 6), and the remainder of them would, sooner or later, have done so too, if left to the mutability of their own wills. So also it proved with Adam and Eve: both of them evidenced the mutability of their wills by apostatizing. Accordingly, God foreseeing all of this from the beginning, made a "reserve" (Rom. 11:4—explained in v. 5 as "election), determining to have a remnant who should be blessed of Him and who would everlastingly bless Him in return. Election and preserving grace are never to be severed.

We have thus far pointed out, first that divine justice is of an entirely different order and character than human justice; second that divine justice is grounded upon God's sovereign dominion over all the works of His hands, being the exercise of His own imperial will. Third, that nothing whatever is due the creature from the Creator, not even what He is pleased to give, and that so far from God's being under any obligation to it, it is under lasting obligations to Him. Fourth, that whatever God wills and works is right and must be reverently submitted to, yea, adored by us. Fifth, that it is impossible to charge God with injustice in His electing certain ones to be the objects of His amazing grace, since that apart from it, *all* had eternally perished. Let us now descend to a lower and simpler level, and contemplate God's election in connection with the human race fallen in Adam.

If there was no injustice in God's making a choice of some unto special favor and eternal blessing as He viewed His creatures in the glass of His purpose to *create,* then certainly there could be no injustice in His determining to show them mercy as He foreviewed them among the mass of Adam's *ruined* race; for if a sinless creature has no claim whatever upon its maker, being entirely dependent upon His charity, then most assuredly a fallen creature is entitled to nothing good at the hands of its offended judge. And this is the angle from which we must now view our subject. Fallen man is a criminal, an outlaw and if bare justice is to be meted out to him, then he must be left to receive the due reward of his iniquities, and *that* can mean nothing less than eternal punishment, for his transgressions have incurred infinite guilt.

Before enlarging upon what has just been said, it also needs to be pointed out that if the only hope for a *holy* creature lies in God's electing grace, then doubly is this the case with one that is *unholy,* totally depraved. If an holy angel was in constant danger, incapable of maintaining his purity, because of the mutability of his nature and the fickleness of his will, what shall be said of an *unholy* creature? Why, nothing less than this: fallen man has a nature that is confirmed in evil, and therefore his will no longer has any power to turn unto that which is spiritual, yea, it is inveterately steeled against God; hence, his case is utterly and eternally hopeless, unless God, in His sovereign grace, is pleased to save him *from himself.*

Preachers may prate all they please about man's inherent powers, the freedom of his will, and his capacity for good, yet it is useless and madness to ignore the solemn fact of the fall. The difference and disadvantage between our case and that of unfallen Adam's can scarcely be conceived. Instead of a perfect holiness possessing and inclining our minds and wills, as it did his, there is no such vital principle left in our hearts. Instead, there is a thorough disability unto what is spiritual and holy, yea, contrary enmity and opposition thereto. "Men err, not knowing the power of original sin, nor the depth of corruption that is in their own hearts. The will of man now is the prime and proper seat of sin: the throne thereof is seated therein" (Thos. Goodwin). Outward helps and aids are of no account, for nothing short of a new creation is of any avail.

No matter what instruction fallen men receive, what inducements be offered them, the Ethiopian cannot change his skin. Neither light, conviction, nor the general operations of the Holy Spirit, are of any avail, unless God over and above them impart a new principle of holiness to the heart. This has been clearly and fully demonstrated under both Law and Gospel. Read Exodus 20 and Deuteronomy 5 and see the wondrous and awe-inspiring manifestation of Himself which God granted unto Israel at Sinai: did *that* change their hearts and incline their wills to obey Him? Then read through the four Gospels and behold the incarnate Son of God dwelling in the midst of men, not as a judge, but as a benefactor—going about doing good, feeding the hungry, healing the sick, proclaiming the gospel: did *that* melt their hearts and win them to God? No, they hated and crucified Him.

Behold, then, the case of fallen mankind: alienated from the life of God, dead in trespasses and sins, with no heart, no will for spiritual things. In themselves their case is desperate, irretrievable, hopeless. Apart from divine election none would, none could, ever be saved. Election means that God was pleased to reserve a remnant, so that the entire race of Adam should not eternally perish. And *what thanks* does He receive for this? None at all, save from those who have their sin-blinded eyes opened to perceive the inexpressible blessedness of such a fact. Thanks, no; instead, the vast majority even of those in professing Christendom when they hear of this truth, ignorant of their own interests and of the ways of God, quarrel at His election, revile Him for the same, charge Him with gross injustice, and accuse Him of being a merciless tyrant.

Now the great God stands in no need of any defense from us: in due time He will effectually close the mouth of every rebel. But we must address a few more remarks to those believers who are disturbed by such as insist so loudly that God is guilty of injustice when He sovereignly elects some. First, then, we ask these slanderers of Jehovah to *make good* their charge. The burden of proof falls upon them to do so. They affirm that an electing God is unjust, then let them demonstrate *how* such be the case. They cannot. In order to do so they must show that lawbreakers merit something good at the hands of the lawgiver. They must show that the King of kings is morally obliged to smile upon those who have blasphemed His name, desecrated His sabbaths, slighted His Word, reviled His servants, and above all, despised and rejected His Son.

"Is there one man in the whole world who would have the impertinence to say that he merits anything of his Maker? If so, be it known unto you that he shall have all he merits; and his reward will be the flames of hell forever, for *that* is the utmost that any man ever *merited* of God. God is in no debt to man, and at the last great day every man shall have as much love, as much pity, and as much goodness, as he deserves. Even the lost in hell shall have all they deserve; ay, and woe worth the day for them when they shall have the wrath of God, which will be the summit of their deservings. If God gives to every man as much as he merits, is He therefore to be accused of injustice because He gives to some infinitely more than they merit?" (C. H. Spurgeon). How many who now speak of him eulogistically, and refer to him as "beloved Spurgeon," would gnash their teeth and execrate him were they to hear his faithful and plain-spoken preaching.

Second, we would inform these detractors of God that His *salvation* is not a matter of justice, but *of pure grace,* and grace is something that can be claimed by none. Where is the injustice if any one does as he wills with his own? If I am free to disburse my charity as I see fit, shall God be conceded less freedom to bestow His gifts upon whom He pleases! God is indebted to none, and therefore if He grants His favors in a sovereign way who can complain. If God passes thee by, He has not injured thee; but if He enriches thee, then art thou a debtor to His grace, and then wilt thou cease prating about His justice and injustice, and wilt gladly join with those who astonishingly exclaim, "He hath not dealt with us after our sins; nor rewarded us according to our iniquities" (Ps. 103:10). Salvation is God's free gift, and therefore He bestows it on whom He pleases.

Third, we would ask these haughty creatures, to whom has God ever *refused* His mercy when it was sincerely and penitently sought? Does He not freely proclaim the gospel to every creature? Does not His Word bid *all* men to throw down the weapons of their warfare against Him and come to Christ for pardon? Does He not promise to blot out your iniquities if you will turn unto Him in the way of His appointing? If you refuse to do so, if you are so thoroughly in love with sin, so wedded to your lusts that you are determined to destroy your own soul, then who is to blame? Most certainly God is not. His gospel promises are reliable, and anyone is at liberty to prove them for himself. If he does so, if he renounces sin and puts his trust in Christ, then he will discover for himself that he is one of God's chosen ones. On the other hand, if he deliberately spurns the gospel and rejects the Saviour then his blood is on his own head.

This leads us to ask, fourth, You say it is unjust that some should be lost while others are saved: but *who* makes them to be lost that are lost? Whom has God ever caused to sin?—rather doth He warn and exhort against it. Whom has the Holy Spirit ever prompted to a wrong action?—rather doth He uniformly incline against evil. Where do the Scriptures bolster up any in his wickedness?—rather do they constantly condemn it in all its forms. Then is God unjust if He condemns those who wilfully disobey Him? Is He unrighteous if He punishes those who defiantly disregard His danger-signals and expostulations?

Assuredly not. To each such one God will yet say, "Thou hast destroyed thyself" (Hos. 13:9). It is the creature who commits moral suicide. It is the creature who breaks through every restraint and hurls himself into the precipice of eternal woe. In the last great day it will appear that God is *justified* when He speaks, and *clear* when He judges (Ps. 51:4).

Election is the taking of one and leaving of another, and implies freedom on the part of the elector to choose or refuse. Hence the choosing of one does no injury to the other which is not chosen. If I select one out of a hundred men to a position of honor and profit, I do no injury to the ninety and nine not elected. If I take two from a score of ragged and hungry children, and adopt them as my son and daughter, feed and clothe, house and educate them, I do them an immense benefit; but while disbursing my bounty as I choose and making two happy, I do no injury to the eighteen who are left. True, they remain ragged, ill-fed, and uneducated, yet they are in no worse condition for my having shown favor to their late companions—they only continue precisely in the situation in which they were.

Again; if among ten convicts justly sentenced to death, the king of England was pleased to choose five to be the recipients of his sovereign mercy, pardoned and released them, they would owe their very lives to his royal favor; nevertheless, by extending kindness to them, no injury is done to the other five: they are left to suffer the righteous penalty of the law, due to them for their transgressions. They only suffer what they *would* have suffered if the king's mercy had *not* been extended toward their fellows. Who, then, can fail to see that it would be a misuse of terms, a grievous slander of the king, to charge him with injustice, because he was pleased to exercise his royal prerogative and evidence his favor in this discriminating manner.

Our Saviour definitely expressed *this* idea of election when He said, "Then shall two be in the field; the one shall be taken, and the other left" (Matt. 24:40). If both had been "left," then both had perished: hence the "taking" of the one did no injury to his fellow. "Two women shall be grinding at the mill; the one shall be taken, and the other left" (Matt. 24:41). The taking of the one was a great favor to her, but the leaving of her companion did her no wrong. Divine election, then, is a choice to favor from among those who have *no claims* upon God. It therefore does no injustice to them that are passed by, for they only continue as and where they were, and as and where they would have been if none had been taken from among them. In the exercise of His electing grace God has mercy upon whom He will have mercy, and in the bestowment of His favor He does what He wills with His own.

It is not difficult to perceive the ground upon which the false reasoning of God's detractors rests: behind all the murmurings of objectors against the Divine justice lies the concept that God is *under obligation* to provide salvation for all His fallen creatures. But such reasoning (?) fails to see that if such a contention were valid, then *no thanks* could be returned to God. How could we praise Him for redeeming those whom He was bound to redeem? If salvation be a *debt* which God owes man for allowing him to fall, then salvation cannot be a matter of *mercy*. But we must not expect that those whose eyes are blinded by pride should understand anything of the infinite demerits of sin, of their own utter unworthiness and vileness; and therefore it is impossible that they should form any true concept of Divine grace, and perceive that when *grace* is exercised it is necessarily exercised in a *sovereign* manner.

But after all that has been pointed out above some will be ready to sneeringly ask, "Does not the Bible declare that God is 'no respecter of persons': how then can He make a selection from among men?" The calumniators of Divine predestination suppose that either the Scriptures are inconsistent with themselves, or that in His election God has regard to merits. Let us first quote from Calvin: "The Scripture denies that God is a respecter of persons, in a different sense from that in which *they* understand it; for by the word *person* it signifies not a man, but those things in a man which, being conspicuous to the eyes, usually conciliate favor, honor, and dignity, or attract hatred, contempt, and disgrace. Such are riches, power, nobility, magistracy, country, elegance of form, on the one hand; and on the other hand, poverty, necessity, ignoble birth, slovenliness, contempt, and the like. Thus Peter and Paul declare that God is not a respecter of persons because He makes no difference between the Jew and Greek, to reject one and receive the other, merely on account of his nation (Acts 10:34, Rom. 2:11). So James uses the same language when he asserts that God in His judgment pays no regard to riches (2:5).

"There will, therefore, be no contradiction in our affirming, that according to the good pleasures of His will, God chooses whom He will as His children, irrespective of all merit, while He rejects and reprobates others. Yet, for the sake of further satisfaction, the matter may be explained in the following manner. They ask how it happens, that of two persons distinguished from each other by no merit, God, in His election, leaves one and takes another. I, on the other hand, ask them, whether they suppose him that is taken to possess any thing that can *attract* the favor of God? If they confess that he has not, as indeed they must, it will follow, that God looks not at man, but derives His motive to favor him from His own goodness. God's election of one man, therefore, while He rejects another, proceeds not from any respect of man, but solely from His own mercy; which may freely display and exert itself wherever and whenever it pleases."

To have "respect of persons" is to regard and treat them differently on account of some supposed or real difference in them or their circumstances, which is no warrantable ground or reason for such preferential regard and treatment. This character of a respecter of persons belongs rather to one who examines and rewards others according to their characters and works. Thus, for a judge to justify and reward one rather than another because he is rich and the other poor, or because he has given him a bribe, or is a near relative or an intimate friend, while the character and conduct of the other is more upright and his cause more just. But such a denomination is inapplicable to a disburser of charity, who is granting his favors and bestowing freely undeserved gifts to one rather than to another, doing so without any consideration of personal merit. The benefactor has a perfect right to do what he will with his own, and those who are neglected by him have no valid ground for complaint.

Even if this expression be taken in its more popular acceptation, nothing so strikingly evidences that God *is* "no respecter of persons" than *the character* of the ones He has chosen. When the angels sinned and fell God provided no Saviour for them, yet when the human race sinned and fell a Saviour was provided for many of them. Let the unfriendly critic carefully weigh this fact: had God been a "respecter of persons" would He not have selected the angels and passed by men? The fact that He did the very reverse clears Him of this calumny. Take again that nation which God chose to be the recipients of earthly and temporal favors above all others during the last two thousand years of Old Testament history. What sort of characters were they? Why, an unappreciative and murmuring, stiffnecked and hardhearted, rebellious and impenitent people, from the beginning of their history until the end. Had God been a respecter of persons He surely had never singled out *the Jews* for such favor and blessing!

The very character, then, of those whom God chooses refutes this silly objection. The same is equally apparent in the New Testament. "Hath not God chosen the poor of this world" (James 2:5): blessed be His name, that it is so, for had He chosen the wealthy it had fared ill with many of us, had it not? God did not pick out magnates and millionaires, financiers and bankers, to be objects of His grace. Nor are those of royal blood or the peers of the realm, the wise, the gifted, the influential of this world, for few among *them* have their names written in the Lamb's Book of Life. No, it is the despised, the weak, the base, the non-entities of this world, whom God has chosen (I Cor.

1:26-29), and this, in order that "no flesh should glory in his presence." Pharisees passed by and publicans and harlots brought in! "Jacob have I loved": and what was there in him *to* love!—and echo still asks "what?" Had God been "a respecter of persons" He certainly had never chosen worthless *me!*

6 Its Nature

It has been well said that, "The reason why any one believes in election is, that he finds it in the Bible. No man could ever imagine such a doctrine—for it is, in itself, contrary to the thinkings and the wishes of the human heart. Every one, at first, opposes the doctrine, and it is only after many struggles, under the working of the Spirit of God, that we are made to receive it. A perfect acquiescence in this doctrine—an absolute lying still, in adoring wonder, at the footstool of God's sovereignty, is the last attainment of the sanctified soul in this life, as it is the beginning of Heaven. The reason why any one believes in election is just this, and *only* this, that *God* has made it known. Had the Bible been a counterfeit it never could have contained the doctrine of election, for men are too averse to such a thought to give it expression, much more to give it prominence." (G. S. Bishop).

Thus far, in our exposition of this blessed truth, we have shown that the *source* of election is the will of God, for nothing exists or can exist apart from that. Next, we have seen, that the *Grand Original* of election is the man Christ Jesus, who was ordained unto union with the second person in the Godhead. Then, in order to clear the way for a more detailed examination of this truth as it bears upon us, we demonstrated the *verity* and then the *justice* of it, seeking to remove from the minds of Christian readers the defiling and disturbing effects of the principal objection which is made against divine election by its enemies. And now we shall endeavor to point out the principal elements which enter into election.

First, it is *an act by God.* True it is that there comes a day when each of the elect chooses God for his absolute Lord and supreme Good, but this is the effect and in no sense the cause of the former. Our choosing of Him is in time, His choosing of us was before time began; and certain it is that unless He had first chosen us, we would never choose Him at all. God, who is a sovereign being, does whatsoever He pleases both in heaven and in earth, having an absolute right to do as He will with His own creatures, and therefore did He choose a certain number of human beings to be His people, His children, His peculiar treasure. Having done this, it is called "election of God" (I Thess. 1:4), for He is the efficient cause of it; and the persons chosen are denominated "His own elect" (Luke 18:7; cf. Rom. 8:33).

This choice of God's is an *absolute* one, being entirely gratuitous, depending on nothing whatever outside of Himself. God elected the ones He did simply because He chose to do so: from no good, merit, or attraction in the creature, and from no foreseen merit or attraction to *be* in the creature. God is absolutely self-sufficient, and therefore He never goes outside of Himself to find a reason for any thing that He does. He cannot be swayed by the works of His own hand. No, He is the One who sways them, as He alone is the One who gave them existence. "In Him we live, and are moved [Greek], and have our being." It was, then, simply out of the spontaneous goodness of His own volition that God singled out from the mass of those He purposed to create a people who should show forth His praises for all eternity, to the glory of His sovereign grace forever and ever.

This choice of God's is an *unchangeable* one. Necessarily so, for it is not founded upon anything in the creature, or grounded upon anything outside of Himself. It is before everything, even before His "foreknowledge." God does not decree because He foreknows, but He foreknows because He has infallibly and irrevocably fixed it—otherwise He would merely guess it. But since He foreknows it, then He does not guess—it is certain; and if certain, then He must have fixed it. Election being the act of God, it is *forever,* for whatever He does in a way of special grace, is irreversible and unalterable. Men may choose some to be their favorites and friends for a while, and then change their minds and choose others in their room. But God does not act such a part: He is of one mind, and none can turn Him; His purpose according to election stands firm, sure, unalterable (Rom. 9:11; II Tim 2:19).

Second, God's act of election is *made in Christ:* "according as he hath chosen us in him" (Eph. 1:4). Election does not find men in Christ, but *puts* them there. It gives them a being in Christ and union to Him, which is the foundation of their manifestative being in Him at conversion. In the infinite mind of God, He willed to love a company of Adam's posterity with an immutable love, and out of the love wherewith He loves them, He chose them in Christ. By this act in His infinite mind, God gave them being and blessedness in Christ from everlasting. Though, while all fell in Adam, yet all did not fall alike.

The non-elect fell so as to be damned, they being left to perish in their sins, because they had no relation to Christ—He was not related to them as the Mediator of union with God.

The non-elect had their all in Adam, their natural head. But the elect had all spiritual blessing bestowed upon them in Christ, their gracious and glorious Head (Eph. 1:3). They could not lose these, because they were secured for them in Christ. God had chosen them as His own: He their God, they His people; He their Father, they His children. He gave them to Christ to be His brethren, His companions, His bride, His partners in all His communicable grace and glory. On the foresight of their fall in Adam, and what would be the effects thereof, the Father proposed to raise them up from the ruins of the fall, upon the consideration of His Son's undertaking to perform all righteousness for them, and as their Surety, bear all their sins in His own body on the tree, making His soul an offering for sin. To carry all of this unto execution, the beloved Son became incarnate.

It was to this that the Lord Jesus referred in His high priestly prayer, when He said to the Father "I have manifested thy name unto the men which thou gavest me out of the world: thine they were, and thou gavest them me" (John 17:6). He was alluding to the whole election of grace. They were the objects of the Father's delight: His jewels, His portion; and in Christ's eyes they were what the Father beheld them to be. How highly, then, did the Father esteem the Mediator, or He would never have bestowed His elect on Him and committed them all to His care and management! And how highly did Christ value this love-gift of the Father's, or He would not have undertaken their salvation at such tremendous cost to Himself! Now the giving of the elect to Christ was a different act, a distinct act from that of their election. The elect were first the Father's by election, who singled out the persons; and then He bestowed them upon Christ as His love-gift: "Thine they were [by election] and thou gavest them me"—in the same way that grace is said to be given us in Christ Jesus before the world began (II Tim. 1:9).

Third, this act of God was irrespective of and *anterior to any foresight of the entrance of sin.* We have somewhat anticipated this branch of our subject, yet as it is one upon which very few today are clear, and one we deem of considerable importance, we propose to give it separate consideration. The particular point which we are now to ponder is, as to whether His people were viewed by God, in His act of election, as fallen or unfallen; as in the corrupt mass through their defection in Adam, or in the pure mass of creaturehood, as to be created. Those who took the former view are known as Sublapsarians; those who took the latter as Supralapsarians, and in the past this question was debated considerably between high and low Calvinists.

This writer unhesitatingly (after prolonged study) takes the Supra-lapsarian position, though he is well aware that few indeed will be ready to follow him.

Sin having drawn a veil over the greatest of all the divine mysteries of grace—that of the divine incarnation alone excepted—renders our present task the more difficult. It is much easier for us to apprehend our misery, and our redemption from it—by the incarnation, obedi-ence, and sacrifice of the Son of God—than it is for us to conceive of the *original* glory, excellency, purity, and dignity of the Church of Christ, as the eternal object of God's thoughts, counsels, and purpose. Nevertheless, if we adhere closely to the Holy Scriptures, it is evident (to the writer, at least) that God's people had a super-creation and spiritual union with Christ before ever they had a creature and natural union with Adam; that they were blessed with all spiritual blessings in the heavenlies in Christ (Eph. 1:3), before they fell in Adam and became subject to all the evils of the curse. First, we will summarize the reasons given by John Gill in support of this.

God's decree of election is to be divided into *two* parts or degrees, namely, His purpose concerning the end and His purpose concerning the means. The first part has to do with the purpose of God in Himself, in which He determined to have an elect people and that for His own glory. The second part has to do with the actual *execution of* the first, by fixing upon the means whereby the end shall be accom-plished. These two parts in the divine decree are neither to be severed nor confounded, but considered distinctly. God's purpose concerning the end means that He ordained a certain people to be the recipients of His special favor, for the glorifying of His sovereign goodness and grace. His purpose concerning the means signifies that He determined to create that people, permit them to fall, and to recover them out of it by Christ's redemption and the Spirit's sanctification. These are not to be regarded as separate decrees, but as component parts and degrees of one purpose. There is an *order* in the divine counsels as real and definite as Genesis 1 shows there was in connection with creation.

As the purpose of the *end* is first in view (in the order of nature) before the determination of the *means,* therefore what is first in intention is last in execution. Now as the glory of God is the last in execution, it necessarily follows that it was first in intention. Where-fore men must be considered in the Divine purpose concerning the end as neither yet created nor fallen, since both their creation and the permission of sin belong to God's counsel concerning the *means.* Is it not obvious that if God first decreed to create men and suffer them to fall, and then out of the fallen mass chose some to grace and glory, that He purposed to create men *without* any end in view? And is not that charging God with what a wise man would never do, for when man determines to do a thing he proposes an end (say the building of an house) and then fixes on ways and means to bring about the end. Can it be thought for a moment that the Omniscient One should act otherwise?

The above distinction between the divine purpose concerning the end and God's appointing of means to secure that end, is clearly borne out by Scripture. For example, "For it became him, for whom are all things, and by whom are all things, in bringing many sons unto glory, to make the captain of their salvation perfect through sufferings" (Heb. 2:10). Here is first the decree concerning the *end*: God ordained His many sons "unto glory"; in His purpose of the *means* God ordained that the captain of their salvation should be made perfect "through sufferings." In like manner was it in connection with Christ Himself. "The Lord said unto my Lord, Sit thou at my right hand" (Ps. 110:1). God decreed that the Mediator should have this high honor conferred upon Him, yet in order thereto it was ordained that "He shall drink of the brook in the way" (v. 7): God, then, decreed that the Redeemer should drink of the fulness of those pleasures which are at His right hand for evermore (Ps. 16:11), but before that He must drain the bitter cup of anguish. So it is with His people: Canaan is their destined portion, but the wilderness is appointed as that through which they shall pass on their way thereto.

God's foreordination of His people unto holiness and glory anterior to His foreview of their fall in Adam, comports far better with the instances given of Jacob and Esau in Romans 9:11 than does the sublapsarian view that His decree contemplated them as sinful creatures. There we read, "(For the children being not yet born, neither having done any good or evil, that the purpose of God according to election might stand, not of works, but of Him that calleth;) It was said unto her, The elder shall serve the younger." The apostle is showing that the preference was given to Jacob independent of all ground of merit, because it was made before the children were born. If it be kept in mind that what God does in time is only a making manifest of what He secretly decreed in eternity, the point we are here pressing will be the more conclusive. God's acts both of election and preterition—choosing and passing by—were entirely *irrespective* of any foreseen "good or evil." Note, too, how this compound expression "the *purpose* of God according to *election*" supports the contention of there being *two* parts to God's decree.

It should also be pointed out that God's foreordination of His people unto everlasting bliss before He contemplated them as sinful creatures, agrees far better than does the sublapsarian idea, with the *unformed* clay of the Potter: "Hath not the potter power [the right] over the clay; of the same lump to make one vessel unto honor and another unto dishonor?" (Rom. 9:21). Upon this Beza (co-pastor with Calvin of the church at Geneva) remarked that "if the apostle had considered mankind as corrupted, he would *not* have said that some vessels were made unto honor and some unto dishonor, but rather that seeing all the vessels were fit for dishonor, some were *left in* that dishonor, and others *translated from* dishonor to honor."

But leaving inferences and deductions, let us turn now to something more express and definite. In Ephesians 1:11 we are told, "Being predestinated according to the purpose of Him who worketh all things after the counsel of His own will." Now a careful study of what precedes reveals a clear distinction in the "all things" which God works "according to the counsel of His own will," or, to state it in another way, the spiritual blessings which God bestows upon His people are divided into *two* distinct classes, according as He contemplated them first in an unfallen state and then in a fallen. The first and highest class of blessings are enumerated in verses 4-6 and have to do with God's decree concerning the *end;* the second and subordinate class of blessings are described in verses 7-9 and have to do with God's decree concerning the *means* which He has appointed for the accomplishment of that end.

These two parts in the mystery of God's will towards His people from everlasting are clearly marked by the change of tense which is used: the past tense of "he *hath* chosen us" (v. 4), "*having predestinated* us unto the adoption of children" (v. 5) and "*hath* made us accepted in the beloved" (v. 6), becomes the present tense in verse 7: "in whom we *have* redemption through His blood." The benefits spoken of in verses 4-6 are such as in no way depended upon a consideration of the fall, but follow from our being chosen in Christ, being given upon grounds higher and distinct from that of His being our Redeemer. God's choice of us in Christ our Head, that we should be "holy" signifies not that imperfect holiness which we have in this life, but a perfect and immutable one such as even the unfallen angels had not by nature; and our predestination to adoption denotes an immediate communion with God Himself—blessings which had been ours had sin never entered.

As Thomas Goodwin pointed out in his unrivalled exposition of Ephesians 1, "The first source of blessings—perfect holiness, adoption, etc.—were ordained us *without* consideration of the Fall, though not *before* the consideration of the Fall; for all the things which God decrees are at once in His mind; they were all, both one another, ordained to our persons. But God in the decrees about these first sort of blessings viewed us as *creatures* which He could and would make so and so glorious. . . . But the second sort of blessings were ordained us merely upon consideration of the fall, and to our persons considered as *sinners* and unbelievers. The first sort were to the 'praise of God's grace,' taking grace for the freeness of love; whereas the latter sort are to 'the praise of the glory of his grace,' taking grace for free mercy.''

The first and higher blessings are to have their full accomplishment in heaven, being suited to that state into which we shall then be installed, and as in God's primary intention they are before the other and are said to have been "before the foundation of the world" (Eph. 1:4), so they are to be realized *after* this world is ended—the "adoption" to which we are predestinated (Eph. 1:5) we still await (Rom. 8:23); whereas the second blessings are bestowed upon us in the lower world, for it is here and now we receive "forgiveness of sins" through the blood of Christ. Again; the first blessings are founded solely upon our relation to the *person* of Christ, as is evident from "chosen in Him. . . . accepted in the beloved"; but the second sort are grounded upon His *work*, redemption issuing from Christ's sacrifice. Thus the latter blessings are but the removing of those obstacles which by reason of sin stand in our way of that intended glory.

Again; this distinction of blessings which we receive in Christ as creatures, and through Christ as sinners, is confirmed by the *twofold office* which He sustains toward us. This is clearly expressed in "for the husband is the head of the wife, even as Christ is the head of the church, and he is the saviour of the body" (Eph. 5:23). Notice carefully the *order* of those titles: Christ is first as head and husband to us, which lays the foundation of that relation to God of being His adopted children—as by marriage with His Son. Second, He is our "Saviour," which necessarily respects sin. With Ephesians 5:23 should be compared Colossians 1:18-20, where the same order is set forth: in verses 18 and 19 we learn of what Christ is absolutely ordained to and His church with Him, by which He is the founder of that state we shall enter after the resurrection: and then in verse 20 we see Him as redeemer and reconciler: first the "head" of His Church, and then its "Saviour!" From this twofold relation of Christ to the elect arises a *double glory* which He is ordained unto: the one intrinsical, due to Him as the Son of God dwelling in human nature and being therein the head of a glorious Church (see John 17:5); and the other more extrinsical, as acquired by His work of redemption and purchased with the agony of His soul (see Phil. 2:8-10)!

We have called attention to the fact that the only reason why any God-fearing soul believes in the doctrine of election is because he finds it clearly and prominently revealed in God's Word, and hence it follows that our only source of information thereon is the Word itself. Yet, what has just been said is much too general to be of specific help to the earnest inquirer. In turning to the Scriptures for light upon the mystery of election, it is most essential that we should bear in mind that *Christ* is the key to every part of them: "In the volume of the Book it is written of me" He declares, and therefore if we attempt to study this subject apart from Him we are certain to err. In preceding chapters we have evidenced that Christ is the grand original of election, and it is from that starting point we must proceed if we are to make any right advance.

What has just been pointed out holds good not only in the general, but in the particular: for instance, in connection with that special branch of our subject which was discussed we will now follow up from this particular viewpoint. If we go right back to the beginning itself then it will appear that God was pleased, and so resolved, to go forth into creature communion, which is to say that He determined to bring into existence creatures who should enjoy fellowship with Himself. His own glory was alone the supreme end in this determination, for "the Lord hath made all things for himself" (Prov. 16:4). We repeat, that His own glory was the sole and sufficient motive which induced God to create at all: "Who hath first given to him, and it shall be recompensed unto him again? For of him, and through him and to him, are all things: to whom be glory forever. Amen" (Rom. 11:35, 36).

The principal glory which God designed to Himself in election was the manifestation of *the glory of His grace*. This is irrefutably established by "Having predestinated us unto the adoption of children through [Greek] Jesus Christ to himself, according to the good pleasure of his will, to the praise of the glory of his grace" (Eph. 1:5, 6). Grace is one of those illustrious perfections in the divine character, which is glorious in itself, and had ever remained so though no creature had been formed; but God has so displayed this attribute in election that His people will praise and render glory to it throughout the endless ages yet to be. God showed His holiness in the giving of the Law, His power in the making of the world, His justice in casting the wicked into hell, but His grace shines forth especially in predestination and what His elect are predestinated unto. So, too, when it is said to God "that he might make known the riches of his glory on the vessels of mercy, which he had afore prepared unto glory" (Rom. 9:23), the prime reference is to His *grace* as Ephesians 1:7 shows.

The second person in the Trinity was predestinated to be God-man, being first decreed, for we are "chosen in Him" (Eph. 1:4), which presupposes Him to be chosen first, as the soil in which we are set. We are predestinated unto the adoption of children, yet it is "through Jesus Christ" (Eph. 1:5). So we read "Who verily was foreordained [as "Christ"—see previous verse] before the foundation of the world" (I Peter 1:20); as we shall show later that expression "before the foundation of the world" is not merely a note of time, but chiefly one of eminence or preference, that God had *Christ* in His view before His intention to create the world for Him and His people. Now we have shown that Christ was ordained to be God-man for much higher ends than our salvation, namely, for God's own self to delight in, to behold the perfect image of Himself in a creature, and by that union to communicate Himself to that man in a manner and degree not possible to any mere creature as such.

Together with the Son's being predestinated to be God-man, there falls unto His glorious person, as His inheritance, to be the sovereign end of all things else which God should make and the end of whatever His intelligent creatures He should be pleased to choose unto glory. This is clear from "For all things are yours . . . and ye are Christ's, and Christ is God's" (I Cor. 3:21-23), which is spoken of in reference of endship. As you, the saints, are the end for which all things were ordained, so Christ is the end of you, and Christ is God's *end or design* in acting. We say that Christ is "the sovereign end," and not the supreme end, for God Himself is above and over all; but Christ is the sovereign end unto all creation, having joint-authority with God, under God. So it is declared that "by Him" and "for Him" were all things created (Col. 1:16), as it is said of God in Romans 11:36. Thus this sovereign end in creation fell to Him as the inheritance of the Mediator: "The Father loveth the Son, and hath given all things into His hand" (John 3:35).

In the presdestination of the Son of man unto union with the Son of God, and in the constituting of Him through that union to be the sovereign end of us and of all things, there was conferred upon the man Christ Jesus thus exalted the highest possible favor, immeasurably transcending all the grace shown unto the elect any way considered, so that if the election of *us* be to the praise of the glory of God's grace, *His* much more so. More honor has been conferred upon "that holy thing" born of the virgin than upon all the members of His mystical body put together; and it was *grace* pure and simple, sovereign grace, which bestowed it. What was there in His humanity, simply considered, which entitled it to such an exaltation? nor could there be any desert foreseen which required it, for it must be said of the man Christ Jesus, as of every other creature, "for who maketh thee to differ from another? and what hast thou that thou didst not receive?" (I Cor. 4:7).

Let it not be forgotten that in decreeing the Son of man into union
with the second person of the Trinity, with all the honor and glory
involved therein, that God was prefectly *free,* as in everything else, to
have decreed Him or not decreed Him, as He would; yea, had He
pleased, He could have appointed the arch-angel rather than the seed
of the woman, to that inestimable privilege. It was therefore *free grace*
in God which made that decree, and by how much loftier was the
dignity conferred upon Christ above His fellows, so much greater was
the grace. The predestination of the man Jesus, then, is the highest
example of grace, and thus God's greatest end in predestination *to
manifest His grace* (from whence election hath its title to be styled
"the election of grace": Rom 11:5) was accomplished in Him above
His brethren, that He should be to the praise of the glory of God's
grace, far above what we are.

Since in the case of Christ we have both the pattern and example of
election—the grand original—it is quite evident that grace is *not* to be
limited or understood only of the divine favor toward creatures that
are *fallen* and are delivered out of ruin and misery. Grace does not
necessarily presuppose sin in the objects it is shown unto, for the
highest instance of all, that of the grace bestowed upon the man Christ
Jesus, was conferred upon One who had no sin and was incapable of
it. Grace is favor shown to the *undeserving,* for the human nature in
the God-man merited not the distinction conferred upon it. When
extended to fallen creatures, it *is* favor shown to the *ill-deserving* and
Hell-deserving, yet this is not implied in the term itself, as may further
be seen in the case of divine grace being extended to the unfallen
angels. Thus, as Christ is the pattern to whom God has predestinated
His people to be conformed, His election of them to everlasting glory
was under His view of them as *unfallen* and not as corrupt creatures.

God having thus absolutely chosen the Son of man and therewith
endowed Him with such royalty as to be the sovereign end of all
whom He should create or elect to glory, it therefore follows that
those who were chosen of us men were intended by the very ordination of God in our choice *to be for Christ's glory* as the end of our
election, as well as for God's own glory. We were not absolutely
ordained—as Christ in His unique predestination was in the first design
of it—but from the first of ours the intention of God concerning us
was that we should *be Christ's* and have our glory from Him who is
"the Lord of glory" (I Cor. 2:8). Here, as everywhere, Christ has the
pre-eminence, for the person of Christ, God-man, was predestinated
for the dignity of Himself, but we for the glory of God and of Christ.
Though God the Father, first and alone, designed who the favored

ones should be, yet that there should be an election of any was for Christ's sake, as well as His own.

In our election God had His Son in view as God-man, and in His design of Him as our end, He chose us for His sake, that we might be His "fellows" or companions (Ps. 45:7), that as He was God's delight (Isa. 42:1), so we might be His delight (Prov. 8:31). Thus we were given to Christ first, not as sinners to be saved by Him, but as sinless members to a sinless Head, as a sovereign gift to His person, for His honor and pleasure, and to be partakers of a supernatural glory with Him and from Him. "And the glory which thou gavest me [as the God-man] I have given them" as concurring with Thy election of them and Thy giving of them to Me to be Mine. Thou hast loved them as Thou hast loved Me (i.e., with an everlasting love in election), yea, thou gavest them to me for my glory as their end, and for which chiefly Thou lovest them (John 17:22, 23).

And what immediately follows in John 17? This, "Father, I will that they also, whom thou hast given me, be with me where I am; that they may behold my glory, which thou hast given me: for Thou lovedst me before the foundation of the world" (v. 24). Christ was loved in His election from everlasting, and out of God's love for Him His people were given to Him—with what intent? Even to behold, admire, and adore Him in His person and glory, as being that very thing they were ordained for, more than for their own glory, for *their* glory arises from beholding *His* (II Cor. 3:18). And what is this glory which Christ was ordained unto? The glory of His *person* first absolutely decreed Him which is the height of His glory in heaven, where it is we are ordained to behold it. And observe how He here (John 17:24) reveals the main motive to God in this: *"for* thou lovedst me"—Christ's being chosen first in the intention of God, the members were chosen and given to Him so that they should redound to His glory.

We being chosen for Christ's glory as our end, and for His sake, as well as to the glory of God's grace towards us, God did ordain a *double relation* of Christ unto us for His glory, additional unto that absolute glory of His person. First the relation of an "Head," wherein we were given to Him as members of His body, and as a spouse unto her husband to be her head. Second, the relation of a "Saviour" and Redeemer, which is in addition to His headship; and both of these for the further glory of Christ, and also for the demonstration of God's grace towards us. These two relations are quite distinct and must not be confounded. "For the husband is the head of the wife, even as Christ is the head of the church; and he is the Saviour of the body"

(Eph. 5:23): each of those offices were appointed Him by the good pleasure of God's will. This same twofold relation of Christ to His people is set forth again in Colossians 1:18-20: this double *official* honor conferred upon Him is further and above the absolute royalties of His *person* as the God-man.

Now that twofold relation of Christ to His people has, answerably a double and distinct aspect and consideration upon us and of us in our election by God, which was not absolute as Christ's was, but *relative unto* His two principal offices. The first concerns our persons without the consideration of our fall in Adam, whereby we were contemplated in the pure lump of creatureship as to be created, and in that consideration God ordained us unto ultimate glory, under relation to Christ as an "Head": whether as members of His body or as His bride, or rather both as He is the Head of the Church; of either or both which our persons were fully capable of before or *without* any consideration of our fall. Second, of our persons viewed as fallen, as corrupt and sinful, and therefore as objects to be saved and redeemed from the thraldom thereof, under our relation to Him as a "Saviour."

Each of these relations was for the glory of God's *grace*. First, in His design to advance us, considered purely as creatures, to an higher glory by His Christ than was attainable by the law of creation. To ordain us unto this glory was pure grace, no less so than to redeem us from sin and misery when fallen; for it was wholly independent of works or merit, even as Christ's election (which is the pattern of ours) was apart from the consideration of works of any kind: as He declared, "my goodness extendeth not to thee" (Ps. 16:2). "Although the life-work and death-agony of the Son did reflect unparalleled lustre upon every attribute of God, yet the most blessed and infinitely happy God stood in no need of the obedience and death of His Son: it was for our sakes that the work of redemption was undertaken" (C. H. Spurgeon). It is to this *original grace* that II Timothy 1:9 refers: grace alone moving God to redeem and call us, apart from works, "according to" that mother grace whereby we were ordained to glory from the beginning.

In that original grace lay God's grand and ultimate design, for it will have its accomplishment last of all, and as the perfection of all. God might immediately, upon our first creation, have taken us up into that glory. But second, for the further magnifying of Christ and the ampler demonstration of His grace—to extend it to its utmost reach: as the word in the Hebrew is "draw out at length thy lovingkindness" (Ps. 36:10)—He was not pleased to bring us unto the full possession of our inheritance in beholding the personal glory of Christ our head; but permissively ordained that we should fall into sin, and therefore decreed to create us in mutable condition (as the law of creation required), which made way for the abounding of His grace (Rom. 5:15). This is confirmed by, "But God, who is rich in mercy [a term which denotes our *ill-desert*], for his great love wherewith he loved us" (Eph. 2:4): first God loved us, viewed as sinless creatures; and this became the foundation of "mercy" to us considered as sinners.

It was upon this divine determination that the elect should not immediately upon their creation enter into the glory unto which they were ordained, but should first be suffered to fall into sin and wretchedness and then be delivered out of the same, that Christ had for His great and further glory the office of Redeemer and Saviour superadded to His election of Headship. It is our being sinful and miserable which occupies our present and immediate concern, as that which we are most solicitous about while left in this world, and therefore it is that the Scriptures do principally set forth Christ as Redeemer and *Saviour*. We say "principally" for as we have seen they are by no means silent upon the higher glory of His *headship;* yea, sufficient is said thereon to draw out our thoughts, affections and hopes unto the beholding Him in His grandest glory.

In bringing to a close this outline of the divine order of Christ's election, and of ours, as it is represented in Scripture, let it be pointed out that we are not to suppose an interval of time between God's foreordination of Christ as Head and of Him as Saviour, for all was simultaneous in the mind of God; but the distinction is in the order of nature, and for our better understanding thereof. Christ could not be the "Head" without the correlate of His mystical "body," as He could not be our "Saviour" except we had fallen. "Behold my servant, whom I uphold; mine elect, in whom my soul delighteth" (Isa. 42:1): Christ was first God's elect and delight and then His servant—upheld by Him in the work of redeeming. Absolutely and primarily Christ as God-man was ordained for Himself, for His own glory; relatively and secondarily, He was chosen for us and our salvation.

The glory of the person of the God-man, absolutely considered, was the primo-primitive design of God, that upon which He set His heart; next unto this was His ordination of Christ to be an Head unto us and we a body to Him that by our union to Him as our Head, He was the sufficient and efficient author of such blessings as our becoming immutably holy, of sonship from His Sonship, and the gracious acceptance of our persons in Him as the chief Beloved, and heirs of the same glory with Him—all of which we were capable of in God's considering us as pure creatures through our union with Christ, and needed not His death to have purchased them for us, being quite distinct from the blessing of redemption as Ephesians 1:7 (following vv. 3-6) clearly enough shows. As this was the first in God's design, so it is the last in execution, being greater than all "salvation" blessings, the crown of all, when we shall be "forever with the Lord."

Descending to a much lower level, let it be pointed out that most certainly the holy angels could not be regarded in the corrupt mass when they were chosen, since they never fell; therefore it is most reasonable to suppose *we* were regarded by God as in the same pure mass of creatureship, when He elected us. Thus it was with the human nature of Christ, which is the object of election, for it never fell in Adam, nor ever came into a corrupt state, yet it was "chosen out of the people" (Ps. 89:19), and consequently the people out of which it was chosen must be considered as yet *unfallen*. This alone agrees with the type of Eve (the Church) being given to Adam (Christ) *before* sin entered. So God's double ordination of the elect to glory and then to salvation (in view of the fall) agrees with the double ordination of the non-elect: preterition as creatures and condemnation as sinners.

N.B. For most of the above we are indebted to Thomas Goodwin. In some places we have purposely repeated ourselves in this chapter, as much of the ground gone over is entirely new to most of our readers.

7 *Its Design*

In the last chapter we have sought to go right back to the very beginning of all things and trace out the *order* of God's counsels in connection with His eternal decree in election, so far as they are revealed in Holy Writ. Now we shall seek to project our thoughts forward to the future, and contemplate God's grand design, or *what it was* He ordained His people *unto*. Here we shall be on more familiar ground to many of our readers, yet we must not overlook the fact that even this phase of our subject will be entirely new to quite a few of those who will scan these lines, and for their sakes especially it will behoove us to proceed slowly, taking nothing for granted, but furnishing clear Scriptural proof for what we advance. That which is to be before us is inexpressibly blessed, O that it may please God to so quicken the hearts of both writer and reader that we may actually rejoice and adore.

1. God's design in our election was that we should *be holy:* "According as he hath chosen us in him before the foundation of the world, that we should be holy and without blame before him" (Eph. 1:4). There has been much difference of opinion among the commentators as to whether this refers to that imperfect holiness of grace which we have in this world, or to that perfect holiness of glory which will be ours in the world to come. Personally, we believe that both are included, but that the latter is chiefly intended; and so we shall expound it. First, of that perfect holiness is heaven. That this is the prime reference appears from the amplifying clause "and without blame before him": it is *such* a holiness that God Himself can find no flaw in. Now the imperfect holiness which the saints have personally in this life, though it be a holiness before God in truth and sincerity,

yet it is not one "without blame": it is not one God can fully delight in.

Second, as God hath ordained us to perfect holiness in the world to come, so He hath ordained us to an evangelical holiness in this world, or else we shall never come to heaven: unless we be made pure in heart here, we shall never see God there. Holiness is the image of God upon the soul, a likeness to Him which makes us capable of communion with Him; and therefore the apostle declares that we should "follow holiness, whithout which no man shall see the Lord" (Heb. 12:14). As reason is the foundation of learning, no man being able to attain it unless he hath reason, so we cannot reach the glory of Heaven unless the principle of holiness be divinely communicated to us. Therefore, as God's first design in our election was that we should be holy before Him. let us now make this *our* paramount concern. Here too is solid comfort for those who find indwelling sin to be their heaviest burden: though thy holiness be most imperfect in this life, yet is it the earnest of a perfect holiness in the life to come.

Holiness must needs be the fruit of our being chosen in Christ, for it is essential to our having a being in Him. It would be a contradiction in terms to say that God chose a man to be in Christ and did not make him to be holy. If God ordains a man to be in Christ, then He ordains him to be a *member* of Christ, and there must be conformity between Head and members. The election of grace was given to Christ as His spouse, and husband and wife must be of the same kind and image. When Adam was to have a wife she must be the same specie: none of the beasts was fit to be a partner for him. God brought them all before him, but among them all "For Adam was not found a help *meet* for him" (Gen. 2:20), because they had not the same image and kind. So if God chooses a man in Christ—the Holy One—he must necessarily be holy, and this is the reason why our holiness is annexed to our being chosen in Him (Eph. 1:4).

God, then, has decreed that His people shall be perfectly holy before Him, that they shall be in His presence forever, there to enjoy Him everlastingly, and delight themselves in that enjoyment, for as the Psalmist tells us "in thy presence is fulness of joy." Therein is revealed to us *of what consists* the ineffable bliss of our eternal inheritance: it is perfect holiness, perfect love to God; this is the essence of celestial glory. If the entire apostolate had spent the whole of their remaining lifetime in an attempt to depict and describe what heaven is, they could have done no more than enlarge upon these words: perfect holiness in God's presence, perfect love to Him, perfect enjoyment of Him, even as we are beloved by Him. This is heaven, and this is what God has decreed to bring His people unto. This is His first design in our election: to bring us into an unblemished holiness before Him.

2. God's design in our election was that we should be *His sons:*
"Having foreordained us unto adoption as sons through Jesus Christ
unto Himself according to the good pleasure of His will" (Eph. 1:5
ASV.). Holiness is that which *fits* us for heaven, for an unholy person
could not possibly enjoy heaven: were he to enter it, he would be
altogether out of his native element. Holiness, then, is that which
constitutes the saints meetness for their inheritance in light (Col.
1:12). But adoption is that which gives *the right to* the glory of
heaven, being bestowed upon them as a dignity or prerogative (John
1:12). As we have pointed out on other occasions, the last two words
of Ephesians 1:4 belong properly to verse 5: "In love having predestinated us unto the adoption." God's love unto His dear Son was so
great that, having chosen us in Him, His heart went out toward us as
one with Christ, and therefore did He ordain us unto this further
honor and privilege. This agrees perfectly with "Behold, what manner
of *love* the Father hath bestowed upon us, that we should be called
the sons of God" (I John 3:1).

God might have made us perfectly holy in Christ and added no
further blessing to it. "Ye have your fruits unto holiness" says the
apostle (Rom. 6:22), and precious fruit that is; but he did not stop
there—"and the end everlasting life:" that is added as a further fruit
and privilege. In like manner, God added adoption to holiness: as the
Psalmist says "the Lord will give grace and glory" (84:11). As our
God, He chose us to holiness, according to that express saying "ye
shall be holy: for I the Lord your God am holy" (Lev. 19:2). But as
He became our *Father* in Christ, He predestinated us unto the adoption of *sons.* Here, then, is the twofold relation which the Most High
sustains to His people in and through Christ, and there is the consequent twofold blessing of our persons because of Christ. Observe how
minutely this corresponds with "Blessed be the God *and Father* of our
Lord Jesus Christ, who hath blessed us with all spiritual blessings in
the heavenly places in Christ" (Eph. 1:3).

By adoption we become God's sons *in law,* as by regeneration we
are made His children *in nature.* By the new birth we become (experimentally) members of God's family; by adoption we have the legal
status of sons, with all the high privileges that relationship involves:
"Because ye are sons, God hath sent forth the Spirit of his Son into
your hearts" (Gal. 4:6). Adoption makes known the high prerogatives
and blessings which are ours by virtue of union with Christ, the legal
right which we have unto all the blessings we enjoy, both here and
hereafter. As the apostle reminds us, if we are children then are we
"heirs," co-heirs with Christ; yea, heirs of God (Rom. 8:17)—to
possess and enjoy God as Christ doth. "Seemeth it to you a light thing
to be a king's *son-in-law?*" exlaimed David (I Sam. 18:23), when it

was suggested that he marry Michal: you may haply be the king's favorite and he may make you great, but to become his son-in-law is the highest honor of all. This is why we are told immediately after I John 3:1, "Beloved, now are we the sons of God, and it doth not yet appear what we shall be: but we know that when he shall appear, we shall be like him" (v. 2)—like Him in our proportion: as He perfectly enjoys God, so shall we.

Let it be duly noted that it is "through Jesus Christ" we are sons and heirs of God. Christ is our pattern in election, the One to whose image we are predestinated to be conformed. Christ is God's natural Son, and we become (by union with Christ) God's legal sons. "That he might be the firstborn among many brethren" (Rom. 8:29) signifies that God did set up Christ as the prototype and masterpiece, and made us to be so many little copies and models of Him. Every dignity we possess, every blessing we enjoy—save our election when God chose us in Him—we owe to Christ. He is the virtual cause of our adoption. Christ, as we have said, is God's natural Son; how, then, do we become His sons? Thus: God gave us to Christ to be married to Him, and He betrothed us to Him from everlasting, and so we become sons-in-law unto God, even as a woman comes to be a man's daughter-in-law by marrying his son.

We owe our adoption to our relation unto Christ's person, and not to His atoning work. Our adoption as originally it was in predestination bestowed upon us, was not founded upon redemption or Christ's obedience, but on Christ's being God's natural Son. Our justification is indeed grounded upon Christ's obedience and sufferings: "In whom we have redemption through his blood, the forgiveness of sins" (Eph. 1:7). But our adoption and becoming sons-in-law to God is through Christ's being His natural Son, and we His brethren in relation to *His person*. "God is faithful by whom ye were called unto the fellowship of his Son Jesus Christ our Lord" (I Cor. 1:9). That fellowship or communion involves our participation of His dignities and whatever else in Him we were capable of; just as a woman acquires a legal title unto all the possessions of the man she marries. As Christ being God's natural Son was the foundation of His work possessing infinite worth, so our adoption is founded on our relation to His person, and then our justification upon His meritorious work.

We must, however, add this word of caution to what has just been pointed out: when we fell in Adam we lost all our privileges, and therefore Christ was fain to purchase them anew; and hence it follows that adoption, and all other blessings, are the fruits of His merit so far as their actual *bestowment* is concerned. Thus the apostle tells us Christ became incarnate "to redeem them that were under the law, that we might receive the adoption of sons" (Gal. 4:5)—our sins and bondage under the law and its curse interposing an obstacle against God's actual bestowment of adoption. But mark the minute accuracy of the language used: Christ's redemption is not said to *procure* adoption for us, but only that we might *receive* it. That which procured adoption was our relation to Christ as God's sons-in-law: this being God's purpose from everlasting.

Let us duly consider now the *greatness* of this privilege. Adam was created holy, and Luke 3:38 tells us he was "the son of God," but nowhere is it said that he was the son of God by adoption through Christ. So too in Job 38:7 the angels are called "morning stars" and "sons of God," yet we are never told they are such by adoption through Christ. They were "sons" indeed by creation, for God made them; but not sons-in-law of God by being married unto His Son, which is a grace and dignity peculiar to believers. Thus we excel the angels by our special relation to the Son of God's love: Christ nowhere calls the angels His "brethren," as He doth us! This is borne out by Hebrews 12:22 where, in contrast from the angels mentioned previously, we read of "the Church of the firstborn," a title denoting superiority (Gen. 49:3): we being related to God's "Firstborn," have higher privilege of sonship than the angels have.

"A figure may perhaps help us here. A father chooses a bride for his son, as Abraham chose one of his own kin for Isaac, and gives her a goodly dowry, besides presenting her with bridal ornaments, such as Eliezer put upon Rebekah. But on becoming the spouse of his son, she becomes his daughter, and now his affections flow forth to her, not only as a suitable bride for his dear son; not only does he admire her beauty and grace, and is charmed with the sweetness of her disposition, but he is moved also with fatherly love towards her as adopted unto himself, and thus occupying a newer and nearer relationship. Figures are, of course, necessarily imperfect, and as such must not be pressed too far; but if the one which we have adduced at all help us to a clearer understanding of the wondrous love of God in the adoption of us unto Himself, it will not be out of place. We thus see that predestination to the adoption of children, is a higher, richer, and greater blessing than being chosen unto holiness, and may thus be said to follow upon it as an additional and special fruit of God's love.

"But the love of God, in predestinating the church unto the adoption of children by Jesus Christ to Himself, has even a deeper root than viewing her as the bride of His dear Son. It springs out of and is most closely and intimately connected with the true, real, and eternal sonship of Jesus. Being chosen in Christ, the elect become the sons of God. Why? Because He is the true, real, and essential Son of the Father; and thus, as in union with Him, who is the Son of God by nature, they become the sons of God by adoption. Were He a Son merely by office, or by incarnation, this would not be the case, for He would then only be a Son by adoption Himself. But being the Son of God by eternal subsistence, He can say, 'Behold I and the children which Thou hast given Me: I Thy Son by nature, they Thy sons by adoption.' We see, then, that so great, so special was the love of God to His only begotten Son, that, viewing the Church in union with Him, His heart embraced Her with the same love as that wherewith He loved Him" (J. C. Philpot).

3. God's design in our election was that we should be *saved:* saved from the fall and its effects, from sin and its attendant consequences. This particular ordination of God was upon His foreview of our defection in Adam, who was our natural head and representative; for as pointed out in previous chapters, God decreed to permit the fall of His people in order to the greater manifestation of His own grace and increased glory of the Mediator. Obviously the very term "salvation" implies sin, and that in turn presupposes the fall. But this determination of God to suffer His people to fall into sin and then deliver them from it, was entirely subservient to His prime design concerning the elect and the ultimate glory to which He ordained them. The subordination of this third design of God in our election to those we have already considered appears in "who hath saved us, and called us with a holy calling, not according to our works, but *according to* His own purpose and grace, which was given us in Christ Jesus before the world began" (II Tim. 1:9).

If the above Scripture be carefully analyzed it will be seen, first, that God formed a "purpose" concerning His people and that "grace" was given them in Christ Jesus "before the world began" either historically or in the mind of God: the reference being to His sovereign act in singling them out from the pure mass of creatureship, giving them being in Christ, and bestowing upon them the grace of sonship. Second, that God "hath saved us" (the reference being to believers) and "called us with a holy calling," which refers to what takes place in time when He brings us forth from our death in sin by an effectual call unto holiness (cf. Titus 3:5). Third, that this saving and calling for us was "not according to our works" either actual or foreseen, but "according to His own purpose," i.e., was based upon His *original intention* that we should be His sons. Neither our merits (for we have none), nor our misery, moved God to save us, but His having given us to Christ from the beginning.

As we have previously pointed out, God assigned unto Christ a *double relation* to His people: "Christ is the head of the church: and he is the saviour of the Body" (Eph. 5:23). In the same Epistle He is seen first as the Head in whom we were orginally "blessed with all spiritual blessings in the heavenly places" (1:3); later, He is presented as Saviour, as the One who "loved the church and gave himself for it; that he might sanctify and *cleanse* it" (5:25, 26). In speaking of Him as "the Saviour of the Body" it is intimated that He is the Saviour of none else, which is clearly confirmed by "therefore I endure all things for the elect's sake, that *they* may also obtain the salvation which is in Christ Jesus with eternal glory" (II Tim. 2:10): note, not merely, "Salvation" indefinitely, but *"the* salvation" decreed by God for *His own.* Nor does "we trust in the living God, who is the Saviour of all men, specially of those that believe" (I Tim. 4:10) in anywise clash with this: the "living God" has reference to the Father, and "Saviour" is more correctly rendered "Preserver" in Baxter's Interlinear.

Now this "salvation" which God has decreed for His elect, viewed as fallen in Adam, may be summed up under two heads: from the guilt and penalty of sin, and from its dominion and power, these having to do, respectively, with the legal and experimental sides. They are accomplished in time by what Christ did *for* us, and by what the Spirit works *in* us. Of the former it is written, "For God hath not appointed us to wrath, but to obtain salvation by our Lord Jesus Christ" (I Thess. 5:9); of the latter we read "God hath from the beginning chosen you to salvation through sanctification of the Spirit and belief of the truth" (I Thess. 2:13). It is by the latter we obtain evidence and assurance of the former: "Knowing, brethren beloved, your election of God. For our gospel came not unto you in word only, but also in power and in the Holy Ghost" (I Thess. 1:4, 5). When our salvation from sin is consummated we shall be delivered from the very presence of it.

4. God's design in our election was that we should be *for Christ:* "All things were created by him, and for him," (Col. 1:16). God not only chose us in Christ and predestinated us unto sonship through Him, but gave us to Him, so that Christ was likewise the end of God's purpose in choosing to perfect holiness and adoption. God having a natural Son, the second person in the Trinity, whom He designed to make visible in human nature, through an union of it to His Son, did decree for His greater glory to ordain us unto the adoption of sons to Him and as brethren unto Him, so that He should not be alone, but rather "the firstborn among many brethren." As in Zechariah 13:7 the man Christ Jesus is designated Jehovah's *"fellow,"* so from Psalm 45:7 we learn that God predestinated others to be for his Son, to be His companions: "Hath anointed thee above *thy fellows.*

The subject of the divine decrees is so vast in its range (whether we look backward or forward) and so comprehensive in its scope (when we contemplate all that is involved and included in it), that it is far from being an easy task to present a summarized sketch (which is as high as this writer aspires) of the same; and when attempt is made to furnish an orderly outline and deal separately with its most essential and distinctive features, it is almost impossible to prevent a measure of overlapping; yet if such repetition renders it easier for the reader to take in the prime aspects, our object will be accomplished. Part of what we now wish to contemplate in connection with God's design in our election was somewhat anticipated—unavoidably so—in the chapter on the nature of election, when, in showing that God's original intention was anterior to His foreview of our fall, we touched upon the positive side of His design.

We have sought to point out the infinite distance between the creature and the Creator, the high and lofty One, and that because of the *mutability* of our first estate by nature there was a necessity of *super* creation grace if the condition and standing of either men or angels was to be immutably fixed, which God was pleased to appoint by an election of grace. And therefore did God by that election also ordain those whom He singled out unto a super-creation union with Himself and communication of Himself, as our highest and ultimate end, which is far above that relation we had to Him by mere creation; *this* being accomplished by and through *Christ.* "Yet to us there is one God, the Father, of whom are all things, and we unto Him and one Lord, Jesus Christ, through whom are all things, and we through Him" (I Cor. 8:6, ASV.). Let us note first the discriminating language used in this verse: there is a pointed difference made here between the "us" and the "all things," as of a select and special company, which is repeated in the second half of the verse.

We and all other things are from the Father—"of Him" or by His will and power, as the originating cause: this is common to "us" and all of His creatures. But the "we" He speaks of as a severed remnant, set apart to some higher excellency and dignity, and this special company is also referred to as "*we* through Him" (the Lord Jesus) in contrast from the "through whom are *all* things." The A.V. gives "one God, the Father, of whom are all things, and we *in* (Greek *eis*) Him," which is quite warrantable, the reference there being to God's taking us into Himself out of a special love and by a special union with Himself: compare "the church of the Thessalonians which is *in* God the Father" (I Thess. 1:1). But the Greek also imports our being singled out unto His glory, "*for* Him": our being *in* Him is the foundation of our being *for* Him .

The distinction to which we have just adverted receives further illustration and confirmation in "One God and Father of all, who is above all, and through all, and in *you* all" (Eph. 4:6). Here again we find the same difference used about the phrases of the *all things* and the *us*. Of the all things God is said to be "above all," whereby we understand the sublimity and transcendency of the divine nature and essence as being infinitely superior to that being which all creatures have by participation from Him. Yet, second, the transcendent One is also imminent, near to, piercing "through" all creatures. He is present with all, yet holding a different being from all—as the air permeates all our dwellings, be they palaces or hovels. But third, when it comes to the saints, it is *"in you* all": this is sovereign grace making them to differ from all the rest. God is so united to them as to be made one with them, in a special manner and by a special relationship.

How amazing is that grace which has taken such creatures as we are into union with One so elevated and ineffable as God is! This is the very summit of our privilege and happiness. If we compare Isaiah 57:15 with 66:1, 2 we shall see how God Himself has there emphasized both the sublimity and the transendency of His own person and the marvel and measure of His grace toward us. In the former God speaks of Himself as "the high and lofty One that inhabiteth eternity, whose name is holy; I dwell in the high and holy place, with him also that is of a contrite and humble spirit"; while in the other He declares "The heaven is my throne and the earth is my footstood . . . but to this man will I look even to him that is poor and of a contrite spirit." How this demonstrates the infinite condescension of His favor that picks up animated dust, indwells us, communicates Himself to us as to none others: we have a participation of Him such as the angels have not!

Before proceeding further with our exposition of I Corinthians 8:6 so far as it bears upon our present subject, perhaps we should digress for a moment and make a brief remark upon the words "But to us there is but one God, the Father," which has been grossly perverted by those who deny a trinity of persons in the Godhead. The term "Father" here (as in Matt. 5:16; James 3:9, etc.) is not used of the first person in contradistinction to the second and third, but refers to God as God, to the Divine nature as such. If it could be shown from this verse that Christ is not God in the most absolute sense (see Titus 2:13), then by parity of reason it necessarily follows that "one Lord" would deny the Father is Lord, giving the lie to Revelation 11:15, etc. The main thought of I Corinthians 8:6 becomes quite intelligible when we perceive that this verse furnishes a perfect antithesis and opposition to the false devices of the heathen religion mentioned in verse 5.

Among the pagans there were many "gods" or supreme deities and many "lords" or middle persons and mediators. But Christians have only one supreme Deity, the Triune God, and only one Mediator, the

Lord Jesus Christ (cf. John 17:3). Christ has a *double* "Lordship."
First a natural, essential, underived one, belonging to Him considered
simply as the second person of the Trinity. Second (to which I Cor.
8:6 refers), a derived, economical and dispensatory Lordship, received
by commission from God, considered as God-man. It was to this
allusion was made previously, wherein it was stated that God decreed
the man Christ Jesus should be taken into union with His Son, and so
appointed Him His "sovereign end." The administration of the universe has been placed under Him: all power is committed to Him
(John 5:22, 27; Acts 2:36; Heb. 1:2). Christ as God-man has equal
authority with God (John 5:23), yet under Him, as Corinthians 3:23,
"ask of Me" (Ps. 2:8), Philippians 2:11 shows.

The next thing in I Corinthians 8:6 we would dwell upon is the
clause "and we in Him" (Greek) or as the margin has it "we for Him."
Such a supernatural union with God and communication of God is His
ultimate design towards us in His choosing of us. Hence it is that we so
often read that "for the Lord hath chosen Jacob *unto Himself,* and
Israel for His peculiar treasure" (Ps. 135:4). "This people have I
formed *for myself*" (Isa. 43:21). "I have reserved to myself seven
thousand men" (Rom. 11:4). This choosing of us is not merely a
setting apart from all others to be His peculiar treasure (Exod. 19:5),
nor only that God hath separated us for His peculiar worship and
service to be holy unto Himself (Jer. 2:3), nor only that we should
show forth His praise (Isa. 43:21), for even the wicked shall do that
(Prov. 16:4; Phil. 2:11); but we are peculiarly for Himself and His
glory, wholly in a way of grace and loving kindness.

All that which grace can do for us in communicating God Himself
to us, and all that He will do for us unto the magnifying of His glory,
arises wholly out of the *free favor* He shows us. In other words, God
will have no more glory in us and on us, than arises out of what He
bestows in grace upon us, so that our happiness as the effect will
extend as far as His own glory as the end. How wondrous, how grand,
how inexpressibly blessed, that God's glory in us should not be
severed in anything from our good: God has so ordered things that not
only are the two things inseparable, but co-extensive. If, therefore,
God has designed to have a manifestative glory unto the uttermost, He
will show forth unto us grace unto the uttermost. It is not merely that
God bestows gifts, showers blessings, but communicates to us *Himself*
to the utmost that we as creatures are capacitated for.

This is so far above poor human reason that nothing but faith can
apprehend it, that we are yet to be "filled with all the fulness of
God" (Eph. 3:19). In communicating Himself, God communicates *the*
whole of Himself, whether of His divine perfections so far as to bless

us therewith, or of all three persons, Father, Son, and Holy Spirit, for us to enjoy and have fellowship with. All in God shall as truly serve to make the elect blessed (according to a creature capacity) as serves to make Him blessed in His own immense infinity. If we have God Himself, and the whole of Himself, then are we "heirs of God" (Rom. 8:17), for we are "joint heirs with Christ"; and that God Himself is Christ's inheritance is proved by His own declaration "the Lord is the portion of mine inheritance" (Ps. 16:5). More than this we cannot have or wish: "He that overcometh shall inherit *all* things; and I will be his *God,* and he shall be my son" (Rev. 21:7).

In consequence of having chosen us for Himself, God *reserves Himself for us,* and all that is in Him. If Romans 11:4 speaks of God's having "reserved to himself" the elect (see v. 5 and note the "also"), so I Peter 1:4 tells that God is "reserved in heaven for us" as is clear from the fact that God Himself is our "inheritance," and none shall share in this wondrous inheritance but the destined heirs. And there He waits, as it were, till such time as we are gathered to Himself. There He has waited throughout the centuries, suffering the great ones of each generation to pass by, reserving Himself (as in election He did design) for His saints—"as if a great prince in a dream or vision should see the image of a woman yet to be born, and should so fall in love with his foreview of her that he should reserve himself till she is born and grown up, and will not think of or entertain any other love" (T. Goodwin). Christian reader, if God hath such love for thee, what ought to be thy love to Him! If He hath given Himself wholly to thee, how entire should be thy dedication unto Him!

When God hath brought us safely through all the trials and troubles of this lower world to heaven, then will He make it manifest that His first and ultimate design in electing us was for Himself, and therefore our first welcome there will be a presenting of us to Himself: "Now unto him that is able to keep you from falling, and to present you faultless before the presence of His glory with exceeding joy" (Jude 24), which is here mentioned that we might praise and give Him glory beforehand. The reference here is (we believe) not to Christ (*that* we have in Eph. 5:27; Heb. 2:13), but to the *Father* Himself, as "the presence of his glory" intimates, that being what we are "presented" before. It is the same Person who presents us to Himself whose glory it is. This is further borne out by "to the only wise God our Saviour [note the "Father" is distinctly called "our Saviour" in Titus 3:4] be glory and majesty, dominion and power, now and ever. Amen" (v. 25), all which attributes are those of God the Father in the usual current of doxologies.

God will present us to Himself "with exceeding joy." This "presentation" takes place at the first coming of each individual saint into heaven, though it will be more formally repeated when the entire election of grace arrive there. As we on our part—and with good reason—shall rejoice, so God on His part, too. He is pleased to present us with great joy to Himself, as making our entrance into Heaven more His own concern than it is ours. This presenting us to Himself "before the presence of His glory" is a matter of great joy to Himself to have us so with Himself: as parents are overjoyed when children long absent return home to them—compare the joy of the Father in Luke 15. It is because His purpose is accomplished, His eternal design realized, His glory secured, that He rejoices. With this agrees, "He will rejoice over thee with joy; he will rest in his love: he will joy over thee with singing" (Zeph. 3:17). It was for Himself God first chose us as His ultimate end, and this is now perfected.

Another Scripture which teaches that God has chosen His people *for Himself* is "Having predestinated us unto the adoption of children by Christ *to himself*" (Eph. 1:5). The Greek word rendered "to Himself" may as indifferently (with a variation of the aspirate) be rendered "for Him," so that with equal warrant and propriety we may understand it, first, as relating to God the Father, He having predestinated us to Himself as His ultimate end of this adoption; or second, to Jesus Christ, who is also one end in God thus predestinating us unto adoption. That the preposition *eis* often signifies "for" as denoting the end or final cause, appears from many places: for example, in the very next verse, "to [or "for"] the praise of the glory of His grace" as His grand design; so too in Romans 11:36 "to Him" (or "for Him") are all things." We shall therefore take this expression in its most comprehensive sense and give it a twofold meaning according to its context and the analogy of faith.

God's having predestinated us "to Himself" is not to be understood as referring primarily or alone to adopting us as sons to Himself, but as denoting distinctly and immediately His having elected and predestinated us to His own great and glorious self, and for His great and blessed Son. In other words, the clause we are now considering points to another and larger end of His predestinating us than simply our adoption; although that be mentioned as a special end, yet it is but a lower and subordinate end in comparison with God's predestinating us *to Himself.* First, He chose us in Christ unto an impeccable holiness which would satisfy His own nature; in addition, He predestinated us unto the honor and glory of adoption; but over and above all, His grace reached to the utmost extent by predestinating us to Himself— the meaning and marvel of which we have already dwelt upon.

God's having predestinated us "to Himself" denotes a *special pro-*

priety in us. The cattle upon a thousand hills are His, and they honor Him in their kind (Isa. 43:20), but the Church is His peculiar treasure and medium of glory. The elect are consecrated to Him out of the whole in a peculiar way: "Israel was holiness unto the Lord, and the first fruits of his increase" (Jer. 2:3), which denotes His consecrating them to Himself, as the type in Numbers 18 explains it. Christ made a great matter of this in God's taking us to be His: "I pray not for the world, but for them which thou hast given me; for they are *thine*" (John 17:9); so too the apostle Paul emphasized the same note in "The Lord knoweth them that are *his*" (II Tim. 2:19). It denotes too a choosing of us *to be holy* before Him, as consecrating us unto His service and worship, which is specially instanced in Romans 11:4, where the "I have reserved to Myself" is in contrast from the rest which He left to the worshipping of Baal. But above all, it imports His taking us into the *nearest oneness* and communion with and participation of Himself.

Consider now the phrase in Ephesians 1:5 as meaning "for Him," that is, for Jesus Christ. The Greek words *autos* and *hautos* are used promiscuously, either for "him" or "himself," so that we are not straining it at all in rendering "for Him." It is in the prepositions which are used with reference to Christ in connection with the Church's relation to Him that His glory is told out: they are in Him, through Him, for Him. Each of these is employed here in Ephesians 1:4, 5 and in that order: we were chosen *in* Him as our Head, predestinated to adoption *through* Him as the means of our sonship, and appointed *for* Him as an end—the honor of Christ as well as the glory of His own grace was made God's aim in His predestinating of us. The same three things are attributed to Christ in connection with creation and providence: see Greek of Colossians 1:16. But it is of God the Father alone, as the fountain, we read "of Him" (the Originator) (Rom. 11:36; I Cor. 8:6; II Cor. 5:18).

First God decreed that His own dear Son should be made visibly glorious in a human nature, through an union with it to His own person; and then for His greater glory God decreed us to be adopted sons through Him, as brethren unto Him, for God would not His Son in humanity should be alone, but have "fellows" or companions to enhance His glory. First, by His comparison with them, for He is "anointed *above* His fellows" (Ps. 45:7), being "the firstborn among many brethren" (Rom. 8:29). Second, God gave to His Son an unique honor and matchless glory by ordaining Him to be God-man, and for the enhancing of the same He ordained that there should be those about Him who might see His glory and magnify Him for the same (John 17:24). Third, God ordained us to adoption that Christ might be the means of all the glory of our sonship, which we have through Him, for He is not only our pattern in predestination, but the virtual cause of it.

Now in God's councils of election, the consideration of Christ's assumption of man's nature was not founded upon the supposition or foresight of the Fall, as our being predestinated *for Him* as the end intimates. Surely, this is obvious. Why, to bring Christ into the world only on account of sin and for the work of redemption were to *subject Him unto us,* making our interests the end of His becoming incarnate! That is indeed to get things upside down, for Christ, as God-man is *the end of us,* and of all things else. Moreover, this were to subordinate the infinite value of His *person* to the benefits we receive from His *work;* whereas redemption is far inferior to the gift of Himself unto us and we unto Him. It might also be shown that redemption itself was designed by God first for Christ's own glory rather than to meet our need.

N.B. We are again indebted to the invaluable writings of Thomas Goodwin.

8 Its Manifestation

By His electing act God took the Church into a definite and personal relation to Himself, so that He reckons and regards its members as His own dear children and people. Consequently, even while they are in a state of nature, before their regneration, He views and owns them as such. This is very blessed and wonderful, though alas it is a truth which is almost unknown in present-day Christendom. It is now commonly assumed that we only become the children of God when we are born again, that we have no relation to Christ until we have embraced Him with the arms of faith. But with the Scriptures in our hands there is no excuse for such ignorance, and woe be unto those who deliberately repudiate their plain testimony: to their divine Author will they yet have to answer for such wickedness.

It seems strange that the very ones who are foremost in propagating (unwittingly, we would feign believe) the error alluded to above, are they who have probably said and written more upon the typical teaching of the Book of Exodus than any one else. We would ask such, Were not the Hebrews definitely owned by God as belonging to Him *before* He sent Moses to deliver them from the house of bondage, before the blood of the paschal lamb was shed, yea, while they were utterly idolatrous (Ezek. 20:5-9)? Verily, for to Moses He declared, "I have surely seen the affliction of *my people* which are in Egypt, and have heard their cry by reason of their taskmasters; for I know their sorrows" (Exod. 3:7); and of Pharaoh He demanded, "Thus saith the Lord God of Israel, Let *my people* go, that they may hold a feast unto me in the wilderness" (5:1). And the Hebrews were a divinely or-dained type of the Israel of God, the spiritual election of grace!

It is quite true that God's elect are "*by nature* the children of wrath, even as others" (Eph. 2:3), nevertheless their *persons* have been

91

loved by Him with an everlasting love. Consequently, before the Spirit is sent to quicken them into newness of life, the Lord God contemplates and speaks of them as His own. As this is now so little known, we will pause and offer proof from the Word. First, God calls them *His children:* "All thy children shall be taught of the Lord" (Isa. 54:13)—His children *before* taught by Him; and again, "He should gather together in one the children of God that were scattered abroad" (John 11:52)—His children *before* "gathered" by Him. Second, He designates them *His people.* "Thy people shall be willing in the day of thy power" (Ps. 110:3)—His people before "made willing," "I am with thee, and no man shall set on thee to hurt thee, for I *have* much people in this city" (Acts 18:10)—before Paul preached the gospel in that heathen center.

Third, Christ denominates God's elect *His sheep* before they are brought into the fold: "And other sheep I have, which are not of this fold: them also I must bring" (John 10:16)—who were those "other sheep" but those of His elect among the Gentiles? Fourth, the elect are spoken of as *the tabernacle of David* while they are in the ruins of the fall: "God at the first did visit the Gentiles to take out of them a people for his name. And to this agree the words of the prophets; as it is written, after this I will return, and will build again the tabernacle of David, which is fallen down" (Acts 15:14-16). In the apostolic age God began to take out of the Gentiles a people for His name, and concerning this Amos had prophesied of old: "The tabernacle of David, that is, the elect of God, once stood in Adam with the non-elect, and with them they fell; but the Lord will set up His elect again, not in the first Adam, but in the second Adam, in whom they shall be for an habitation of God through the Spirit" (James Wells).

Love in the heart of God was a secret in Himself from everlasting, being wholly unknown before the world began, except to Christ, God-man, yet it has been exercised towards the whole election of grace. Though they were beloved with such a love as contained the uttermost of God's good will unto them, and to the uttermost of blessing, grace and glory, yet it was in such a way and manner that for a season they were altogether unacquainted with the same. Though the acts of God's will in Christ's Person concerning them and upon them were such as could never cease, nevertheless they were to be in a state for a season in the which none of them were to be opened and made known to them. All was in the incomprehensible mind of Jehovah from everlasting, and the same it will be to everlasting; but the revelation and manifestation of the same has been made at different times and in various degrees.

The various conditions in which God's elect find themselves not only exhibit the manifold wisdom of God, but illustrate our last remark above. The elect were to be in a creature state of purity and holiness; as such they were made naturally in Adam. From that they fell into a state of sin and misery, sharing the guilt and depravity of their federal head. They were to be brought therefrom into a redeemed state by the atoning work of Christ, and given a knowledge of this through the quickening and sanctifying operations of the Spirit. After their earthly course is finished they are brought into a sinless state, while they rest from their labors and await the consummation of their salvation. In due course they shall be brought into the resurrection state, and from thence into the state of everlasting glory and unutterable bliss.

In like manner there are different stages in the unfolding of God's eternal purpose concerning His people. The principle of divine election has operated from the beginning of human history. No sooner did the Fall take place than the Lord announced the line of distinction which was drawn between the woman's seed and the seed of the Serpent, first exemplified in the clear-cut case of Cain and Abel (I John 3:12). In an earlier chapter we called attention to the continuous operation of this selective principle, as was seen in the families of Noah, Abraham, Isaac and Jacob, and later still more conspicuously in the separating of Israel from all other nations, as the people of Jehovah's choice and the objects of His special favor. But what we would now consider is not so much the operation of God's eternal purpose of grace, as the *manifestation* of it.

In all these states through which the elect are ordained to pass the love of God is exercised and displayed toward them and upon them, agreeably to the good pleasure of His will. The secret and everlasting love of God to His chosen and His open disclosure of the same, though distinct parts, are one and the same love. The first act of God's love to the persons of those whom He chose in Christ consisted in giving them being in Christ, well being in Christ from everlasting: *that* was the fundamental act of all grace and glory for God then "blessed them with all spiritual blessings in heavenly places in Christ" (Eph. 1:3). The love of God in His own heart towards the person of Christ, the Head of the whole election of grace, cannot be expressed, and His love towards the persons of the elect in Christ is so great and infinite that the Scriptures themselves declare "it passeth knowledge." The open expression and manifestation of this love it is now our design to ponder.

First, *the incarnation and mission of Christ:* "In this was *manifested* the love of God toward us, because that God sent his only-begotten Son into the world, that we might live through him" (I John 4:9).

Take notice of *the persons* unto whom the love of God was thus manifested, expressed in the word "us." This is a term made use of by the sacred writers to include and express the saints of God by. It is a distinguishing excellency of the apostles that they bring home their subjects with all their energy to the minds of saints, and then apply them so that hereby the truth might be felt in all its vast importance. Let the subject be election, redemption, effectual calling or glorification, and most generally they use the term "us," as thereby including themselves and all the believers to whom they wrote. This serves fitly to evince that all of them are alike interested in all the blessings and benefits of grace, which opens the way for them to appropriate and enjoy the good of them in the Scriptures.

To illustrate what has just been pointed out: "Blessed be the God and Father of our Lord Jesus Christ, who hath blessed *us* with all spiritual blessings in the heavenly places in Christ: according as he hath chosen *us* in Him before the foundation of the world, that we should be holy and without blame before him in love: having predestinated *us* unto the adoption of children by Jesus Christ . . . to the praise of the glory of his grace, wherein he hath made *us* accepted in the beloved" (Eph. 1:3-6). In that passage the repeated "us" shows the interest which *all* the saints have in their eternal election in Christ. With respect to effectual calling the apostle uses the word "us" in Romans 9:24. So in connection with salvation (note the "us" in II Tim. 1:9) and glorification (see Eph. 2:7; Rom. 8:18). Let it be carefully observed that whereas this repeated "us" in the Epistles includes the whole election of grace, yet it excludes all other and cannot with any truth or propriety be applied to any but the called of God in Christ Jesus.

We next consider in what this open manifestation of the love of God consisted, namely, in the incarnation and mission of Christ. In the infinite mind of Jehovah all His love concerning the persons of the elect was conceived from everlasting, with the various ways and means by which the same should be displayed and made known in a time state, so that the Church might be the more sensibly taken therewith. As it pleased the Lord, notwithstanding His eternal love to His people in Christ, to will their fall from a state of creature purity into depravity, so also their redemption from the same was predetermined. An everlasting covenant transaction took place between the Father and the Son, wherein the latter engaged to assume human nature and act as their Surety and Redeemer. His incarnation, life and death were fixed upon as the means of their salvation. This became the subject of Old Testament prophecy: that Christ was to be manifested in the flesh, with what He was to do and suffer, in order to take away sin and bring in everlasting righteousness.

That which was revealed in the Scriptures of the prophets concerning Christ made it fully evident that it was of God that the whole of it was originally council-transaction in Heaven before time began, the fruit of consultation between Jehovah and the Branch, of which the eternal Spirit was witness, He communicating the same to holy men, who spake as they were moved by Him, for He searcheth all things, even the deep things of God. In the person of Immanuel, God with us, by His open incarnation and the salvation He wrought out and most honorably completed, all the love of the blessed Trinity is reflected most gloriously. God has shone forth in all the greatness and majesty of His love upon His Church in Christ, and thus displayed His everlasting good will unto them. He has so loved them as to give His only begotten Son. This is clearly set forth in His Word, so that it is all-sufficient to keep up a lively sense thereof in our minds, as the Spirit is pleased to maintain a believing knowledge of it in our hearts.

A brief word upon the *end* of this manifestation of the love of God as spoken of in I John 4:9: it is "that we might live through him." "It is through the incarnation and mediation of the Lord Jesus Christ that we live through Him a life of justification, peace, pardon, acceptance, and access to God. The elect of God in their fallen state were all sin, corruption, misery, and death; in these circumstances God commended His love toward them, in that while they were yet sinners Christ died for them. He by His death removed their sins from them. He loved them and washed them from their sins in His own blood, and brought them nigh unto God, so that herein the Father's everlasting love of them is most distinctly evidenced" (S. E. Pierce, to whose lovely sermon on I John 4:9 we here gladly acknowledge our indebtedness).

A most striking parallel with the Scripture we have looked at above is the statement made by the Lord to His Father in John 17:6: "I have *manifested* thy name unto the men which thou gavest me out of the world: thine they were, and thou gavest them me." The manifesting of the name of God, or the secret mystery of His mind and will, could only be performed by Christ, who had been in the bosom of the Father from everlasting, who became incarnate in order to make visible Him who is invisible. It was the office and work of the Messiah to open the "hidden wisdom" (I Cor. 2:7), to unlock the holy of holies, to declare what had been kept secret from the foundation of the world; and here in John 17 He declares that He had faithfully discharged it. But mark well how the "us" of I John 4:9 is here defined as "the men which thou gavest me out of the world." Yes, it was to them Christ manifested God's ineffable name.

In John 17 Christ opened the whole heart of God, making known His everlasting love as was never revealed before. Therein He ex-

pounded the good will which the Father bore to the elect in Christ
Jesus, in a manner sufficient to fill the spiritual mind with knowledge
and understanding, even such as was calculated to lead to an entire
trust and confidence in the Lord for all the blessings of this life and
that which is to come. And who could give this information but
Himself? He came down from heaven with this express end and design.
He was the great Prophet over the House of God. He had the key of all
the treasury of grace and glory. In Him personally was "hid all the
treasures of wisdom and knowledge" (Col. 2:3). By the "Name" of
God is meant all that He is in a manifestative and communicative way.
It is His love to the Church, His covenant relation to His people in
Christ, the eternal delight of His heart to them, which Christ has been
pleased to so fully reveal.

It is by the Lord's admitting us into the knowledge of Himself that
we are led to know our election of God. The true apprehension of this
is a ground for joy, therefore did Christ say, "Rejoice, because your
names are written in heaven" (Luke 10:20). As we cannot know that
we are the beloved of God but by believing on His Son, so this is the
fruit of spiritual knowledge. Christ has the key of knowledge and
opens the door of faith, so that we receive Him as revealed in the
Word. It is He, who by His Spirit, is pleased to shed abroad the love of
God in the heart. He gives the Spirit to make a revelation of the
everlasting covenant to our minds, and thereby we are made to know
and feel the love of God to be the fountain and spring of all grace and
everlasting consolation. As Jehovah caused all His goodness to pass
before Moses and showed him His glory (Exod. 33:19), so He admits
us into the knowledge of Himself as "The Lord God merciful and
gracious."

Second, *by a supernatural call.* We have somewhat anticipated this
in the last two paragraphs, but must now consider it more distinctly.
A saint's being called is the first immediate fruit and breaking forth of
God's purpose of electing grace. "The river ran under ground from
eternity and rises and bubbles up therein first, and then runs above
ground to everlasting. It is the initial and grand difference which God
puts between man and man, the first mark which He sets upon His
sheep, whereby He owns them and visibly signifies that they are His"
(T. Goodwin). "Whom He did predestinate, them he also called"
(Rom. 8:30). The original benefit was His predestination of us, and
the next blessing is His calling of us. The same order is observed in
"Who hath saved us, and called us . . . according to his own purpose
and grace which was given us in Christ Jesus before the world began"
(II Tim. 1:9). The eternal purpose is made evident in time by a divine
call.

Another Scripture which presents this same truth are those well-known words "give diligence to make your calling and election sure" (II Peter 1:10). It is not our faith nor our justification which is here specifically singled out, but our *"calling,"* which we are bidden to "make sure," for thereby our election will be attested to us, that is, confirmed to our faith. It is not that election is not sure without it, for "the foundation of God [His eternal decree] standeth sure" (II Tim. 2:19) before our calling; but hereby it is certified unto our faith. Thus the apostles speak one uniform language, and therefore when writing to believers show that the two terms are co-extensive. Thus, Paul "unto the church of God which is at Corinth . . . *called* to be saints"—saints by calling (I Cor. 1:2). Peter unto "the church that is at Babylon, *elected* together with you" (I Peter 5:13). The terms are equivalent, the apostles acknowledging none other to be true "calling" but what was the immediate proof of election, being commensurate to the same persons.

It is indeed blessed to observe—so graciously has the Spirit condescended to stoop to and help our infirmity—how frequently this precious truth is iterated in the Word, so that there might be no room whatever for doubt on the point. "The Lord hath appeared of old unto me, saying, Yea, I have loved thee with an everlasting love: therefore with loving-kindness have I drawn thee" (Jer. 31:3). Two things are here affirmed, and the intimate and inseparable relation between them is emphatically stated. First, the everlasting love of God unto His own; second, the effect and showing forth of the same. It is by the Spirit's effectual call the elect are brought out of their natural state of alienation and drawn to God in Christ. That supernatural call or drawing is here expressly attributed to the Lord's "loving kindness," and the connection between this and His everlasting love for them is pointed by the "therefore." Thus, it is by means of God's reconciling us to Himself that we obtain proof of His everlasting good will toward us.

The everlasting love and grace of the triune God unto His chosen ones is made apparent to them in this world by means of the fruit or immediate effects of the same: that which was secret in the heart of Jehovah is gradually brought into open manifestation through His own wondrous works unto the Church. It cannot be expected that the world of the ungodly should take any interest in these transactions, but to the regenerate they must be a source of unfailing and ever-increasing delight. As we pointed out earlier, the electing love of God was evidenced, first, in the incarnation and mission of His own dear Son, who was ordained to accomplish the redemption of His people that had fallen in Adam. Second, the eternal purpose of God's grace is revealed in and through a divine call which the elect receive while here on earth. We must now consider more definitely what this divine call really is.

First of all we must distinguish carefully between this call which is received by the elect and that which comes to all who are under the sound of the Word: the one is particular, the other general. Whosoever comes under the sound of the Word, yea, all who have it in their hands in its written form, are called by God to forsake their sins and seek His mercy in Christ. This general call comes to the elect and non-elect alike: but alas, it is *refused* by all of them. It is described in such passages as, "Unto you, O men, I call; and my voice is to the sons of man" (Prov. 8:4), "many [are] called, but few chosen" (Matt. 20:16). Their rejection of the same is depicted thus: "Because I have called, and ye refused; I have stretched out my hand, and no man regarded" (Prov. 1:24), "They all with one consent began to make excuse" (Luke 14:18). But it is with the special and particular call, of which the elect alone are the subjects, that we are now concerned.

Second, then, this calling of the elect is an individual and *inward one,* falling not upon the outward ear, but penetrating to their very hearts. It is the Word of God's *power,* reaching them in their natural state of spiritual death and quickening them into newness of life. It is the Good Shepherd seeking and saving His lost sheep and restoring them to His Father: as it is written, "He calleth His own sheep by name, and leadeth them out. And when He putteth forth His own sheep, He goeth before them, and the sheep follow Him; for they know His voice" (John 10:3, 4). From the legal side of things the salvation of God's elect became an accomplished fact when Christ died and rose again, but not until the Spirit of God's Son is sent into their hearts— "whereby they cry Abba, Father"—is it made good in their actual experience. It is by the Spirit alone that we are given a saving knowledge of the Truth, being led by Him into a right apprehension thereof: The Spirit so shines upon our understanding that we are enabled to take in the *spiritual* knowledge of God and His Son Jesus Christ.

Third, then, it is an *effectual* call, being accomplished by the supernatural operations of the Spirit. It holds equally good of the new creation as of the old that, "He [God] spake, and it was done; He commanded, and it stood fast" (Ps. 33:9). It is in such passages as "Thy people shall be willing in the day of Thy power" (Ps. 110:3), this effectual call is referred to—their natural unwillingness to surrender themselves completely to the Lord's claims is sweetly melted down by the communication of an overwhelming sense of God's grace and love to them. Again; "All Thy children shall be taught of the Lord" (Isa. 54:13), so taught that He "hath given us an understanding, that we may *know Him* that is true" (I John 5:20). Once more, this effectual call is God's making good the promises of the new covenant: "I will put My laws into their mind, and write them in their hearts: and I will be to them a God, and they shall be to me a people" (Heb. 8:10).

Theologians have wisely designated this the "effectual call" so as to distinguish it from the general and outward one which comes to all who hear the gospel. This effectual call is not an invitation, but is the actual *bestowment* of life and light. It is the immediate fruit of God's wondrous and infinite love to our persons when we are altogether unlovely, yea, the subjects of nothing but what renders us repulsive and hateful (see Ezek. 16:4-8!). It is then that the Holy Spirit is given to the elect—given to make good *in* them what Christ wrought out *for* them. Let it be clearly recognized and thankfully owned that the gift of the Spirit to us is as great and grand a gift as the gift of Christ for us. By the Spirit's inhabiting us we are sanctified and sealed unto the day of redemption. By the Spirit's indwelling of us we become the temples of the living God, His dwelling-place on earth.

It is not sufficiently recognized that all covenant mercies are in the hand of the blessed Holy Spirit, whose office and work it is to bring home the elect (by effectual calling) to Christ, and to make known and apply to their souls the salvation which the Lord Jesus has fulfilled and wrought out for them. He comes from Heaven in consequence of Christ's atonement and ascension, and proclaims salvation from the Lord for wretched sinners. He enters their hearts of sin and woe and makes known the salvation of God. He puts them by believing on the person and work of Christ into possession of the things that accompany salvation, and then He becomes a Comforter to them. Such do not pray for the Spirit to come and regenerate them, for they have already received Him as a life-giving and sanctifying Spirit. What they must now do it pray for grace to receive Him as the Spirit of adoption, that He may witness with their spirit that they are the children of God.

Now this effectual call is a necessary and proper consequence and effect of God's eternal election, for none are the recipients of this supernatural vocation but His chosen ones. Wherever predestination unto everlasting glory goes before concerning any person, then effectual calling unto faith and holiness infallibly follows. "God hath from the beginning chosen you to salvation through sanctification of the Spirit and belief of the truth" (II Thess. 2:13). The elect are chosen unto salvation by the free and sovereign grace of God; but how is that salvation actually obtained? How are His favored ones brought into the personal possession of it? Through sanctification of the Spirit and belief of the truth, and not otherwise. God's decree of election is an ordination unto everlasting life and glory, and it is evident by holiness being effectually wrought in its objects by the regenerating and sanctifying operations of the Spirit. It is thereby that the Spirit communicates what Christ purchased for them.

"And that He might make known the riches of His glory on the vessels of mercy, which He had afore prepared unto glory, even us, whom He hath called, not of the Jews only, but also of the Gentiles" (Rom. 9:23, 24). In the verses immediately preceding the apostle had treated of the unspeakably solemn subject of how God shows His wrath and makes known His power in connection with the non-elect, but here he takes up the blessed theme of how God discovers the riches of His glory on the vessels of mercy. This is by the effectual call which is received individually by His people. That call is what serves to make manifest God's everlasting grace toward us: as Romans 8:28 expresses it we are "the called according to His purpose"; in other words, the Spirit is given to us in order to the accomplishment of God's decree, or to put it in another way, through his effectual call the believer may look upward to the eternal love of God unto him, much as he might through a chink in his wall peer through to the shining of the sun in the heavens.

As the love of God the Father is chiefly spoken of under the act of election and expressed by Him giving His only begotten Son to be our Head and Mediator, and as the love of God the Son shines forth brightest in His incarnation, obedience, and laying down His life for us, so the love of God the Spirit is displayed in His *revealing* in the Word the eternal transactions between the Father and the Son and by *enlightening* our minds into a true, vital, and spiritual knowledge of the Father and the Son. It is at effectual calling that the Spirit is pleased to make an inward revelation and application of the salvation of Christ to the soul, which is indeed heaven dawning upon us, for by it dead sinners are quickened, hard hearts softened, stubborn wills rendered pliable, great sins manifestatively forgiven, and infinite mercy displayed and magnified. It is then that the Holy Spirit, who is the Lord and giver of all spiritual life, enables great sinners to know that God is love.

By His Spirit Christ is pleased to shed abroad the love of God in the heart, and through the gospel He manifests the knowledge of the Father's love to us. He gives the Spirit to make a revelation of this to our minds, and thus we are led to know and feel the love of God to be the foundation of all grace and of everlasting consolation. As the knowledge of our personal election (obtained through our effectual calling) makes it evident to us that we are near and dear to God, so it follows that we perceive we are dear to Christ. As the Spirit imparts to us a knowledge of the Father's love unto us in His dear Son, we are led to search into and study this wondrous subject of election, and the more we know of it, the more we are astonished at it. Hereby, under the influences of the Holy Spirit, we are led to such views of the grace of the Lord Jesus as fills the heart with holy contentment and delight.

Third, the eternal purpose of God's grace unto us is manifested *by a supernatural change in us.* Strictly speaking this is not a distinct branch of our subject, for the new birth is one and the same as our effectual calling; nevertheless, for the sake of clarity and to resolve those doubts which the regenerate are the subjects of, we deem it well to give the same a separate consideration. When a sincere soul learns that there is both a general and external call, and a particular and inward one, he is deeply concerned to ascertain which of these he has received, or rather, whether he has been favored with the *latter,* for it is only the supernatural call of the Spirit which is effectual unto salvation. It is on this point that many of God's dear people are so deeply perplexed and exercised: to ascertain and make sure that they have passed from death unto life and been brought into a vital union with Christ.

In seeking to clear this point the writer has to guard against infringing too much upon the next branch of our subject, namely, the *knowledge of* our election. At present we are treating of the *manifestation* of it, particularly as it is seen in that supernatural change which is wrought in its subjects at the moment they receive God's effectual call. We shall therefore content ourselves here with endeavoring to describe some of the principal features of this supernatural change. That supernatural change is described in general terms in, "If any man be in Christ, he is a new creature" (II Cor. 5:17). Another passage treating of the same thing is, "According as His divine power [he] hath given unto us all things that pertain unto life and godliness, through the knowledge of him that hath called us unto glory and virtue" (II Peter 1:3). It will at once appear that this verse is very much to the point, for it refers specifically to our effectual call and attributes the same to God's Divine power."

This supernatural change consists, then, in our being made new creatures in Christ Jesus. That which is brought forth by the Spirit at the new birth, though but a feeble and tiny spiritual babe, is nevertheless "a new creature"; a new life has been imparted, new principles communicated from which new actions proceed. It is then that "Of His [Christ's] fulness have all we received, and grace for grace" (John 1:16), that is, every spiritual grace in the Head is transmitted to His members; every grace from Christ in the Christian is now complete for parts: "grace for grace" as a child receives limb for limb from its parents. At our effectual calling divine power gives to us "all things pertaining to life and godliness": what they comprise we must now briefly consider.

First, *a spiritual understanding.* The natural man can neither perceive nor receive spiritual things in a spiritual way (though he can ponder them in a natural and intellectual way), because he is devoid of spiritual discernment (I Cor. 2:14). But when we are effectually called God gives us "an understanding that we may know him that is true." Hence it is II Peter 1:3 declares that the all things pertaining to life and godliness are given us "through the knowledge of Him that has called us." The first light which the soul receives when the Spirit enters his heart is a new view of God, and in that light we begin to see what sin is, as it is in itself against a holy God, and thus perceive what holiness is. It is this new and spiritual knowledge of God Himself which constitutes the very core and essence of the blessing and work of the new covenant of grace: "They shall not teach every man his neighbor, and every man his brother, saying, Know the Lord: for all *shall know Me,* from the least to the greatest" (Heb. 8:11). This spiritual knowledge of God, then, is the germ and root of the spiritual change which accompanies the effectual call.

Second, *a principle of holiness* is wrought in the soul. God chose His people in Christ that they should be "holy" (Eph. 1:4), and therefore does He call them "with a holy calling" (II Tim. 1:9). Thereby we are made "meet to be partakers of the inheritance of the saints in light" (Col. 1:12). Our *title* to heaven rests upon what Christ did for us, but our *fitness* for heaven consists of the image of Christ being wrought in us. This principle of holiness is planted in the heart by the Spirit, and is termed "the new nature" by some writers. It evidences itself by the mind's pondering again and again that God is a holy God, whose pure eyes can endure no iniquity, and by the heart's cleaving to Him under *this* apprehension of Him. Here, then, is the test by which we are to examine and measure ourselves: do I—notwithstanding so much in my heart and life which humbles me and causes me to mourn as contrary to divine holiness—*approve* of all God's commands as holy and good, though opposite to my lusts? And is it my constant longing for God to make me, increasingly, a partaker of this holiness?

Third, *a love for spiritual objects and things.* Not only is a "new heart" communicated at our effectual calling, but there is such a divine renewing of our will that it is now enabled to choose what is spiritually good—a power which the natural man has not in his fallen condition. It is the turning of the heart unto and longing after holy objects which carries the will along with it. When the love of God is shed abroad in our hearts we cannot but love Him and all that He loves. A true and sincere love to God is the fruit and effect of His effectual call: the two things are inseparable: "to them that *love* God, to them who are the *called* according to His purpose" (Rom. 8:28).

Alas, our natural lusts still crave that which is unholy, nevertheless, in the renewed heart there is a principle which delights in and seeks after that which is pure and holy: "We know that we have passed from death unto life, because we love the brethren" (I John 3:14). Do you not find (intermingled with other workings in you) true strains of love toward God Himself?

Fourth, *a spiritual principle of faith.* Natural faith suffices for natural objects, but spiritual and supernatural objects require a spiritual and supernatural faith. That spiritual faith is "the gift of God" (Eph. 2:8), wrought in the regenerate by "the operation of God" (Col. 2:12). This faith is the effect and accompaniment of our effectual call: "with lovingkindness have I drawn thee" (Jer. 31:3) signifies, first, that the heart is drawn unto the Lord, so that it rests on His promises, reposes in His love, and responds to His voice. "By *faith* Abraham, when he was *called* to go out into a place which he should after receive for an inheritance, obeyed" (Heb. 11:8): the two things are inseparable—faith responds to God's call. Therefore do we read of "the faith of God's elect" (Titus 1:1), which differs radically from the "faith" of formal religionists and wild enthusiasts. First, because it is a divine gift and not the working of a natural principle. Second, because it receives with childlike simplicity whatever is states in the Word, quibbling not at "difficulties" therein. Third, because its possessor realizes that only God can sustain and maintain that faith in his soul, for it lies not in the power of the creature to either exercise or increase it.

In conclusion, let us point out that this supernatural change wrought in the elect at their effectual call, this working in them a spiritual understanding that they may know God, the imparting to them of a principle of holiness, of love and of faith, is the *foundation* of all the actings of grace which do follow. Every acting of grace, to the end of the believer's life, evidences this first work of effectual calling to be sound and saving. At regeneration God endows the soul with all the principles and seeds of all graces, and the future life of the Christian and his growth in grace (through the conflict between the "flesh" and "spirit") is but a calling of them into operation and manifestation.

We will now treat God's making known in time that purpose of grace which He formed concerning the Church in eternity past. The everlasting love of God unto His chosen people is discovered in a variety of ways and means, chief among them being the inestimable gifts of His Son for them and of His Spirit to them. Thus, we have so far dwelt upon, first, the incarnation and mission of Christ as the principal opening of the Father's heart unto His own, for while the glorification of the Godhead was His chief design therein, yet inseparably connected therewith was the blessing of His saints. Second, God's gracious design is manifested by the communication of the Spirit unto the elect, whereby they are made the subjects of a supernatural call. Third, this is made still further evident by the supernatural change wrought in them by the Spirit's regeneration and sanctification.

Fourth, *by Divine preservation.* "But the God of all grace, who hath called us unto His eternal glory by Christ Jesus, after that ye have suffered a while, make you perfect, stablish, strengthen, settle you" (I Peter 5:10). This verse sets forth the wondrous and mighty grace of God dispensed to His elect in effectually calling them, in preserving them from temptation and sin, in strengthening and enabling them to persevere unto the end, and—notwithstanding all the opposition of the flesh, the world, and the devil—bring them at last securely unto eternal glory; for as Romans 8:30 declares, "Whom He called, them He also justified, and whom he justified, them he also glorified." Once again we shall draw freely from the most excellent writings of the Puritan, Thomas Goodwin, first because his works are now out of print and unknown to our generation, and second because having personally received so much help therefrom, we wish to share the same with our readers.

It is to be duly noted that in the immediate context (I Peter 5:8) the Devil is set forth in all his terribleness: as our "adversary" for malice, likened unto "a lion" for strength, unto a "roaring lion" for dread, "walking about seeking" such is his unwearied diligence; "whom he may devour" if God prevent not. Now observe the blessed and consolatory contrast: "But God": the Almighty, the self-sufficient and all sufficient One; "the God of grace": how comforting is the singling out of *this* attribute when we have to do with Satan in point of temptation. If the God of grace be for us, who can be against us? When Paul was under temptation a messenger (or angel) from Satan being sent to buffet him, what was it that God did immediately set before him for relief? This: "My *grace* is sufficient for thee" (II Cor. 12:9)—the grace in God's heart toward him and the grace working in his own heart, both to assist him effectually.

But there is something yet more precious here in I Peter 5:10: "the God of *all* grace," which has reference first to the exceeding riches of grace that are in His nature, then to the benevolent designs which He has toward His own, and then to His gracious dealings with them. The grace in His nature is the fountain, the grace of His purpose or counsels is the wellhead, and the grace in His dispensations or dealings with us are the streams. God is an all-gracious God in Himself, even as He is the Almighty, which is an essential attribute. There is a limitless ocean of grace in Himself to feed all streams in which His purposes and designs of grace are to issue forth. Our consolation from hence is, that all the grace which is in the nature of God is in the promise of His being "the God of all grace" to His Church, declared to be so engaged as to afford supplies unto them, yea, to the utmost expenditure of these riches as their needs shall require.

Nor is God known to be such only by His people in the New Testament era. David, who was the greatest subject as well as adorer of this grace that we find in the Old Testament, apprehended and acknowledged the same. "According to Thine own heart, hast thou done all this greatness, in making known all these great things" (I Chron. 17:19). And mark what immediately follows, "O Lord, there is none like thee, neither is there any God beside thee": that is, Thou art the God of all grace, for it was a point of *grace*, high grace, David is there extolling, namely, God's covenant of grace with him in Christ, just revealed to him. "What can David say more?" (v. 18); such divine favor is beyond him; just as Paul in Romans 8:31, "what shall we then say to these things?" When God pardons, He does so after the manner of a great God, full of all grace: He will "*abundantly* pardon" (Isa. 55:7), not according to our thoughts saith He (v. 8) but according to His own.

That to which the old divines referred when they spoke of God's purposing grace was the ocean thereof in His own nature, from which flow those beneficent designs which He hath toward His people, designs which the prophet described as "thoughts of peace" (Jer. 29:11), which He took up unto them or which He "thinks toward" them. It would be impossible to speak of all these thoughts, for as David declares, "Many, O Lord my God, are thy wonderful works which thou hast done, and thy thoughts which are to us-ward: they cannot be reckoned up in order" (Ps. 40:5). We must then summarize them and dwell only on those particulars which directly serve to the point before us, namely, our preservation, or God's carrying us safely through all temptations unto everlasting glory.

First Peter 5:10 manifestly speaks of God's *purposing* grace, that grace which was in His heart toward His people before He calls them, from which in fact that call proceeds and which moved Him thereunto, as it is expressly affirmed in II Timothy 1:9. The first act of His purposing grace was in His choosing of us, His singling out of those persons whom He designed to be a God of grace unto. Choice of their persons is therefore styled "the election of grace" (Rom. 11:5), that being the fundamental act of grace, upon which all others are built. To be a God of grace unto His Church is to love its members merely because He chose to love them, for grace is the *freeness* of love.

"Receive us graciously" is the prayer of the Church (Hos. 14:2); "I will love them *freely* (v. 4) is the Lord's response. Divine grace and human merits are as far apart as the poles: as Romans 11:6 shows, the one mutually excludes the other.

For God to be the God of all grace unto His people is for Him to resolve to love them, and that forever; to be unchanging in His love and never to have His heart taken from off them. This is clearly denoted in the language of I Peter 5:10, for He "called us unto His eternal glory." It is not simply that He hath called us into His grace or favor, but into glory, and that, "*eternal* glory": that is, by the effectual call He estates us into the whole and full *right* thereof forever. What can this mean but that God called us out of such grace and love as He did and doth resolve to be the God of all grace to us for everlasting, and therefore calls us beyond recall (Rom. 11:29). This is clearly borne out by what immediately follows: "after that ye have suffered awhile, make you perfect, stablish, strengthen, settle you."

This grace thus fixed in the divine will is the most sovereign and predominating principle in the heart of God, overruling all other things He willeth, so as to effectually carry on and carry out His resolution of free grace. Grace, as it is the most resolute, so it is the most absolute principle in the heart of God; for unto it belongeth the dominion. What else means "the *throne* of grace" (Heb. 4:16)? Why else is grace said to "reign . . . unto eternal life" (Rom. 5:21)? The same thing appears in the context of I Peter 5:10: "Humble yourselves [or submit to] therefore under the mighty hand of God [that is, to His sovereign power] that He may exalt you in due time" (v. 6): He "careth for you" (v. 7); all of which is carried down to "the God of all grace" in verse 10; which is followed by "To *Him* be glory and dominion for ever and ever. Amen" (v. 11), that is, to Him *as* "the God of all grace."

But it is as the God of all grace by way of execution or *performance* that we must now contemplate Him in His gracious dispensations of all sorts, which are *the effects* of the ocean of grace in His nature and the purpose of grace in His heart. We may turn back for a moment to I Peter 5:5: "God giveth grace to the humble," which refers to His actual bestowment of grace. In like manner, James declares, "He giveth more grace" (4:6), where he quotes the same passage as Peter's. In James it is spoken of in reference to subduing His people's lusts, particularly lusting after envy. Truly this is grace indeed, that when lust is raging, the grace of God should move Him to give more grace whereby He subdueth; unto them that humble themselves for their lusts, He giveth more grace.

It will help us to a better understanding of this divine title "the God

of all grace" if we compare it with "the God of all comfort" in II
Corinthians 1:3. Now that is spoken of in relation to *effects of*
comfort: as the Psalmist says "He is good, and doeth good"; so
immediately after He is spoken of as "the God of all comfort" it
follows, "who comforteth us in all our tribulations." He is "the God
of all comfort" in relation unto all sorts of distresses, which the saints
at any time have; in like manner, He is the God of all grace in respect
of its gracious effects. Yet this may be added—for the due magnifying
of free grace—that the two are not commensurate, for the dispensations of His grace are *wider* than the dispensations of His comfort.
God often gives grace where He does not bestow comfort, so that He
is the God of all grace to a larger extent than He is of all comfort.

Now since there is a fulness, an ocean, *all* dispensatory grace to
be given forth by God, what necessarily follows? This, first, that there
is no temptation that doth or can befall a saint that is under the
dominion of free grace, but God hath a grace prepared to be applied
when His hour arrives. It clearly implies that God hath a grace fitted
and suited as every need and occasion should arise. There is no sore in
the heart but He hath a plaster ready for it, to be laid thereon in due
season. The very word "grace" is a relative to need and temptation,
and so "*all* grace" must be a relative to *all* or any needs whatsoever. If
there were any want in the large subjects of free grace of which they
are capable, and God had not a special grace for it, He were not the
God of *all* grace. But it can never be said that the misery of His people
is more extensive than the scope of God's grace.

As God hath grace for all the manifold needs of His people, so He
is the God of all grace in giving forth help as their occasions require,
for such is the season for grace to be displayed. "Let us therefore
come boldly unto the throne of grace, that we may obtain mercy, and
find grace to help *in time of need*" (Heb. 4:16). So again, "that He
maintain the cause of his servant, and the cause of his people Israel at
all times, *as the matter shall require*" (I Kings 8:59), which is to be
viewed as a type of the intercession of the antitypical Solomon, the
Prince of peace. Thus God's favor is manifested unto His people at all
times of need and in all manner of ways. If God were to fail His
people in any one season and help them not in any one need, then He
were not the God of *all* grace, for it is the chiefest part of being
gracious to relieve in time of greatest need.

The fact that He is the God of all grace in respect to dispensing the
same, demonstrates that He takes not this title upon Himself potentially, but that He is so *actually*, it is merely that He has in Himself
sufficient grace to meet all the varied needs of His people, but also
that He really *does* so. By instances of all sorts, God gives full proof of

the same. In the day to come, He will have the honor of being not only the God of all grace potentially, but really so in the performance of it, for it will then be seen that He fully made good that word, "There hath no temptation taken you but such as is common to man: but God is faithful, who will not suffer you to be tempted above that ye are able; but will with the temptation also make a way to escape, that ye may be able to bear it" (I Cor. 10:13). The greatest and acutest need of the Christian springs out of his *indwelling* sin, yet ample provision is made here, too, for "Where sin abounded, grace did much more abound" (Rom. 5:20).

This superabounding of divine grace is gloriously displayed when God effectually calls His people. Let us mention one or two eminent details in proof. First, God then shows Himself to be the God of all grace in the *pardon* He bestows. Consider what an incalculable debt of sinning we had incurred! From the earliest infancy the carnal mind is enmity against God: "The wicked are estranged from the womb: they go astray as soon as they be born, speaking lies" (Ps. 58:3). Every thought from the first dawning of reason has been only evil continually. Our sins were more in number than the hairs of our head. Suppose, Christian reader, thou hadst lived for twenty or thirty years before God effectually called thee: during all that time thou hadst done no good—not a single act acceptable to the thrice holy God; instead, all thy ways were abominable to Him. Nor hadst thou any concern about God's being so grievously dishonored, nor the fearfulness of thine estate. And then, lo!—wonder of wonders—by one act, in a single moment, God blotted out all thy sins: "having forgiven you *all* trespasses" (Col. 2:13).

Second, God showed Himself to be the God of all grace in bestowing on thee a *righteousness* which met every requirement of His holy Law: a perfect righteousness, even the righteousness of Christ, which contained in it all obedience. That infinitely meritorious righteousness was imputed to thy account wholly and at once: not piecemeal, abit at a time, but in one entire gift. "For if by one man's offence death reigned by one; much more they which receive abundance of grace and of the gift of righteousness shall reign in life by one, Jesus Christ" (Rom. 5:17). Verily, that was indeed "*abundance* of grace." That perfect righteousness of Christ is fully commensurate with all the designs of grace in God's heart toward thee, and the whole of this thou receivest at thy calling, so that thou mayest exclaim, "I will greatly rejoice in the Lord, my soul shall be joyful in my God; for he hath clothed me with the garments of salvation, he hath covered me with the robe of righteousness, as a bridegroom decketh himself with ornaments, and as a bride adorneth herself with her jewels" (Isa. 61:10). It was the realization of this which moved Paul to extol the grace bestowed on him at his first conversion: "And the grace of our Lord was *exceeding abundant*" (I Tim. 1:14).

Third, God showed Himself to be the God of all grace in *sanctifying* thee. This includes first and foremost the bestowment of the Holy Spirit, who takes up His residence in the heart, so that thy body is the temple of God, whereby thou art set apart and consecrated to Him. In consequence of this, mortifying grace was bestowed, so that every lust then received is death-wound: "They that are Christ's have crucified the flesh with the affections and lusts" (Gal. 5:24). Quickening grace was also imparted, whereby the spirit is enabled to resist the flesh: "According as his divine power hath given unto us all things that pertain unto life and godliness, through the knowledge of him that hath called us to glory and virtue" (II Peter 1:3). Justification and sanctification are inseparably conjoined: as the former provides an inalienable standing for us, so the latter secures our state; and thereby is the foundation laid for our glorification.

These inestimable blessings were the pledges and earnests of thy preservation, for "He which hath begun a good work in you will perform it until the day of Jesus Christ" (Phil 1:6). It is in no wise a question of thy worthiness, but solely a matter of divine grace: "I know that, whatsoever God doeth, it shall be for ever: nothing can be put to it, nor any thing taken from it" (Eccl. 3:14). True, sin is still left within thee—to further humble thy heart—and thy lusts are ever active; nevertheless, you may be fully assured with David "The Lord *will perfect* that which concerneth me; Thy mercy, O Lord, endureth forever" (Ps. 138:8). True, thou hast a most inadequate appreciation of such wondrous favor being shown thee, and to thine unutterable shame thou must confess that your daily conduct is utterly unworthy thereof; nevertheless, that too serves to bring out the amazing grace which bears with so ungrateful and vile a creature.

Before looking at some of the obstacles which might be supposed to stand in the way of the believer being carried safely through all temptation into eternal glory, we must guard against a possible misconception. It is not the prerogative of divine grace to save men who continue how they will in sin, to save out of an absolute sovereignty because it will save them. No indeed: God saves none without rule, much less against rule. The very verse which speaks of Him being the "God of all grace" adds "who hath *called* us" and as II Timothy 1:9 declares, God calls us "with an *holy* calling . . . according to his own purpose and grace"; for "without holiness no man shall see the Lord." The monarchy of grace hath fundamental laws, as all well-regulated monarchies have. Let the foundation of God be never so sure that "the Lord knoweth [loveth] them that are his," yet it is added "Let everyone that nameth the name of Christ depart from iniquity" (II Tim. 2:19).

On the other hand, we do unhesitatingly declare the Scriptures teach that the saving grace of God is an effectual, all-powerful, infallible principle in the hearts of the regenerate, enabling them to keep those rules that are set them as essentially requisite to salvation. The one thing which Arminians suppose stands in the way of this is man's free will—as if God had made a creature which He was unable to rule. We are not ashamed to affirm that there is such a supremacy in divine grace that it engages all in God to its triumphant issue. If on the one hand grace complies with divine wisdom, justice, and holiness in setting rules; on the other hand grace draws all other attributes of God into an engagement for the preserving of us, keeping our otherwise perverse wills within the compass of those rules, and overcoming all opposition to the contrary. Hence it is that God makes so absolute a covenant: "I will not turn away from them, to do them good, . . . they shall not depart from me" (Jer. 32:40).

We now desire to point out the arguments of comfort and support which may be drawn from this grand truth that the God of all grace will safely carry His people through all temptations. Having begun as the God of all grace in justifying them after this manner, and in sanctifying them at their effectual call, what is there which should divert and hinder Him from conducting them to eternal glory? Is it the *guilt* of sin, incurred by transgressions after calling? or the *power* of sin again recovering its strength in them? If neither of these, then nothing else remains. As both of them, at times, acutely distress the consciences and minds of Christians, it is advisable for us to point out that there is nothing in either of them which can even begin to turn God's heart from off His beloved children. May the Lord graciously help us to make this quite clear.

If any thing was calculated to provoke God not to continue His grace unto the Christian it would be the guilt of those sins committed after his calling. But that shall *not* be able to so do. If God justified them at the first from sins mountain high, and thereby became engaged to continue a God of all grace ever after to them, then surely He will not fail to pardon their after-sins. Compare matters as they stood in this respect afore calling with the state thereof after. First, at thy calling God pardoned a continued course of sinning for many years, wherein there had been laid up a multitude too great for thee to number; but a pardoning thy sins after conversion it is at worst but of backslidings, and those repaired by many sincere repentings coming between. If then, God pardoned an entire course of sinning, will He not much more easily continue to pardon backsliding intermingled with repentings, even though they are sins committed again and again?

"Turn, O backsliding children, saith the Lord; for I am *married* unto you" (Jer. 3:14). Married Israel had been to God afore, but she had gone a-whoring from Him. At his first conversion God is espoused to the believer and He did then give up Himself to be a God of all grace to him. How marvelous is such grace to His unfaithful spouse! "Return, thou backsliding Israel, saith the Lord; and I will not cause mine anger to fall upon you: for I am *merciful,* saith the Lord" (Jer. 3:12). So merciful is He and He pardons on the lowest terms we could desire: "Only *acknowledge* thine iniquity, that thou hast transgressed against the Lord thy God, and hast scattered thy ways to the strangers under every green tree, and ye have not obeyed my voice" (v. 13). The same is found again in Isaiah 57:17, 18 and Hosea 14:4, where He promises to heal their backsliding.

Now if the God of all grace picked us up out of the mire when our hearts were wholly hard and impenitent, broke them, and forgave us all our years of sinning: then shall He not continue to melt our hearts when we backslide and recover us? Then, He forgave thee all thy past sins in one immeasurable lump; now He distributes His pardon, daily as thou humblest thyself for transgressions. That fountain opened "for sin and for uncleanness" (Zech. 13:1) is constantly available for us. Dost thou not confess thy sins, plead the blood of Christ, seek for mercy at the throne of grace, and beg forgiveness through Christ's intercession? If so, thou shalt not seek in vain; for though God pardoneth not because of thy humblings and seekings (as they are thy doings), yet in this course runs His pardoning grace.

But will not those who have been effectually called, reply: Alas, my sins since conversion have been greater and grosser than any I committed before. Answer: first, thou mayest have been very young when first converted: since then, as you have developed according to the course of nature, lusts too have grown, and you are more conscious of them than in early youth. Second, thy circumstances may account for them, though not excuse them. Some do sin worse after conversion than before: Job and Jeremiah sinned more grievously in later life than during their earlier years, for their temptations grew much higher. Third, consider not only thine awful sins, but thy sincere repentings too—thy earnest cryings to God against them, which were not disregarded by Him—demonstrating again that He *is* "the God of all grace."

One other thing which might be supposed to obstruct the course of God's grace begun in us at effectual calling, causing His heart to be diverted from us, is the *power* and ragings of sin within the Christian. But if He did sanctify us at the first as the God of all grace, then surely that affords a sure ground of confirmation that, notwithstanding the hazards with which our remaining corruptions might seem to threaten us, He will assuredly preserve grace in us despite all the temptations we are subject to. At his sanctification God laid in the soul of the Christian the seeds of every grace and gracious disposition that he shall ever possess: is He not well able to nourish and preserve this garden of His own planting? Listen to His most precious promise, "I the Lord do keep it; I will water it every moment; lest any hurt it, I will keep it night and day" (Isa. 27:3).

"Do ye think that the Scripture saith in vain, The spirit that dwelleth in us lusteth to envy? But He giveth more grace. Wherefore He saith, God resisteth the proud, but giveth grace unto the humble" (James 4:5, 6). This clearly denotes that our fiercest and most perilous conflicts are with some particular lust or temptation, for so the apostle's instance here carries it—the lust of envy. But when a regenerated soul is conscious of this corruption and doth humble himself under it and for it, bewailing the same before God, this shows that a contrary grace is working within him opposing the activities of that lust, *resisting* that envy (and the pride from which it springs), and therefore it is that he seeks for humility (the contrary grace to pride); and the Lord as the God of all grace giveth him "more grace."

But many a poor soul will reply: alas, I greatly fear that my condition is far worse now than ever it was previously. Answer: take the very worst condition that you have ever been in since conversion, and consider the frame of your heart therein, and then compare it with the best mood you were ever in before conversion. Honestly, dare you exchange this now for that then? Before conversion you had not the least iota of holy affection in thee, no aim at the glory of God; but since conversion thou hast (take the whole course of your Christian life) had an eye unto God and sought to please Him. True, like David, you must say, "I have gone astray like [not a sow but] a lost sheep"; yet can you also add with him "seek thy servant; for I do not forget thy commandments" (Ps. 119:176).

Before thy conversion thou never callest upon God, unless a formality; but now thou often criest unto Him unfeignedly. Before, you had no real hatred of sin and no pursuit after holiness; but now thou hast though falling far short of what thou wouldest be. Thou talkest of lusts harrying thee with temptations; yes, but once thou hadst the Devil dwelling within thee, as in his own house, in peace, and taking thee captive at his will. You complain of coldness in the performance of spiritual duties; yes, but once thou wast wholly dead. It may be thy graces are not shining, and yet there are in thee longings after God, desires to fear His name. There is, then, a living spiritual creature in thee, which, like the mole underground, is working up towards the air, heaving up the earth.

A further proof (in I Peter 5:10) that the God of all grace will carry safely through all suffering and temptations into heaven those whom he has called, is contained in the words "called us unto His *eternal glory.*" Though we are not yet in actual possession and full enjoyment thereof, nevertheless God has already invested us with a full and indefeasible right thereunto. This "glory" was the firstborn of all God's thoughts and intentions concerning us, for it was the end or upshot of His gracious designs with us. Said the Lord Jesus, "Fear not, little flock: for it is your Father's good pleasure to give you the kingdom" (Luke 12:32), and He will exclaim in the day to come, "Come, ye blessed of my Father, inherit the kingdom prepared for you from the foundation of the world" (Matt. 25:34), which refers unto heaven itself, where God reigns as undisputed King.

Now God's heart is so set upon this glory as His first and last end for His people that, when His electing grace is made known at our calling, He does then give us a full right thereto. Though He suspends the giving us the full possession of it for some years, yet He does not suspend the complete title thereto, for the whole of salvation is then stated upon them. A beautiful (and designed) type of this is found in I Samuel 16:18. In the open view of his brethren, God sent Samuel to David while he was yet young, and anointed him king, thereby investing him unto a sure right to the kingdom of Israel—that anointing being the earnest and pledge of all the rest. But for many years David's possession of the kingdom was delayed, and during that time he suffered much at the hands of Saul; nevertheless, God miracuously preserved him and brought him safely into it.

But note well that God has not only called us unto His glory, but unto "His *eternal* glory," whereby is implied not simply that the glory is eternal as an adjunct of it, but that our calling and estate thereby is into the eternity of that glory, as well as unto the glory itself. This implies two things. First, he that is called of God hath a spiritual life or glory begun in his soul which is eternal—note how the image of Christ wrought in the believer in this life is termed "glory" in II Corinthians 3:18. This glory of spiritual life in the Christian is indestructible; "Whosoever liveth and believeth in me shall never die" (John 11:25). Second, it imports that when a man is called, he is put into possession of an eternal right of glory—not a present right to glory only, but a perpetual right; a present right that reaches to eternity. We are "made heirs according to the hope of eternal life" (Titus 3:7).

There is yet one other phrase in I Peter 5:10 which remains to be considered: "by Jesus Christ." There is a security which Jesus Christ

gives, as well as that of the Father's, to confirm the believer's faith
that he shall be strengthened and enabled to persevere. God is the God
of all grace to us *by Jesus Christ:* all His acts of grace towards us are in
and through Him: He elected us at first and then loved us only as
considered in Jesus Christ. God having thus laid Christ as Mediator, or
rather as the foundation of His grace, it is a sure ground of its
continuance to us. All God's purposes of grace were made in Christ,
and all His promises are established and performed in and through
Him.

There are two persons engaged for the preservation of saints unto
glory: God the Father and Jesus Christ. We have seen what confirmation to our faith the interests that God the Father hath to us doth
afford; equally full and strong is that supplied by the interest which
Jesus Christ hath to them. The making of our salvation sure and
steadfast against all opposition is directly founded upon Him and
committed to Him. Concerning Jesus Christ God says, "Behold, I lay
in Zion for a foundation of stone, a tried stone, a precious corner-
stone, *a sure foundation:* he that believeth shall not make haste" (Isa.
28:16), or as the apostle explains it "shall not be confounded" (I
Peter 2:6). We are "the called of Jesus Christ" (Rom. 1:6). We have
"eternal life through Jesus Christ our Lord" (Rom. 6:23). God "stab-
lisheth us with you in Christ" (II Cor. 1:21).

Little space remains for us to consider the security which a due
contemplation of Christ's person, His relation to us, and office for us,
affords to our faith that we shall be divinely strengthened to persevere
unto the end. Only a few details can therefore be mentioned. First, *His
redemptive work.* This is of such infinite worth that it not only
purchased for us our first calling unto grace (Rom. 5:2), but together
therewith, our continuance in that grace. Christ meritoriously bought
off all our temptations and an ability in Himself to succor and
establish us to the end. "Who gave Himself for our sins, that He might
deliver us from this present evil world" (Gal. 1:4). "Who gave Himself
for us, that He might redeem us from all iniquity, and purify us unto
Himself a peculiar people, zealous of good works" (Titus 2:14). While
His precious blood retains its infinite value in the esteem of God, not
one of His sheep can perish.

Second, Christ's *tender pity.* "For in that he himself hath suffered
being tempted, he is able to succor them that are tempted" (Heb.
2:18). In the previous verse it is declared that He is a "merciful High
Priest" to pity us, so that He hath a heart and willingness to help His
people; but in verse 18 it is added that He is able so to do. And mark,
it is not affirmed that He is able in respect of His personal power, as
He is God, but there is a further and acquired ability as He is man. He

was made a frail man, subject to temptations, and the painful experiences through which He passed in the days of His humiliation engages His heart to pity us when in distress, and because of this acquired tenderness, He is able to succor us in temptation.

Third, *His intercession.* "For if, when we were enemies, we were reconciled to God by the death of His Son, much more, being reconciled, we shall be saved by His life" (Rom. 5:10), that is, by His life for us in heaven. "Wherefore He is able also to save them to the uttermost that come unto God by him, seeing he ever liveth to make intercession for them" (Heb. 7:25). If, then, thou hast come unto God by Him, Christ's intercession effectually secures thine uttermost salvation. Because He hath taken thee into His heart, He has taken thee into His prayers. Once Christ takes us into His prayers, He will never leave us out, but prevail for us, whatever be our case or whatever we fall into (I John 2:1)—clear proof of this was furnished by the case of Peter. A man may be cast out of the prayers of a saint, as Saul was out of Samuel's; but none was ever cast out of Christ's prayers whom He once took in. His prayers will prevail to prevent thee from falling into such sins as God will not forgive.

Fourth, *Christ's interest in that glory* we are called unto and our interest in Christ's glory, for they are one. "God is faithful, by whom ye were called unto the fellowship of his Son, Jesus Christ our Lord" (I Cor. 1:9); that is, to be partakers of the same things (in our measure) that *He* is partaker of. "For if we have been planted together in the likeness of his death, we shall be also in the likeness of his resurrection" (Rom. 6:5). The apostle declares that God "calls you by our gospel to the obtaining of the glory of our Lord Jesus Christ" (II Thess. 2:14). It is Christ's own glory—the reward of that wondrous work by which He so illustriously magnified the Father—which His people are brought into, for nothing short of this would satisfy the heart of Christ: "Father, I will that they also, whom thou hast given me, be with me where I am; that they may behold my glory" (John 17:24).

Here, then, is how the secret election of God in eternity past is openly manifested unto His people in this time state: by a supernatural call, and by miraculously bringing them through a world which is as hostile to their souls as Babylon's furnace was to the bodies of the three Hebrews.

9 Its Perception

Thus far we have dwelt mainly upon the *doctrinal* side of election; now we turn more directly to its experimental and practical aspect. The entire doctrine of Scripture is a perfect and harmonious unit, yet for our clearer apprehension thereof it may be considered distinctively in its component parts. Strictly speaking it is inadmissible to talk of "the doctrines of grace," for there is but one grand and divine doctrine of grace, though that precious diamond has many facets in it. We are not warranted by the language of Holy Writ to employ the expression the doctrines of election, regeneration, justification, and sanctification, for in reality they are but parts of one doctrine; yet it is not easy to find an alternative term. When the plural "doctrines" is used in the Word of God, it alludes to what is false and erroneous: "doctrines of men" (Col. 2:22), "doctrines of devils" (I Tim. 4:1), "divers and strange doctrines" (Heb. 13:9)—"divers" because there is not agreement among them.

In contrast from the false and conflicting doctrines of men, the truth of God is one grand and consistent whole, and it is uniformly spoken of as "the doctrine" (I Tim. 4:16), "sound doctrine" (Titus 2:1). Its distinctive mark is described as "the doctrine which is according to godliness" (I Tim. 6:3)—the doctrine which produces and promotes godliness. Every part of that doctrine is intensely practical and experimental in all its bearings. It is no mere abstraction addressed to the intellect, but, when duly apprehended, exerts a spiritual influence upon the heart and life. Thus it is with that particular phase of God's doctrine which is now before us. The blessed truth of election is revealed not for carnal speculation and controversy, but to yield the lovely fruits of holiness. The choice is God's, but the salutary effects are in us. True that doctrine must be applied by the power of the Holy Spirit to the soul before those effects are produced; for here, as everywhere, we are entirely dependent upon His gracious operations.

The first effect produced in the soul by the Spirit's application of the truth of divine election is the promotion of true *humility*. Pride and presumption now receive their death wound: self-complacency is shattered, and the subject of this experience is shaken to his very foundations. He may for years past have made a Christian profession, and entertained no serious doubts of the sincerity and genuineness thereof. He may have had a strong and unshaken assurance that he was journeying to heaven; and during that time he was utterly ignorant of the truth of election. But what a change has come over him! Now that he learns God has made an eternal choice from among the children of men, he is deeply concerned to ascertain whether or not *he* is one of heaven's favorites. Realizing something of the tremendous issues involved, and painfully conscious of his own utter depravity, he is filled with fear and trembling. This is most painful and unsettling, for as yet he knows not that such exercises of soul are a healthy sign.

It is just because the preaching of election, when accompanied by the power of the Holy Spirit (and what preaching is more calculated to *have* His blessing than that which most magnifies God and abases man!) produces such an harrowing of heart, that is so distasteful to those who wish to be "at ease in Zion." Nothing is more calculated to expose an empty profession, to arouse the slumbering victims of Satan. But alas, those who have nothing better than a fleshly assurance do not wish to have their false peace disturbed, and consequently *they* are the very ones who are the loudest in their outcries against the proclamation of discriminating grace. But the howling and snapping of dogs is no reason why the children of God should be deprived of their necessary bread. And no matter how unpleasant be the first effects produced in him by the heart's reception of this truth, it will not be long before the humbled one will be truly thankful for that which causes him to dig more deeply and make sure that his hope is founded on the Rock of ages.

Divine chastisement is a painful thing; nevertheless, to them that are exercised thereby, it afterwards yieldeth the peaceable fruits of righteousness (Heb. 12:11). So it is a grievous thing for our complacency to be rudely shattered, but if the sequel be that we exchange a false confidence for a Scripturally grounded assurance, we have indeed cause for fervent praise. To discover that God's purpose of grace is restricted to an elect people, is alarming to one who has imagined that He loves all mankind alike. To be made to seriously wonder if I am one of those whom God chose in Christ before the foundation of the world, raises a question which it is not easy to answer satisfactorily; and to be made to diligently inquire into my actual state, to solemnly examine myself before God, is a task which no hypocrite will prosecute; yet is it one which the regenerate will not shrink from, but on the contrary will pursue it with earnest zeal and fervent prayers to God for help therein.

It is not (as some foolishly suppose) that the one who is now so seriously concerned about his spiritual condition and eternal destiny is in such alarm because he doubts God's Word. Far from it: it is just because he *believes* God's Word that he *doubts himself*, doubts the validity of his Christian profession. It is because he believes the Scriptures when they declare the Lord's flock is a "very little one" (Greek, Luke 12:32), he is fearful that he belongs not to it. It is because he believes God when He says, "There is a generation that are pure in their own eyes, and yet is not washed from their filthiness" (Prov. 30:12), and that finding so much filth in his own soul, he trembles lest that be true of him. It is because he believes God when He says "the heart is deceitful above all things, and desperately wicked" (Jer. 17:9), that he is deeply exercised lest *he* be fatally deluded. Ah, my reader, the more firmly we believe God's Word, the more cause have we to doubt ourselves.

To obtain assurance that they have received a supernatural call from God, which has brought them from death unto life, is a matter of paramount concern to those who really value their souls. Those to whom God has imparted an honest heart abhor hypocrisy, refuse to take anything for granted, and greatly fear lest they impose upon themselves by passing a more favorable verdict than is warranted. Others may laugh at their concern and mock at their fears, but this moves them not. Too much is at stake for such a matter to be lightly and hurriedly dismissed. They know full well that it is one which must be settled in the presence *of God,* and if they are deceived, they beg Him to make them aware of it. It is God who has wounded them, and He alone can heal; it is God who has disturbed their carnal complacency, and none but He can bestow real spiritual rest.

Is it possible for a person, in this life, to really ascertain his eternal election of God? Papists reply dogmatically that no man can certainly know his own election unless he is certified thereof by some special, immediate, and personal revelation from God. But this is manifestly false and erroneous. When the disciples of Christ returned from their preaching tour and reported to Him the wonders they had wrought and being elated that even the demons were subject to them, He bade them "notwithstanding in this rejoice not, that the spirits are subject unto you; but rather rejoice, because your names *are written in heaven"* (Luke 10:20). Is it not perfectly plain in these words of our Saviour that men *may* attain unto a sure knowledge of their eternal election? Surely we cannot, nor do we, rejoice in things which are unknown or even in things uncertain.

Did not Paul bid the Corinthians "Examine yourselves, whether ye be in the faith, prove your own selves" (II Cor. 13:5). Here it is certainly taken for granted that he who hath faith may know that he hath it, and therefore may also know his election, for saving faith is an infallible mark of election: "As many as were ordained to eternal life believed" (Acts 13:48). Would that more ministers took a page out of the apostle's book and urged their hearers to real self-examination: true, it would not increase their present popularity, but it would probably result in thanksgiving from some of their hearers in a future day. Did not another of the apostles exhort his readers, "Give diligence to make your calling and election sure" (II Peter 1:10)? But what force would such an injunction possess if assurance be unattainable in this life? It would be utterly vain to use diligence if knowledge of our election is impossible without an extraordinary revelation from God.

But how may a man come to know his election? Certainly it is not by ascending up as it were into heaven, there to search into the counsels of God, and afterwards come down to himself. None of us can obtain access to the Lamb's book of life: God's decrees are secret. Nevertheless it *is* possible for the saints to know they are among that company whom God has predestinated to be conformed to the image of His Son. But *how*? Not by some extraordinary revelation from God, for Scripture nowhere promises any such thing to exercised souls. Spurgeon put it bluntly when he said, "We know of some who imagine themselves to be elect because of the vision they have seen when they were asleep, or when they were awake—for men have waking dreams; but these are as much value as cobwebs would be for a garment, they will be of as much service to them at the day of judgment as a thief's convictions would be to him if he were in need of a character to commend him to mercy" (from Sermon on I Thess. 1:4-6).

In order to ascertain our election we have to descend into our own hearts, and then go up from ourselves as it were by Jacob's ladder to God's eternal purpose. It is by the signs and testimonies described in the Scriptures, which we are to search for within ourselves, and from them discover the counsel of God concerning our salvation. In making this assertion we are not unmindful of the satirical comment which it is likely to meet with in certain quarters. There is a class of professing Christians who entertain no doubts whatever about their salvation, who are fond of saying, as well look to an iceberg for heat or into a grave to find the tokens of life, as search within ourselves for proofs of the new birth. But is it not akin to blasphemy to suggest that God the Spirit can take up His residence in a person and yet for there to be no definite evidences of His presence.

There are two testifiers to the believer from which he may assuredly learn the eternal counsels of God respecting his salvation: the witness of God's Spirit and the witness of his own spirit (Rom. 8:16). By what means does God's Spirit furnish testimony to a Christian conscience from the Word, but rather by His application of the promises of the Gospel in the form of a syllogism: whosoever believeth in Christ is chosen to everlasting life. That proposition is clearly set forth in God's Word, and is expressly propounded by His ministers of the gospel. The Spirit of God accompanies their preaching with effectual power, so that the hearts of God's elect are opened to receive the truth, their eyes enlightened to perceive its blessedness, and their wills moved to renounce all other dependencies and give up themselves to the mercy of God in Christ.

But the question arises, how may I distinguish between the witness of the Spirit and Satan's delusive imitation thereof? for as there is a sure persuasion of God's favor from His Spirit, so there are frauds of the Devil whereby he. flatters and soothes men in their sins. Moreover, there is in all men natural presumption which is often mistaken for faith, in fact there is far more of this mock-faith in the world than there is of true faith. It is really tragic to find what multitudes there are in the religious world today who are carried away by the "strange fire" of wild enthusiasm, supposing that the exciting of their animal spirits and emotions is sure proof that they have received the Spirit's "baptism" and thus are certain of heaven. At the other extreme is a large company who disdain and discredit all religious feelings and pin their faith to an "I am resting on John 5:24," and boast that they have not had a doubt of their salvation for many years past.

Now the true witness of the Spirit may be discerned from natural presumption and Satanic deception *by its effects and fruits.* First, the Spirit bestows upon God's elect *praying hearts.* "Shall not God avenge his own elect, which cry day and night unto him" (Luke 18:7). Notice how right after making that statement the Lord Jesus went on to give an illustration of the *nature* of their praying. It is true that formalists and hypocrites pray, but vastly different is that from the crying of the sin-conscious, guilt-burdened, distressed people of God, as appears from the vivid contrast between the pharisee and publican. Ah, it is not until we are brought to feel our utter unworthiness and Hell-deservingness, our ruin and wretchedness, our abject poverty and absolute dependency on God's sovereign bounty, that we begin to "cry" unto Him and that, "day and night"—to pray experimentally, to pray perseveringly, to pray with "groanings which cannot be uttered," and thus, to pray effectually.

Let us look for a moment at a prayer of one of God's people, "Remember me, O Lord, with the favor that thou bearest unto thy people: O visit me with thy salvation" (Ps. 106:4). Now my reader, you are either earnestly seeking that favor by which the Lord remembers His people, or you are not. It is only when we are brought to the place where we are pressed down with a sense of our sinfulness and vileness that we can say in our souls before God, "O visit me with thy salvation." But the Psalmist did not stop there, no more must we: he went on to say, "That I may see the good of *thy chosen,* that I may rejoice in the gladness of thy nation, that I may glory with thine inheritance" (v. 5). God's elect pray for and seek after that which no other men pray for and seek after: they long to *see* the good of God's chosen, they seek to be saved with His salvation, and to dwell in the order of His everlasting covenant and eternal establishment.

A second effect of the Spirit's witness is a bringing of us to *submit to God's sovereignty.* Not only do God's elect pray for something which no other men pray for, but they do so in a different manner from all others. They approach the Almighty not as equals, but as beggars; they make "requests" of Him, and not demands; and they present their requests in strict subserviency to His own imperial will. How utterly different are their humble petitions from the arrogancy and dictatorialness of empty professors. They know they have no claims upon the Lord, that they deserve no mercy at His hands, and therefore they raise no outcry against His express assertion, "I will have mercy on whom I will have mercy, and I will have compassion on whom I will have compassion" (Rom. 9:15). That person whose heart is indwelt by the Spirit of God takes his place in the dust, and says with pious Eli, "It is the Lord: let him do what seemeth him good" (I Sam. 3:18).

We read in Matthew 20:3 of a number of men "standing idle in the marketplace," which we understand to signify that they were not actively engaged in the Devil's service, but that they had not yet enetered God's service. Their attitude was indicative of a desire to be religious. Very well, said the Lord, go and work in My vineyard. But a little later the Lord of the vineyard displayed His *sovereignty,* and they were highly displeased. The Lord gave unto the last even as unto the first, and they murmured. The Lord answered "I do thee no wrong. . . . Is it not lawful for me to do what I will with mine own?" (v. 15). That was what offended them; they would not submit to His sovereignty, yet He exercised it notwithstanding. "Is thine eye evil, because I am good?" He asked and still asks to every one who in the pride and unbelief of his heart rises up against God's discriminating grace. But not so with God's elect: they bow before His throne and leave themselves entirely in His hands.

Third, God's elect have imparted to them a *filial spirit* so that they have the affections of dutiful children to their heavenly Father. It inspires them with an awe of His majesty, so that they are conscious of every evil way. It draws out their hearts in love to God, so that they crave for the conscious enjoyment of His smiling countenance, esteeming fellowship with Him high above all other privileges. That filial spirit produces confidence toward God so that they plead His promises, count on His mercy, and rely on His goodness. His high authority is respected and they tremble at His Word. That filial spirit produces subjection to God, so that they desire to obey Him in all things, and sincerely endeavor to walk according to His commandments and precepts. True, they are yet very far from being that they *should* be, and what they *would* be could their earnest longings be realized; nevertheless, it is their fervent desire *to* please Him in all their ways.

"The Spirit himself beareth witness with our spirit, that we are the children of God" (Rom 8:16). The office of a "witness" is to give testimony or supply evidence for the purpose of adducing proof, either of innocence or guilt. This may be seen from "which show the work of the law written in their hearts, their conscience also bearing witness, and their thoughts the mean while accusing or else excusing one another" (Rom. 2:15). Though the heathen had not received a written revelation from God (as was the case with the Jews), nevertheless they were His creatures, accountable to Him, subject to His authority, and will yet be judged by Him. The grounds on which their responsibility rest are: the revelation which God has made of Himself in nature which renders them "without excuse" (Rom. 1:19, 20) and the work of the law written on their hearts, which is rationality or "the light of nature." Their moral instincts instruct them in the difference between right and wrong and warn of a future day of reckoning. While their conscience also "bears witness," supplies evidence that God is their governor and judge.

Now the Christian has a renewed conscience, and it supplies the proof that he is a renewed person, and consequently, one of God's elect. "We trust we have a good conscience, in all things willing to live honestly" (Heb. 13:18): the bent of his heart was for God and obedience to Him. Not only does the Christian sincerely desire to honor God and be honest with his fellows, but he makes a genuine endeavor thereunto: "Herein do I exercise myself, to have always a conscience void of offence toward God and toward men" (Acts

24:16). And it is the office of a good conscience to witness favorably for us and unto us. To it the Christian may appeal. Paul did so again and again, for example, in Romans 9:1 we find him declaring, "I say the truth in Christ, I lie not, my conscience also bearing me witness in the Holy Ghost," which means that his conscience testified to his sincerity in the matter. Thus we see again how Scripture interprets Scripture: Romans 2:15 and 9:1 define the meaning of "our spirit bearing witness"—adducing evidence, establishing the verity of a case.

Romans 8:16 declares that our spirit (supported by the Holy Spirit) furnishes proof that we are "the children of God," and, as the apostle goes on to show, if children, "then heirs" (v. 17) and "God's elect" (v. 33). Now this witness of our spirit is the testimony of our heart and conscience, purged and sanctified by the blood of Christ. It testifies in two ways, by inward tokens in itself, and by outward proofs. As this is so little understood to-day, we must enlarge thereon. Those inward tokens are certain special graces implanted in our spirit at the new birth, whereby a person may be certainly assured of His divine adoption, and therefore of his election to salvation. Those tokens regard first our sins, and second the mercy of God in Christ. And for the sake of clarity we will consider the former in connection with our sins past, present, and to come.

The token or sign in our "spirit" or heart which concerns *sins past* is "godly sorrow" (II Cor. 7:10), which is really a mother grace of many other gifts and graces of God. The nature of it may the better be conceived if we compare it with its opposite. Worldly sorrow issues from sin, and is nothing else but *terror* of conscience and an apprehension of the wrath of God for the same; whereas godly sorrow though it be indeed occasioned by our sins, springs from a *grief* of conscience caused by a sense of the goodness and grace of God. Worldly sorrow is horror only in respect of the punishment, whereas godly sorrow is grief for sin as sin, which is increased by the realization that there will be no personal punishment for it, since that was inflicted upon Christ in my stead. In order that no one may deceive himself in discerning this "godly sorrow," the Holy Spirit in II Corinthians 7:11 has given seven marks by which it may be identified.

The first is "For behold this selfsame thing ["godly sorrow"] that ye sorrowed after a godly sort, what carefulness it wrought in you." The word for "carefulness" signifies first "haste" and then diligence—the opposite of negligence and indifference. There is not only mourning over, but going to work with a will so as to rectify the misconduct. Second, "yea, what clearing of yourselves": the Greek word signifies "to apologize," seeking forgiveness: it is the reverse of self-extenuation. Third, yea, "what indignation," instead of unconcern: the penitent one is exceedingly angry with himself for committing such offenses. Fourth, "yea, what fear," lest there be any repetition of the same: it is an anxiety of mind against a further lapse. Fifth, "yea what vehement desire": for divine assistance and strength against any recurrence of it. Sixth, "yea, what zeal," in performing the holy duties which are the opposite of those sins. Seventh, "yea what revenge," upon himself, by daily mortifying his members. When a man finds these fruits in himself, he need not doubt the "godliness" of his repentance.

The token in our spirit with respect of sins *present* is the resistance made by the new nature against the old, or the principle of holiness against that of evil (see Gal. 5:17). This is proper to the regenerate as they are dual creatures—children of men and children of God. It is far more than the checks of conscience which all men, both good and bad, find in themselves as often as they offend God. No; it is that striving and fighting of the mind, affections, and will *with themselves,* whereby as far as they are renewed and sanctified they carry the man one way, and as they are still corrupt they carry him the flat contrary. It is this painful and protracted warfare which the Christian discovers to be going on within himself, which evidences him to be a new creature in Christ. If he reviews and recalls the past, he will find in his experience nothing like this before his regeneration.

Everything in the natural adumbrates spiritual realities, did we but have eyes to see and understandings to properly interpret them. There is a disease called ephilites which causes its victims when they are half asleep to feel as though some heavy weight was lying across their chest, bearing them down; and they strive with hands and feet, with all their might, to remove that weight, but cannot. Such is the case of the genuine Christian: he is conscious of something within that drags him down, which clips the wings of faith and hope, which hinders his affections being set upon things above. It oppresses him and he wrestles with it, but in vain. It is the "flesh," his inborn corruptions, indwelling sin, against which all the graces of the new nature strive and struggle. It is an intolerable burden which disturbs his rest, and prevents him doing the things which he would.

The token in our spirit which respects *sins to come* is an earnest care to prevent them. That this is a mark of God's children appears from "We know that whosoever is born of God sinneth not: but he that is begotten of God keepeth himself, and that wicked one toucheth him not" (I John 5:18). Note carefully the tense of the verb, it is not, "he doth not sin," but "sinneth not" as a regular practice and constant course. From that he "keepeth himself." This carefulness consists not only in the ordering of our outward conduct, but extends to the very thoughts of the heart. It was to this the apostle referred when he said "I keep under my body, and bring it into subjection" (I Cor. 9:27)—not his physical body, but the body of sin within him. The more we are conscious of evil thoughts and unlawful imaginations, the more we sit in judgment upon our motives, the less likely is our external behavior to be displeasing unto God.

We turn now to consider the tokens or signs in the Christian's spirit with respect to *God's mercy,* tokens which evidence him to be one of God's elect. The first one is when a man feels himself to be heavily burdened and deeply disturbed with the guilt and pollution of his iniquities, and when he apprehends the heavy displeasure of God in his conscience for them. This far outweighs any physical ills or temporal calamities which he may be subject to. Sin is now his greatest burden of all, making him quite unable to enjoy worldly pleasures or relish the society of worldly companions. Now it is that he feels his urgent need of Christ, and pants after Him as the parched hart does for the refreshing stream. Carnal ambitions and worldly hopes fade into utter insignificance before this overwhelming yearning for reconciliation with God through the merits of the Redeemer. "Give me Christ or else I die" is now his agonizing cry.

Now to all such sin-sick, conscience-tormented, Spirit-convicted souls, Christ has made some exceedingly great and precious promises, promises which pertain unto none but the quickened elect of God. "If any man thirst, let him come unto me, and drink. He that believeth on me, as the scripture hath said, out of his belly shall flow rivers of living water" (John 7:37, 38). Is not that exactly suited to the deep needs of one who feels the flames of hell upon his conscience? He hungers and thirsts after righteousness, for he knows that he has none of his own. He thirsts for peace, for he has none night or day. He thirsts for pardon and cleansing for he sees himself to be a leprous felon. Then come to Me, says Christ, and I will meet your every need. "I will give unto him that is athirst of the fountain of the water of life freely" (Rev. 21:6). And mark what follows his thus coming to Christ: "Whosoever drinketh of this water that I shall give him shall never thirst" (John 4:14).

The second token is *a new affection* which is implanted in the heart by the Holy Spirit, whereby a man doth so esteem and value and set such a high price upon the blood and righteousness of Christ that he accounts the most precious things of this world as but dross and dung in comparison. This affection was evidenced by Paul (see Phil. 3:7, 8). Now it is true that almost every professor will *say* that he values the person and work of Christ high above all the things of this world, when the fact is that the vast majority of them are of Esau's mind, preferring a mess of pottage to Jacob's portion. With very, very few exceptions those who bear the name of Christians much prefer the fleshpots of Egypt to the blessings of God in the land of promise. Their actions, their lives demonstrate it, for where a man's treasure is there is his heart also.

That no man may deceive himself in connection with this particular sign of regeneration and election, God has given us two identifying and corroboratory marks. First, when there is a genuine prizing of and delighting in Christ above all other objects, there is an unfeigned love for *His members.* "We know that we have passed from death unto life, because we love the brethren" (I John 3:14): that is, such as are members of the mystical body of Christ, and because they are so. Those who are dear to God must be dear to His people. No matter what differences there may be between them in nationality, social position, personal temperament, there is a spiritual bond which unites them. If Christ be dwelling in my heart, then my affections will necessarily be drawn forth unto all in whom I perceive, however faintly, the lineaments of His holy image. And just so far as I allow the spirit of animosity to alienate me from them, will my evidence of election be overclouded.

The second corroboratory mark of a genuine valuing of Christ is a love and longing for *His coming:* whether it be by death, or by His second advent. Though nature shrinks from physical dissolution, and though the sin which indwells the Christian renders him uneasy at the thought of being ushered into the immediate presence of the Holy One of God, nevertheless, the actings of the new nature carries the soul above these obstacles. A renewed heart cannot rest satisfied with its present, fitful, and imperfect communion with his beloved. He yearns for full and complete fellowship with Him. This was clearly the case with Paul: "Having a desire to depart, and to be with Christ; which is far better" (Phil. 1:23). That this was not peculiar to himself, but something which is common to the entire election of grace, appears from his word "Henceforth there is laid up for me a crown of righteousness, which the Lord, the righteous judge, shall give me at that day: and not to me only, but unto *all* them that *love* His appearing" (II Tim. 4:8).

Next we turn to the *external* token of our adoption. This is evangelical obedience, whereby the believer sincerely endeavors to obey God's commands in his daily life. *"Hereby we do know* that we know Him, if we keep His commandments" (I John 2:3). God does not judge disobedience by the rigor of the Law for then it would be no token of grace but a means of damnation. Rather does God esteem and consider that obedience according to the tenor of the new covenant. Concerning those who fear Him the Lord declares, "I will spare them, as a man spareth his own son that serveth him" (Mal. 3:17). God regards the things done not by their effects or absolute doing of them, but by *the affection* of the doer. It is at the heart God chiefly looks. And yet, lest any be deceived on this point, let the following qualifications be prayerfully pondered.

That external obedience which God requires of His children and which for Christ's sake He accepts from them is not one which has respect to only a few of the divine commands, but unto all without exception. Herod heard the Baptist gladly, and did many things (Mark 6:20), but he drew the line at complying with the seventh commandment to leave his brother Philip's wife. Judas forsook the world for Christ, and became a preacher of the gospel, yet he failed to mortify the lust of covetousness, and perished. On the contrary David exclaimed, "Then shall I not be ashamed, when I have respect unto *all* thy commandments" (Ps. 119:6). He that repents of one sin truly repents of all sins, and he that lives in any one known sin without repentance, actually repents of no sin at all.

Again, for our external obedience to be acceptable to God, it must extend itself to the whole course of a Christian's life after conversion. We are not to judge ourselves (or any one else) by a few odd actions, but by the general tenor of our lives. As the course of a man's life is, such is the man himself; though he, because of the sin which still indwells him, fails in this or that particular action, yet doth it not prejudice his estate before God, so long as he renews his repentance for his offenses—not lying down in any one sin. Finally, it is required that this external obedience proceed from the whole man: all that is within him is to show forth God praises. At the new birth all the faculties of the soul are renewed, and henceforth are to be employed in the service of God, as formerly they had been in the service of sin.

Let it be said once more that it is most important that the Christian should be quite clear as to exactly *what it is* his spirit bears witness unto. It is not to any improvement in his carnal nature, nor to sin being less active within him; rather is it to the fact that he is a child of God, as is evident from his heart going out after Him, yearning for fellowship with Him, and his sincere endeavor to please Him. Just as an affectionate and dutiful child has within his own bosom proof of the peculiar relationship which he stands in to his father, so the filial inclinations and aspirations of the believer prove that God is his heavenly Father. True, there is still much in him which is constantly rising up in opposition to God, nevertheless there is something else which was not in him by nature.

Let us here anticipate an objection: some say that it is a sin for the Christian to question his acceptance with God because he is still so depraved, or to doubt his salvation because he can perceive little or no holiness within. They say that such doubting is to call God's truth and faithfulness into question, for He has assured us of His love and His readiness to save all who believe in His Son. They deny that it is our duty to examine our hearts and say that we shall never obtain any assurance by so doing; that we must look to Christ alone, and rest on His naked Word. But this is a serious mistake. We *do* rest on His Word when we search for those evidences which that Word itself describes as the marks of a child of God. Said the apostle, "For our rejoicing is this, *the testimony of our conscience* . . . " (II Cor. 1:12). "Let us not love in word, neither in tongue; but in deed and in truth. And *hereby* we know that we are of the truth, and shall assure our hearts before him" (I John 3:18, 19).

But notwithstanding the evidences which a Christian has of his divine sonship, he finds it no easy matter to be assured of his sincerity or to establish solid comfort in his soul. His moods are fitful, his frames variable. It is at this very point the blessed Spirit of God helpeth our infirmities. He adds *His* witness to the testimony of our renewed conscience, so that at times the Christian is assured of his salvation, and can say "*my conscience* is also bearing me witness *in the Holy Spirit*" (Rom. 9:1).

"The sole way of God's appointment whereby we may come to an apprehension of an interest in election is by the *fruits* of it *in our own souls*. Nor is it lawful for us to enquire into it or after it in any other way." With those words of the judicious Owen we are in full accord. For our part, we would not dare to place any reliance of an everlasting hope upon any dream or vision we had received, or any voice we had heard. Even if a celestial being appeared before us and declared that he had seen our name written in the Lamb's book of life, we should place no credence in it, for we would have no means of knowing that it might not be the Devil himself "transformed into an angel of light" (II Cor. 11:14) come to deceive us. Our election must be certified to us by the unerring Word of God, and there we have a sure foundation on which to rest our faith.

The obligation which the gospel puts upon us to believe any thing respects *the order* of the things themselves and the order of our obedience. When it is declared by the gospel that Christ died for sinners, I am not immediately required to believe that Christ died for me in particular—that were to *invert* the divine order of the gospel. The grand and simple message of the evangel of God's grace is, that Christ Jesus came into the world to procure a way of salvation for them who are lost, that He died for the ungodly, that He so perfectly satisfied the claims of the divine justice that God can righteously justify every sinner who truly believes in His Son, Jesus Christ (Rom. 3:26). Consequently since I find myself a member of that class, since I know myself to be a sinner, an ungodly person, lost, then I have full warrant to believe the good news of the gospel. Thus the gospel requires from me faith and obedience and I am under an obligation to render them withal.

Until I believe and obey the gospel I am under no obligation to believe that Christ died for me in particular; but having done so, I *am* warranted to enjoy that assurance. In like manner, I am required to believe the *doctrine* of election upon my first hearing of the gospel, because it is therein clearly declared. But as for my own *personal* election I cannot Scripturally believe it, nor am I obligated to believe it any otherwise, but as God reveals it *by its effects.* No man may justly disbelieve in or deny his election until he be in a condition where it is impossible for the effects of election to be wrought in him. While he is unholy a man can have no evidence that he is elected; so he can have none that he is not elected while it is possible for him to be made holy. Thus, whether men are elected or no, is not that which God calls any immediately to be conversant about: faith, obedience, holiness are what are first required from us.

Before proceeding further let it be pointed out that the elect are usually to be found where the ministers of Christ labor much. Said Paul, "Therefore I endure all things for the elect's sake, that *they* may also obtain the salvation which is in Christ Jesus with eternal glory" (II Tim. 2:10). That illustrates the principle: the apostle knew that in his evangelical labors he was being employed in executing God's purpose in carrying the message of salvation to His people. To that very end was the apostle sustained by divine providence and directed by the Spirit of the Lord. Take a brief specimen of the method in which he was divinely guided. In his second journey publishing the glad tidings in heathen lands, Paul had been led through Phrygia and the region of Galatia, and would have preached the Word in Asia, but was "forbidden of the Holy Spirit" (Acts 16:6)—for what possible reason? but that God had none of His elect there, or if any, that the time had not yet arrived for their spiritual deliverance.

The apostle then essayed to go into Bithynia, but again we are told, "the Spirit *suffered him not*" (Acts 16:7). Very striking indeed is that, though it seems to make little or no impression upon people today. Next we read, "And they *passing by* Mysia [how solemn!] came down to Troas." There the Lord appeared unto him in a vision directing him to go to Macedonia, and from this he assuredly gathered that He had called him to preach the gospel there. He thereupon entered that country and proclaimed the good news, and in consequence, God's elect in Thessalonica obtained salvation. Later, he came to Corinth, where he met with much opposition, and with little success. He seems to have been on the point of departing, when the Lord appeared to him, strengthened his heart, and assured him "I have much people in this city" (Acts 18:10). As the result, he remained there eighteen months and the Corinthian Church was formed.

This grand principle of the Lord's so directing His servants that His elect are caused to hear His gospel from their lips, receives many striking illustrations in the Scriptures. The remarkable way in which Philip was conducted with the word of salvation to the Ethiopian eunuch, and Peter with the same word to Cornelius and his company, are cases in point. Another example, perhaps more striking still, is the way in which the apostles obtained access to the Philippian jailor with the word of life, who, because of his calling, probably found it impossible to hear their public preaching. Most blessedly do these instances exemplify the words of the Saviour who, when referring to that company which the Father had given Him in Gentile lands, declared "And other sheep I have which are not of this fold; them also I must bring, and they shall hear my voice" (John 10:16)—hear His voice through His servants and be quickened by the power of His Spirit.

The Lord Jesus never yet sent His servants to labor where He had not a people, which being given to Him by the Father, were by Him to be brought into the fold. And He never will so send them. But where He has a people, He will there direct His own servants to call that people to Himself, and they like Paul of old will "endure all things for the elect's sake, that they may also obtain the salvation which is in Christ Jesus." Only the day to come will fully reveal how much—by His upholding grace—they did endure so that the elect might be saved. The elect, then, are to be found where the faithful ministers of Christ labor much. Now, my reader, if you are privileged to live in such a place, then in your own midst you may look for the favored people of God. The day of golden opportunity is now yours, and it is your bounden duty to respond and yield to the call made by Christ's servants.

Let us now pass on to something yet more specific. God not only sends His servants to those places where His providence has situated some of His elect, but He clothes His word with power and makes their labors effective. "Knowing, brethren beloved, your election of God. For our gospel came not unto you, in word only, but also in power, and in the Holy Spirit, and in much assurance" (I Thess. 1:4, 5). That passage is very much to the point, and each clause in it calls for our closest attention. It tells us *how* the apostle became assured that the Thessalonian saints were among God's chosen people, and how by parity of reason, they too might know and rejoice in their election. Those details have been placed on record for our instruction, and if the Lord is pleased to grant us a spiritual understanding of them, we shall be on safe and sure ground. But in order for this, we must prayerfully ponder these verses word by word.

"Knowing brethren, beloved, your election of God." How did the apostle know their election of God? Let it be most particularly observed that this assurance of his was obtained *not* by any immediate revelation from Heaven, not by a supernatural vision or angelic message, nor by the Lord Himself, directly informing him to that effect. No; rather was it by what he had witnessed in and from *them*. It was by the *visible fruits* of their election that he perceived them to be "brethren beloved." In other words, he traced back those effects of grace which had been wrought in them at their conversion, to the source thereof in God's eternal purpose of mercy. Those tiny rivulets of grace in their hearts the apostle traced back to the ocean of God's everlasting love from which they proceeded. Therein, he indicated to us the course which we must follow, the method we are to pursue in order to ascertain our predestination to glory.

"For our gospel came not unto you in word only, but also in power." All who pretend to preach the gospel do not actually do so. To allow that they did, would be to grant that there are as many different gospels as there are sects and sentiments in Christendom, all claiming theirs to be the true gospel, to the exclusion of every other. It is therefore a matter of the very highest importance that each of us should know what the gospel of Christ really is, and this must be learned from the Holy Scriptures, under the guidance of God the Spirit. There are numerous counterfeits of it in the world today, and their fraudulency can only be discovered by weighing them in "the balances of the Sanctuary." Equally necessary and important is it that we ascertain how the gospel should be *received* by us if the soul is to be permanently benefited by it, for according to the apostle there is a twofold reception thereof.

"For our gospel came not unto you in word only." For the gospel to come to us "in word only" is for God to leave it to its natural efficacy, or the force of its arguments and persuasion on the human mind. Multitudes, in many places have heard the gospel, yet continue in idoltry and in iniquity, notwithstanding the profession which many of them make. When the gospel comes to us "in word only" it reaches the intellect and understanding, but makes no real impression on the conscience and heart. Consequently, it produces only a feigned and presumptuous faith, a faith which is inferior even to that which the demons have, for they "believe *and tremble*" (James 2:19). It is only when the gospel comes to us "in power and in the Holy Spirit" that it is received with a true and saving faith. How necessary it is then, to test ourselves at this point.

There are two extremes into which men fall through lack of the right receiving of God's Word. The one supposes he is possessed of both will and power to perform works of righteousness sufficient to commend him to the favor of God, and so he becomes "zealously affected, but not well" (Gal. 4:17). He fasts, prays, gives alms, attends church, etc.; and wherein he thinks he fails or comes short, he calls in the merits of Christ as a makeweight for his deficiency. This is but taking a piece of new cloth (Christ's Atonement) and patching into his garment a legal righteousness, hoping thereby to appease a guilty conscience. He continues his religious performances the year round, but never attains to a vital and experimental knowledge of the gospel. All his service is but dead works.

The other extreme is the very reverse of this, but equally dangerous. Instead of toiling to the point of weariness, these work not at all. Being conscious more or less, as all natural men are, that they are sinners, and hearing of free salvation by Jesus Christ, they readily fall in with it, receiving it in their minds but not in their consciences. A superficial and presumptuous faith is begotten, and by a single leap they arrive at a supposed assurance of heaven. But, says Solomon, "An inheritance may be gotten *hastily at the beginning;* but the end thereof shall not be blessed" (Prov. 20:21). These people are great talkers, boast much of their freedom from the law, but are themselves the slaves of sin. They are ever learning, yet never able to come to a knowledge of the truth. They laugh at those who have doubts and fears, yet they themselves have the most cause of all to fear.

Now in marked contrast from both of these classes, are they who receive the gospel not in word only "but in power and in the Holy Spirit." This is a middle way between these two extremes, and one that is hidden from all unregenerate, for "the natural man receiveth not the things of the Spirit of God, for they are foolishness unto him, neither can he know them, because they are *spiritually* discerned" (I Cor. 2:14). When God begins "the work of faith with power" (II Thess. 1:11), and leads that soul in this middle way, he can at first neither see nor understand it. As it was with the father of all who believe, so it is with all his children: when Abraham was effectually called, he "went out, *not knowing* whither he went" (Heb. 11:8). Those born of the Spirit are led forth by "a way that they know not" (Isa. 42:16), and until darkness is made light before them and crooked things straight, they cannot understand the way of the Spirit; but when that *is* done, then the highway is "cast up" for them (Isa. 62:10).

The all-important question, then, is, Has the gospel come to me in word only, or in saving power? If the former, then it has been received *without* anguish, trouble, or distress of conscience, for those are the common marks of divine power working in the sinner's soul. When God's Word comes to us "in power," it comes as a "two-edged sword" (Heb. 4:12), having the same effect on the heart as a sword does when it is thrust into the body. If the wound be deep, the pain and smart will be very acute. So when the Word of God pierces "even to the dividing asunder of soul and spirit, and of the joints and marrow and is a discerner of the thoughts and intents of the heart" it produces real anguish and deep distress. Said Job, "The arrows of the Almighty are within me, the poison whereof drinketh up my spirit [explained in the next words]; the terrors of God do set themselves in array against me" (6:4). And thus, too, David exclaimed, "Thine arrows stick fast in me, and thy hand presseth me sore" (Ps. 38:2).

It was thus in the experience of Paul. Before the Spirit applied the law to his heart, he was alive in his own eyes, though dead in God's; but when the commandment came home to him in divine power, sin revived and he died—in his own esteem (Rom. 7:9). The fact is that he, like every other pharisee, supposed that the law reached no further than the external letter, touching which he considered himself blameless. But when its high demands and searching spirituality was made known to him he found it reached the very thoughts and intents of the heart, and discovered to him the awful depths of depravity in him which was hid before. He found the law was spiritual, but himself carnal, sold under sin. He found—as very, very few do—that his heart was in the very state described by Christ in Mark 7:21, 22. He was compelled to believe what Christ there declared, because he now saw and felt the same within himself.

The first act of faith brings a man to believe that he is in the very state Scripture declares him to be; at enmity against God (Rom. 8:7), a child of wrath (Eph. 2:3), under the curse of a broken law (Gal. 3:10), led captive by the Devil (II Tim. 2:26). A heavy burden of sin lies on his conscience (Ps. 38:4), an active fountain of iniquity like the troubled sea casts up its mire and dirt (Isa. 57:20), which baffles all the efforts of an arm of flesh, bringing him into terrible bondage: "our iniquities, like the wind, have taken us away" (Isa. 64:6). He finds himself bound hand and foot with the cords of his sins, and he cries earnestly to God to take pity upon him, and out of his great mercy loose him. He now needs no set forms of prayer, but night and day he cries "God be merciful to me a sinner."

And *how* does the Lord set him at liberty? By the gospel coming to him "in power and in the Holy Spirit." God exhibits to him in a new light, the sufferings and death of His Son, by whom His justice was satisfied, His law magnified, His wrath appeased, and a way of reconciliation opened between God and sinners. It is the Spirit's office to work faith in the heart and to apply the atoning blood and righteousness of Christ to the conscience, by whom the burden of sin and death is removed, the love of God is made known, peace is imparted to the soul, and joy to the heart. Thus, the same instrument which wounded, brings healing. Therefore did the apostle here add, "For our gospel came not unto you in word only, but also in power, and in the Holy Spirit, *and in much assurance*"—assurance of its divine verity and authority, of its perfect adaptability and suitability to our case, of its ineffable blessedness.

"I remember, too, when the truth came home to my heart, and made me leap for very joy, for it took all my load away; it showed me Christ's power to save. I had known the truth before, but now I *felt* it. I went to Jesus just as I was, I touched the hem of His garment; I was made whole. I found now that the Word was not a fiction—that it was the one reality. I had listened scores of times, and he that spake was as one that played a tune upon an instrument; but now he seemed to be dealing with me, putting his hand right into my heart. He brought me first to God's judgment seat, and there I stood and heard the thunders roll; then he brought me to the mercy seat, and I saw the blood sprinkled on it, and I went home triumphing because sin was washed away" (C. H. Spurgeon).

"Knowing, brethren beloved, your election of God" (I Thess. 1:4). How did the apostle know that those Thessalonians were among God's elect? The next verses tell us: by *the visible fruits* thereof which he perceived in them. Discerning in their lives those effects of grace which had been wrought in them at their conversion, he traced back the same unto God's eternal purpose of mercy concerning them. And, my reader, the way in which Paul knew the Thessalonian believers were "from the beginning chosen . . . to salvation" (II Thess. 2:13) must be the method by which every Christian today is to ascertain his or her election of God.

"For our gospel came not unto you in word only, but also in power, and in the Holy Spirit" (I Thess. 1:5). Everything turns upon *how* the (true) Gospel is received by us: whether it is merely apprehended by the intellect, or whether it really reaches the conscience and heart for only then is it received with a saving faith. When God's Word comes to us "in power," it comes as "a two-edged sword"—cutting, wounding, causing pain and deep distress. When the Word comes to us in power it is not due to any learning or eloquence of the preacher, nor to any pathos which he may employ. The fact that his hearers' emotions are deeply stirred so that they are moved to tears, is no proof whatever that the gospel is come to them in divine efficacy: creature passions are often stirred by the actings of the stage and thousands are moved to weep in the theater. Such superficial emotionalism is but evanescent, having no lasting and spiritual effects. The test is whether we are broken and bowed before *God*.

The same thought is expressed again in the next verse, as though *this* is the particular detail by which we most need to test ourselves: "having received the Word *in much affliction*, with joy of the Holy Ghost" (v. 6). How that exposes the worthlessness of the light and frothy "evangelism" (?) of the day! How solemn it is to remember that Christ described the stony-ground hearer as "he that heareth the Word and anon with *joy* receiveth it; yet hath he not root in himself" (Matt. 13:20, 21). Very different was it with those who were converted on the day of Pentecost, for the first thing recorded of them is, that they were "pricked in their heart" (Acts 2:37). Travail precedes birth, and then comes the rejoicing (see John 16:21). These are the questions to be considered—and answered before God: Has the Word rebuked and condemned me? Has it stripped me of my self-complacency and self-righteousness? Has it cut down my hopes, and brought me to lie as a self-condemned felon before the mercy seat?

"People come and hear sermons in this place, and then they go out and say, 'How did you like it?'—as if *that* signified to anybody. 'How did you like it?' and one says, 'Oh, very well,' and another says 'Oh, not at all.' Do you think we live on the breath of your nostrils? Do you believe that God's servants, if they are really His, care for what *you* think of them? Nay, verily; but if you should reply 'I enjoyed the sermon,' they are inclined to say, 'Then we must have been unfaithful, or else you would have been angry; we must surely have slurred over something, or else the Word would have cut your conscience as with the jagged edges of a knife. You would have said, 'I did not think how I liked it; I was thinking how I liked myself, and about my own state before God; *that* was the matter that exercised me, not whether he preached well, but whether I stood accepted in Christ, or whether I was a castaway.' My dear hearers, Are you learning to hear like that? If you are not, if going to church and to chapel be to you like going to an oratorio, or like listening to some orator who speaks upon temporal matters, then you lack the evidence of election; the Word had not come to your souls with power" (C. H. Spurgeon).

In between the portions quoted above from I Thessalonians 1:5, 6 are two other details: first, "and in much assurance." When the Word comes home in converting power to a man's soul, all his doubts concerning its authenticity and authority are removed, and he needs no human arguments to convince him that its author is *God*. All the skepticism of the rationalists and higher critics would be dispelled like mist before the rising sun, if the Spirit was pleased to effectually apply the Word to their hearts. Those who have been made to feel their dire need of Christ and have perceived His perfect suitability to their desperate condition, have "much assurance" of what the gospel affirms of His person and work. Whatever may have been the case with them formerly, they have no doubt now about His absolute Deity, His virgin birth, His vicarious death, His pre-eminent dignity, as prophet, priest, and king. These all-important things are settled for him, settled forever, and he will declare himself with a positiveness and dogmatism which will shock the sensibilities of the supercilious.

Again it is said, "ye become followers of us and of the Lord." Here is another mark of election: those who are chosen by the Lord *desire to be like Him*. "Ye became followers of us" does not mean that they said, 'I am of Paul, I am of Silas, I am of Timothy,' but that they imitated those eminent evangelists so far as they followed the example which Christ has left us. Ah, *that* is the test my readers. Are we Christlike? or do we honestly wish to be so? Then that is a sure evidence of our election. Do we live by every word of God (Matt. 4:4)?—Christ did. Do we take everything to God in prayer?—Christ did. Do we pray God to bless those who curse us? It is not that we are sinless, perfect; but are we, though often "afar off," really following Christ? If we are, it is not proud boastfulness to acknowledge it, nor is it self-righteousness to derive comfort therefrom, providing we also grieve over our many shortcomings and mourn over our sins.

"With joy of the Holy Spirit." Mark the qualifying language: it is not carnal mirth, but spiritual gladness. And observe too, that this concludes the list, for it is ever the Lord's way to reserve the best wine for the last. Alas, how few professors know anything, experimentally, about this deep, spiritual joy. The religion of the vast majority consists of a slavish attendance upon forms that they delight not in. How many go to some place of worship simply because it is not respectable to stay away, though they often wish it were. Not so with the Christian—when he is in his right mind: he goes to worship the Lord, to hear the voice of his beloved, seeking a fresh love-token from Him, desiring to bask in the sunshine of His presence. And when he is favored with a visit from Christ he exclaims with Jacob, "This is the house of God," a foretaste of heaven.

And now in drawing to a conclusion our remarks upon this fascinating aspect of the subject, there remains one other verse we must ponder: "Wherefore the rather, brethren, give diligence to make your calling and election sure" (II Peter 1:10). Those words have been fearfully wrested by errorists. Enemies of the truth have perverted them to signify that, the divine decree concerning salvation is but provisional, conditional on the sinner's own efforts. They deny that any man's predestination to eternal life is absolute and irrevocable, insisting that it is contingent upon our own personal diligence. In other words, man himself must decide and determine whether God's desire for him is to be realized. Not only is such a concept entirely foreign to the teaching of Holy Writ, but to say that the ratification and realization of God's eternal purpose is left dependent on something from the creature, is sheer blasphemy; and were it true, would not only render our election uncertain, but utterly hopeless.

"Wherefore the rather, brethren, give diligence to make your calling and election sure." These words have also presented a real problem to not a few of God's people. They have been sorely perplexed to understand how any diligence on their part could possibly make God's calling and election sure; and even when that difficulty is cleared up, they are quite at a loss to know what form their diligence is to take. Ah, my friends, God has often expressed Himself in the Scriptures in such a way as to test our faith, humble our hearts, and drive us to our knees. Perhaps it may afford most help if we concentrate on the following points. First, the particular people here addressed. Second, the unusual order of "calling and election. Third, what is the "diligence" here required. Fourth, in what sense can we make our calling and election "sure"?

First, the people addressed. If this simple but essential principle were duly heeded what a mass of erroneous expositions would be avoided. It is the mis-application of Scripture which is responsible for so much faulty interpretation. When the children's bread be cast unto the dogs, the former are robbed and the latter given that which they cannot digest. To take an exhortation which is addressed to believers and appropriate it, or rather misappropriate it, to unbelievers, is an excuseless offense: yet such has often been done with the verse before us. There is no difficulty whatever in ascertaining the addressees of this divine injunction. The opening verse of the epistle tells us that the apostle is here writing to those who had "obtained like precious faith," so that they were *believers;* while in the verse itself they are styled "brethren" and exhorted as such.

This exhortation, then, is addressed to living saints and not to dead sinners. To teach that the unregenerate can do anything at all toward securing their calling and election, is not only colossal ignorance, but it gives the lie of God's Word. When they are delivering a divine message, the first duty of God's ministers is to draw very definitely the line of demarcation between the Church and the world: it is failure at this point which causes so many children of the Devil to claim relationship with the people of God. Attention to the context will almost always make it clear to whom a passage pertains: whether to the children of men in general or to the children of God in particular. The simplest and most effectual way of making this plain to their hearers, is for them to carefully delineate the *characters* (the identifying marks) of the one and of the other—note how the apostle followed this very course in the first four verses of the epistle.

Second, the unusual order that is found here: "your calling and election." Though at first sight this presents a difficulty, yet further study will show it really supplies an important key to the opening of this exhortation. That which puzzles the thoughtful reader is, why "calling" comes *before* "election," for as we have sought so show at length in previous chapters, effectual calling is the consequence of election, as it is also the manifestation thereof. As Romans 8:28 declares believers are "the called according to His purpose": that is, the calling is in pursuance of God's purpose. So too in Romans 8:30 it is said, "Whom He did predestinate, them He also called." Likewise "Who hath saved us and called us with a holy calling, not according to our works, but according to His own purpose" (II Tim. 1:9). Why, then, are these two things inverted in the passage we are now considering?

It is to be carefully noted that Romans 8:28, 30 and II Timothy 1:9 are treating of *God's* acts, whereas II Peter 1:10 mentions calling and election in connection with *our* diligence. It is only by duly noting such distinctions that we can hope to arrive at a right understanding of many of the details of Holy Writ. In Romans 8 the apostle is propounding doctrine, whereas in II Peter 1:10 he is pressing an exhortation, and there is a marked difference between those things. When the ways of God are being expounded, they are presented in their natural or logical order (as in Rom. 8:30), but when Christian *experience* is being dealt with, the order in which we apprehend the truth is the one followed. Thus it is here: we are first to make sure that we have been the recipients of an effectual call, for that in turn will furnish proof of our election. The order of God's thoughts toward us was, election and then calling; but in our experience we apprehend calling before election.

Third, what is the "diligence" here required? There are multitudes who fancy they have received an effectual call from God, but it is merely fancy: instead of prayerfully and diligently devoting themselves to the duty here enjoined, they give themselves the benefit of the doubt. Probably many are quite sincere in their supposition, but they are sincerely mistaken, being led astray by their deceitful hearts. It is far from being sufficient to adopt the doctrine of election as an article of our creed. As one tersely put it:

Though God's election is a truth,
Small comfort there I see,
Till I am told by God's own mouth,
That He hath chosen me.

And I have no right or warrant to expect that He will ever do any such thing, till I have complied with His requirements in the verse now before us.

That to which I am here exhorted is to first make sure my "calling" of God. This is to be done by accumulating and strengthening my evidence that I am His born-again child; and that, in turn, is accomplished by cultivating the character and conduct of a saint. And how is that to be achieved? By using the means of grace which God has provided: such as the daily reading of the Scriptures with spiritual meditation thereon; by secret and fervent prayer for divine succor and grace; by cultivating fellowship with God's people, so far as His providence permits this; by keeping faithful watch over our hearts, disallowing all that is unholy; by the strict denial of self and mortification of our members. But we shall receive most help at this point if we attend unto something yet more specific in the context.

In verses 5-7 we are exhorted, "giving all diligence, add to your faith virtue; and to virtue knowledge; and to knowledge temperance; and to temperance patience; and to patience godliness; and to godliness brotherly kindness; and to brotherly kindness love." Now verse 10 expresses the same duty, but in different words. There is a striking parallelism in this chapter, and it is by noting the repetition (in variation of thought) that we find the chief key to our verse. In verses 5-7 we have an exhortation, and in verse 8 we are shown the result of heeding it. In verse 10 we also have a similar exhortation, and then in verse 11 the result of compliance therewith is shown. Thus our text is to be interpreted in the light of its context. What is the "diligence" here required? Of what does it consist? Verses 5 to 7 tell us. It is by carefully cultivating the spiritual graces therein mentioned that I may ascertain my calling and election.

Fourth, in what sense do we make our calling and election "sure"? First, observe it is *not* "make secure": they are already secured to every saint by the immutability of the divine purpose, for "the gifts and calling of God are without repentance" (Rom. 11:29). It is not the making of our calling and election sure Godwards, but *manwards*. Nor is it something future which is here in view: it is the present *enjoyment* to ourselves of our calling and election, and of *evidencing* the same to our brethren. By heeding the exhortation of verses 5-7 I am to prove my calling and election, and demonstrate the same to the Church. A man may tell me he believes in election and is sure that he has been called of God, but unless I can see in his character and conduct the spiritual graces of verses 5-7 then I have to say of him (as Paul did of the Galatians) "I stand in doubt of you." Here, then, is the meaning: make steadfast in your own conscience your calling and election, and make good to others your profession, by walking as a child of God.

Finally, two *consequences* of complying with those exhortations are pointed out. First, "For if ye do these things, ye shall never fall" (v. 10.) Those who give all diligence to cultivate the spiritual graces mentioned in verses 5-7 (thereby making their calling and election sure, both to themselves and to their brethren), shall never fall from the place of communion with God; shall never fall from the truth into false doctrine and error; shall never fall into grievous sins, and so disgrace their Christian profession; shall never fall into a state of backsliding, so that they lose their relish for spiritual things; shall never fall under sore discipline from God; shall never fall into a despondency so as to lose all assurance; shall never fall into a condition of spiritual uselessness. But, second, "For *so* an entrance shall be ministered unto you *abundantly* into the everlasting kingdom of our Lord and Saviour Jesus Christ" (v. 11): experimentally so here; fully and honorably so in the future. This is the result and reward of "diligence": the Greek word for "ministered" in verse 11 is the same as "added" in verse 5!

And now to summarize. How may a real believer ascertain that he is one of God's elect? Why, the very fact he *is* a genuine Christian evidences it, for a believing into Christ is the sure consequence of God's having ordained him to eternal life (Acts. 13:48). But to be more specific. *How* may I know my election? First, by the Word of God, having come in Divine power to the soul, so that my self-complacency is shattered and my self-righteousness renounced. Second, by the Spirit's having convicted me to my woeful, guilty, and lost condition. Third, by having had revealed to me the suitability and sufficiency of Christ to meet my desperate case, and by a divinely given faith causing me to lay hold of and rest upon Him as my only hope. Fourth, by the marks of the new nature within me: a love for God, an appetite for spiritual things, a longing for holiness, a seeking after conformity to Christ. Fifth, by the resistance which the new nature makes to the old, causing me to hate sin and loathe myself for it. Sixth, by sedulously avoiding everything which is condemned by

God's Word, and by sincerely repenting of and humbly confessing every transgression thereof. Failure at this point will most surely and quickly bring a dark cloud over our assurance, causing the Spirit to withhold His witness. Seventh, by giving all diligence to cultivate the Christian graces, and using all legitimate means to this end. Thus, knowledge of election is cumulative.

10 *Its Blessedness*

First, the doctrine of election *magnifies the character of God*. It exemplifies His *grace*. Election makes known the fact that salvation is God's free gift, gratuitously bestowed upon whom He pleases. This must be so, for those who receive it are themselves no different from and no better than those who receive it not. Election allows some to go to hell, to show that all deserved to perish. But grace comes in like a dragnet and draws out from a ruined humanity a little flock, to be throughout eternity the monument of God's sovereign mercy. It exhibits His omnipotency. Election makes known the fact that God is all powerful, ruling and reigning over the earth, and declares that none can successfully resist His will or thwart His secret purposes. Election reveals God breaking down the opposition of the human heart, subduing the enmity of the carnal mind, and with irresistible power drawing His chosen ones to Christ. Election confesses that "we love him because he first loved us," and that we believe because He made us willing in the day of His power (Ps. 110:3).

The doctrine of election ascribes all the glory to God. It disallows any credit to the creature. It denies that the unregenerate are capable of predicting a right thought, generating a right affection, or originating a right volition. It insists that God must work in us both to will and to do. It declares that repentance and faith are themselves God's gifts, and not something which the sinner contributes towards the price of his salvation. His language is, "Not unto us, not unto us," but "Unto him that loved us and washed us from our sins in his own blood." These paragraphs were written by us almost a quarter of a century since, and today we neither rescind nor modify them.

"The Lord makes distinctions among guilty men according to the sovereignty of His grace. 'I will no more have mercy upon the house of

Israel: but I will have mercy upon the house of Judah.' Had not Judah sinned too? Might not the Lord have given up Judah also? Indeed He might justly have done so, but He delighteth in mercy. Many sin, and righteously bring upon themselves the punishment due to sin: they believe not in Christ, and die in their sins. But God has mercy, according to the greatness of His heart upon many, who could not be saved upon any other footing but that of undeserved mercy. Claiming His royal right He says, 'I will have mercy on whom I will have mercy.' The prerogative of mercy is vested in the sovereignty of God: that prerogative He exercises. He gives where He pleases, and He has a right to do so, since none have any claim upon Him" (C. H. Spurgeon: "The Lord's Own Salvation"—Hos. 1:7).

The above makes it sufficiently plain that it is no light thing to reject this blessed part of eternal truth: nay, it is a most solemn and serious matter so to do. God's Word is not given us to pick and choose from—to single out those portions which appeal to us, and to disdain whatever commends itself not to our reason and sentiments. It is given to us as a whole, and by it each of us must yet be judged. To reject the grand truth we are here treating of is the height of impiety, for to repudiate the election of God is to repudiate the God of election. It is a refusal to bow before His high sovereignty. It is the corrupt preacher opposing himself against the holy Creator. It is presumptuous pride which insists upon being the determiner of its own destiny. It is the spirit of Lucifer, who said, "I will exalt my throne above the stars of God . . . I will be like the Most High" (Isa. 14:13, 14).

Second, the blessedness of this doctrine appears in that *it is all important in the plan of salvation.* Consider this first from the divine side. A Scriptural presentation of this grand truth is indispensable if the distinctive acts of the triune God in salvation matters are to be recognized, honored, and owned. Salvation proceeds not from one divine person only, but equally from the everlasting three. Jehovah has so ordered things that each one in the Godhead should be magnified and glorified alike. The Father is as really and truly the Christian's Saviour as is the Lord Jesus, and so too is the Holy Spirit—note how the Father is expressly designated "God our Saviour" in Titus 3:4, as distinct from "Jesus Christ our Saviour" in verse 5. But this is ignored and lost sight of if this precious doctrine be omitted. Predestination pertains to the Father, propitiation to the Son, regeneration to the Spirit. The Father originated, the Son effectuated our salvation, and by the Spirit it is consummated. To repudiate the former is to take away the very foundation.

Consider it now from the human side: election lies at the very base of a sinner's hope. By nature all are the children of wrath. In practice, all have gone astray. The whole world has become guilty before God, all are exposed to wrath, and if left to themselves would be involved in one common ruin. They are "clay of the same lump," and continuing under nature's forming hand would be all "vessels to dishonor" (Rom. 9:21). That any are saved is of the grace of God (Rom. 11:4-7). Jesus Christ, the redeemer of sinners, is Himself the elect one, as described by the prophet (Isa. 42:1). And all who shall ever be saved are elected in Him, given to Him of the Father, chosen in Him before the foundation of the world. It was to accomplish their salvation that God gave His only begotten Son, and that Jesus Christ assumed our nature and gave His life a ransom.

It is to call the elect that the Scriptures are given, that ministers are sent, that the gospel is preached, and the Holy Spirit is here. It is to accomplish election that men are taught of God, drawn of the Father, regenerated by the Holy Spirit, made partakers of precious faith, endued with the spirit of adoption, the spirit of prayer, and the spirit of holiness. It is in consequence of their election that men are made obedient to the gospel, are sanctified by the Spirit, and become holy and without blame before God. Had there been no divine election, there had been no divine salvation. Nor is this a mere arbitrary assertion of ours: "Except the Lord of Sabbaoth had left us a seed, we had been as Sodom, and been made like unto Gomorrah" (Rom. 9:29). Lost sinners cannot save themselves. God was under no obligation to save them. If He be pleased *to* save, He saves whom He will.

Election not only lies at the foundation of a sinner's hope, but also accompanies every step of the Christian's progress to heaven. It carries to him the glad tidings of salvation. It opens his heart to receive the Saviour. It is seen in every act of faith, in every holy duty, and in every effectual prayer. It calls him. It quickens him in Christ. It beautifies his soul. It crowns him with righteousness and life and glory. It contains within it the precious assurance that "He which hath begun a good work in you will perform it until the day of Jesus Christ" (Phil 1:6). There was nothing in them which moved God to choose His people, and He so deals with them as not to permit anything in or from them as to cause Him to reverse that choice. As Romans 8:30 so definitely intimates, predestination involves glorification, and therefore guarantees the supply of the elect's every need in between the two.

Third, the blessedness of this doctrine appears in *its essential elements.* We will single out three or four of the principal of these. First, the superlative honor of being chosen by God. In all choices the person choosing puts a value on the chosen. To be selected by a king unto an office, or to be called to some employment by the state, how it will dignify a man. Thus it is in spiritual affairs. It was a special commendation of Titus that he had been "chosen of the churches" (II Cor. 8:19). But that the great God, the blessed and only potentate, should choose such poor, contemptible, worthless, and vile creatures as we are, passeth knowledge. Ponder I Corinthians 1:26-29, and see how this is there dwelt upon. How it should amaze us. How it should humble us. Note how this honorable emphasis is put upon the Lord Jesus: "Behold my servant, *whom I have chosen*" (Matt. 12:18); so upon His members too: "The elect's sake, *whom he hath chosen*" (Mark 13:20).

Again; the consequent excellency of this. They are *the elect:* the ones which God hath chosen, and doth not high worth, honor, excellency, necessarily follow from this? The chosen of God must needs be choice: the act of God makes them so. Observe the order in I Peter 2:6, "chief cornerstone, elect, precious"—precious because elect. Take the most eminent of God's saints, and what is their highest title and honor? This: "For David My servant's sake, *whom I chose*" (I Kings 11:34). "Aaron whom He had chosen" (Ps. 105:26). Paul, "he is a chosen vessel unto Me" (Acts 9:15). "Ye are a chosen generation, a peculiar people" (I Peter 2:9), that is, elect. That expression is taken from "Ye shall be a peculiar treasure unto me above all people" (Exod. 19:5). It imports that which is dear to God: "since thou wast precious in my sight, thou hast been honorable" (Isa. 43:4).

Again, mark the *fulness* of such high privilege. "Blessed is the man whom thou choosest, and causest to approach unto thee, that he may dwell in thy courts" (Ps. 65:4); yea, he is "most blessed forever" (Ps. 21:6), or as the Hebrew has it (see mar.) "set for blessings," that is, set apart or appointed for naught but blessings. As the New Testament expresses it, "Blessed be the God and Father of our Lord Jesus Christ, who hath blessed us with *all spiritual blessings* in the heavenly places in Christ: according as he hath chosen us in him" (Eph. 1:3, 4). Election, then, is the treasury-fountain of all blessedness. The elect are chosen unto the nearest approach and union unto God that is possible for creatures, to the highest communion with Himself. Consider too the *time* when He chose us. Paul dates it from "the beginning" (II Thess. 2:13). God hath loved us ever since He was God, and while He is God He will continue to do so. God is from everlasting and He continues to be God to everlasting (Ps. 90:2), and His love to us is as old: "I have loved thee with an everlasting love." And His love is like Himself: causeless, changeless, endless.

The blessedness of election appears again in the comparative *fewness* of the elect. The paucity of men enjoying any privilege magnifies it the more, as in the case of the preservation of Noah and his family:

"The ark ... wherein few, that is, eight souls were saved" (I Peter 3:20). What a contrast was that from the whole world "of the ungodly," which all perished! The same fact and contrast was emphasized by Christ in Luke 12. "For all these things do the nations of the world seek after" (v. 30): that is, the things of time and sense, and God gives such to them. But in opposition thereto, the Lord says, "Fear not, little flock; for it is your Father's good pleasure to give you *the kingdom*" (v. 32). His design was to show the greater mercy of God that so few are reserved unto spiritual and eternal favors, while all others have only material and temporal things as their portion.

How this solemn fact should affect our hearts. Turn your eyes, dear reader, upon the world to-day, and look where you will, what do you behold? Are you not compelled to say of the present generation, in all nations alike, that God has left them to walk "in their own ways?" Must we not mournfully conclude of the men and women of this age that "the whole world lieth in wickedness" (I John 5:19)? The sparce number that are of God, are indeed thinly sown, a small handful of gleaning in comparison with the whole great crop of mankind. And let it not be forgotten that what appears now before our eyes is but the actualization of that which was foreordained in eternity. There is no disappointed and defeated God on the throne of the universe. He has *His* way "in the whirlwind and in the storm" (Nah. 1:3).

And again we say how deeply should this startling contrast affect our hearts. "For a few to be singled forth and saved, when a multitude, yea, a generality of others are suffered to perish; how doth it heighten the mercy and grace of salvation to us; for God in His providence to order many outward means to deliver a few which He denies to others, who perish: how doth this affect the persons that are preserved? How much more when it is 'so great a salvation' " (T. Goodwin). This appears from what were types and mere shadows of it in Old Testament times, as in the case of the one small family of Noah alone being spared from the universal deluge. So, too, by the example of Lot, pulled out of Sodom by the hand of angels. And why? "The Lord being merciful unto him" says Genesis 19:16. Mark what a deep sense of and valuation upon Lot had of the same: "Behold now thy servant hath found grace in thy sight, and thou hast magnified thy mercy, which thou hast showed unto me in saving my life" (Gen. 19:19).

But there is this further to be considered: our being delivered from a condition of like wretchedness and wrath as pertains to the non-elect, which held not in the cases mentioned above. Noah was "A just man, and perfect in his generations" (Gen. 6:9), and Lot was "righteous" and "vexed with the filthy conversation of the wicked" (II

Peter 2:7, 8). They were not guilty of those awful sins because of which God sent the flood and fire upon their fellows. But when *we* were ordained to salvation, we lay before God in a *like condition* of corruption and guilt as all mankind are in. It was only the sovereign decree of a sovereign God which purposed our being brought out of a state of sin and wrath into a state of grace and righteousness. How stupendous, then, was the mercy of God unto *us,* in making this difference (I Cor. 4:7) between those in whom there was "no difference" (Rom. 3:22)! O what love, what whole-hearted obedience, what praise are due unto Him.

Fourth, the blessedness of this doctrine appears in that a true apprehension thereof is *a great promoter of holiness.* According to the divine purpose the elect are destined to a holy calling (II Tim. 1:9). In the accomplishment of that purpose, they are actually and effectually brought to holiness. God separates them from an ungodly world. He writes upon their hearts His Law and affixes to them His seal. They are made partakers of the divine nature, being renewed in the image of Him who created them. They are an habitation of God, their bodies becoming the temple of the Holy Spirit, and they are led by Him. A glorious change is thus wrought in them, transforming their character and conduct. They wash their robes and make them white in the blood of the Lamb. To them, old things are passed away and all things are become new: forgetting the things which are behind, they press forward to the things which are before. They are kings and priests unto God, and shall yet be adorned with crowns of glory.

There are those who, in their ignorance, say that the doctrine of election is a licentious one, that a belief of it is calculated to produce carelessness and a sense of security in sin. Such a charge is a blasphemous reflection upon the divine author of it. This truth, as we have shown at length, occupies a prominent place in the Word of God, and that Word is *holy,* and the whole of it profitable for instruction in *righteousness* (II Tim. 3:16). The apostles one and all believed and taught this doctrine, and they were promoters of piety and not encouragers of loose living. It is true that this doctrine, like every other Scripture, may be *perverted* by wicked men and put to an evil use, but so far as militating against the truth, it only serves to demonstrate the fearful extent of human depravity. We also grant that unregenerate men may intellectually espouse this doctrine and then settle down into a fatalistic inertia. But we emphatically deny that a *heart* reception thereof will produce any such effect.

That faith, obedience, holiness are the inseparable consequences and fruits of election is unmistakably clear from the Scriptures (Acts 13:48; Eph. 1:4; I Thess. 1:4-7; Titus 1:1), and has been fully set forth by us in previous chapters. How can it be otherwise? Election always involves regeneration and sanctification, and when a regenerated and sanctified soul discovers that he owes his spiritual renewal solely to the sovereign predestination of God, how can he but be truly grateful and deeply thankful? And in what other way can he express his gratitude than in a holy course of fruitful obedience? An apprehension of the everlasting love of God for him will of necessity awaken in him a responsive love to God, and wherever *that* exists there will be a sincere effort to please Him in all things. The fact is that a spiritual sense of the distinguishing grace of God is the most powerful constraining motive unto genuine godliness.

Were we to enter into detail upon the principal elements of holiness this chapter would be extended indefinitely. A due consideration of the fact that there was nothing in us which moved God to fix His heart upon us, and that He foresaw us as ruined and hell-deserving creatures, will *humble* our souls as nothing else will. A spiritual realization that all our concerns are entirely at the disposal of God, will work in us a *submission* to His sovereign will as nothing else can. A believing perception that God set His heart upon us from everlasting, choosing us to be His peculiar treasure, will work in us a *contempt of the world*. The knowledge that fellow-Christians are the elect and beloved of God will evoke *love* and *kindness* unto them. The assurance that God's eternal purpose is immutable and guarantees the supply of our every need will impart solid *comfort* in every trial.

11 Its Opposition

Wherever the doctrine of election is Scripturally presented it meets with fierce opposition and bitter declamation. It has been so throughout the entire course of this Christian era, and that, among all races and classes of people. Let the high prerogatives of God be set forth, let the sovereignty of His grace be proclaimed, let men be told they are but clay in the hands of the divine potter to be shaped into vessels of wrath or vessels of mercy as seemeth good in His sight, and at once there is an uproar and outcries of protest. Let the preacher insist that the fallen creature has no claim whatever upon his maker, that he stands before Him as a convicted felon, and is entitled to naught but everlasting judgment, and let him declare that all of Adam's progeny are so utterly depraved that their minds are "enmity against God" and therefore in a state of inveterate insubordination, that their hearts are so corrupt they have no desire for spiritual things, their wills so completely under the domination of evil they cannot turn unto the Lord, and he will be denounced as a heretic.

But this should neither surprise nor stagger the child of God. As he becomes more familiar with the Scriptures, he will find that in every generation the faithful servants of God have been hated and persecuted, some for proclaiming one part of the truth, some for another. When the sun shines on a dunghill, an odious stench is the consequence; when its rays fall upon the stagnant waters of a swamp, disease germs are multiplied. But is the sun to be blamed? Certainly not. So when the sword of the Spirit cuts to the root of human pride, reveals man to be a fallen and foul being, reduces him to an impotent creature, laying him in the dust as a bankrupt pauper, and declares him to be entirely dependent upon the discriminating pleasure of a sovereign God, there is a storm of opposition evoked, and a determined effort is made to silence such flesh-withering teaching.

The method which is usually followed by those who reject this truth is one of *misrepresentation.* The doctrine of election is so grand and glorious that to bear any opposition at all it must be perverted. Those who hate it can neither look upon nor speak of it as it really deserves. Election is treated by them as though it did not include a designation to faith and holiness, as though it was not a conforming of them unto the image of Christ; yea, as though the elect of God might continue to commit all manner of wickedness and yet go to heaven; and that the non-elect, no matter how virtuous they be, or how ardently they long for and strive after righteousness, must assuredly perish. False inferences are drawn, grotesque parodies exhibited, and unscrupulous tactics are employed to create prejudice.

By such devilish efforts do the enemies of God seek to distort and destroy this blessed doctrine. They besmirch it with mire, seek to overwhelm it with things odious, and present it to the indignant gaze of men as something to be repudiated and abominated. A monster of iniquity is thus created and christened "Election," and then presented to the world as something to be cast out as evil. Thereby multitudes have been cheated out of one of the most precious portions of divine truth, and thereby some of God's own people have been sorely perplexed and harassed. That the avowed opponents of Christ should revile a doctrine taught by Him and His apostles is only to be expected; but when those who profess to be His friends and followers join in denouncing this truth, it only serves to demonstrate the cunning of that old serpent the devil, who is never more pleased than when he can persuade nominal Christians to do his vile work for him. Then let not the reader be moved by such opposition.

The vast majority of these opposers have little or no real understanding of that which they set themselves against. They are largely ignorant of what the Scriptures teach thereon, and are too indolent to make any serious study of the subject. Whatever attention they *do* pay to it is mostly neutralized by the veil of prejudice which obstructs their vision. But when such persons examine the doctrine with sufficient diligence to discover that it leads only to holiness—holiness in heart and life—then they redouble their efforts to do away with it. When professing Christians unite with its detractors, charity obliges us to conclude that it is because of failure to properly understand the doctrine. They take a one-sided view of this truth: they view it through distorted lenses: they contemplate it from the wrong angle. They fail to see that election originated in everlasting love, that it is the choosing of a company to eternal salvation, who otherwise would have inevitably perished, and that it makes that company a willing, obedient, and holy people.

We shall not now attempt to cover the whole range of objections which have been brought against the doctrine of election, yet our discussion would be incomplete if we totally ignored them. The workings of unbelief are always endless in number. The child of God needs to be occupied with something more profitable. Yet we feel that we should at least consider briefly the ones which the enemy suppose are the most forceful and formidable. Not that our object is to try and convince them of their errors, but rather with the design of seeking to help fellow-believers who may have been shaken if not stumbled thereby. Our business is not to refute error, but (under God) to establish our readers in the truth. Yet in order to do this, it is sometimes needful to expose the wiles of Satan, show how baseless are the most insidious of his lies, and seek to remove from the Christian's mind any injurious effect they may have had upon him.

Before starting on this unwelcome task let it be pointed out that any lack of ability on our part to refute the calumnies of opponents, is no proof that their position is impregnable. As the renowed Butler pointed out long ago in his masterly "Analogy," "If a truth is established, objections are nothing. The one (i.e., Truth) is founded upon our knowledge, and the other on our ignorance." Once it is established that two and two make four, no quibbling or juggling with figures can disprove it. "We should never suffer what we know to be disturbed by what we know not" said that master of logic, Paley. Once we see anything to be clearly taught in Holy Writ, we must not allow either our own prejudices or the antagonism of others to shake our confidence in or adherence to it. If we are satisfied that we have a "thus saith the Lord" to rest upon, it matters nothing if we be unable to show the sophistry in the arguments brought to bear against it. Be assured that God is true, even if that involves our accounting every man a liar.

The bitterest enemies against the doctrine of election are *the Papists:* This is exactly what might be expected, for the truth of election can never be made to square with the dogma of human merits—the one is diametrically opposed to the other. Every man who loves himself and seeks salvation by his own works, will loathe sovereign grace, and seek to load it with contempt. On the other hand, those who have been effectually humbled by the Holy Spirit and brought to realize that they are utterly dependent upon the discriminating mercy of God, will have no hankerings after nor patience with a system which sets the crown of honor upon the creature. History bears ample testimony that Rome detests the very name of Calvinism. "From all sects there may be some hope of obtaining converts to Rome *except Calvinism*" said the late "Cardinal" Manning. And he

was right, as our own degenerate age bears full witness, for while no
regenerated Calvinist will ever be fatally deceived by the wiles of the
mother of harlots, yet thousands of "Protestant" (?) Arminians are
annually rushing to her arms.

It is an irrefutable fact that as Calvinism has met with less and less
favor in the leading Protestant bodies, as the sovereignty of God and
His electing love have been more and more crowded out of their
pulpits, that Rome has made increasing progress, until today she must
have, both in England and in the U.S.A., a greater number of followers
than any single evangelical denomination. But what is saddest of all is
that, the vast majority of those now occupying so-called Protestant
pulpits are preaching the very things which further Rome's interests.
Their insistence upon the freedom of fallen man's will-to-good must
fill the Papist leaders with delight—in the Council of Trent she anath-
ametized all who affirmed the contrary. To what extent the leaven of
Popery has spread may be seen in that "Evangelical Protestants" (?)
who oppose the doctrine of election are now employing the self-same
objections as were used by the Italian doctors four hundred years ago.

But to come now to some of the objections. First, such a doctrine is
utterly unreasonable. When it suits her purpose Rome makes a big
pretense of appealing to human reason, but at other times she demands that her children close their mental eyes and accept blindly
whatever their unholy "mother" is pleased to palm upon them. Yet
Rome is by no means the only offender at this point: multitudes of
those who regard themselves as Protestants are guilty of the same
thing. So too almost the first response of those who make no religious
profession, when they have this truth presented to their notice, is to
exclaim, "Such a concept does not appeal to me at all. If there is a
God, and if He has anything at all to do with our present lives, I
believe He will give us all an equal chance, balance our good deeds
against our bad, and be merciful unto us. To say that He has favorites
among His creatures, and that He fixed the destiny of every one
before his birth, strikes me as outrageous."

Our first reply to such an objection is that, it is quite beside the
point. The only matter which needs deciding at the outset is, What
saith the Scriptures? If election be clearly taught therein, *that* settles
the matter for the child of God, settles it once and for all. Whether he
understands it or no, he knows that God cannot lie, and that His Word
is "true from the beginning" (Ps. 119:160). If his opponent will not
allow this, then there is no common ground on which they can meet,
and it is utterly futile to discuss the matter with him. Under no
circumstances must the Christian allow himself to be drawn away

from his stand on the impregnable rock of Holy Writ, and descend to the treacherous ground of human reason. Only on that high plane can he successfully withstand the onslaughts of Satan. Reread Matthew 4 and observe how Christ vanquished the tempter.

The holy Word of God does not come to us craving acceptance at the bar of human reason. Instead, it demands that human reason surrender itself to its divine authority and receive unmurmuringly its inerrent contents. It emphatically and repeatedly warns men that if they despise its authority and reject its teachings, it is to their certain eternal undoing. It is by that Word each of us shall be weighed, measured, judged in the day to come; and therefore it is the part of human wisdom to bow to and thankfully receive its inspired declarations. The supreme act of right reason, my reader, is to submit unreservedly unto divine wisdom, and accept with childlike simplicity the revelation which God has graciously given us. Any other, any different attitude thereto, is utterly unreasonable—the derangement of pride. How thankful we should be that the ancient of days condescends to instruct us.

Our second reply to the above objection is that, in a written revelation from heaven we should fully expect to find much that transcends the grasp of our poor earth-bound minds. What was the use of God communicating to us only that which we already knew? Nor are the Scriptures given to us as a field on which reason may be exercised: what they require are *faith and obedience*. And faith is not a blind, unintelligible thing, but confidence in its Author, an assurance that He is too wise to err, too righteous to be unjust; and therefore that He is infinitely worthy of our trust and subjection to His holy will. But just because God's Word is addressed to faith, there is much in it which is contrary to nature, much that is most mysterious, much that leaves us wondering. Faith must be tested—to prove its genuineness. And God delights to honor faith: though His Word be not written to satisfy curiosity, and though many questions are not there fully answered, yet the more faith be exercised, the fuller is the light granted.

God Himself is profoundly mysterious. "Lo, these are parts of His ways: but how little a portion is heard of Him!" (Job 26:14); "How unsearchable are his judgments, and his ways past finding out" (Rom. 11:33). We must therefore expect to find in the Bible much that strikes us as strange: things "hard to be understood" (II Peter 3:16). The creation of the universe out of nothing, at the mere fiat of the Almighty, is beyond the grasp of the finite mind. The divine incarnation transcends human reason: "Great is the mystery of godliness:

God was manifest in the flesh" (II Tim. 3:16): that Christ should be conceived and born of a woman who had known no contact with man, cannot be accounted for by human reason. The resurrection of our bodies, thousands of years after they had gone to dust, is inexplicable. Is it not, then, most unreasonable to reject the truth of election because human reason cannot fathom it!

Second, it is *highly unjust*. Rebels against the supreme sovereign hesitate not to charge Him with unrighteousness because He is pleased to exercise His own rights, and determine the destiny of His creatures. They argue that all men should be dealt with on the same footing, that all should be given an equal opportunity of salvation. They say that if God shows mercy unto one and withholds it from another, such partiality is grossly unfair. To such an objector we reply in the language of Holy Writ: "Nay but, O man, who art thou that repliest against God? Shall the thing formed say to him that formed it, Why hast thou made me thus? Hath not the potter power over the clay of the same lump, to make one vessel unto honour, and another unto dishonour?" (Rom. 9:20, 21). And there we leave him.

But some of the Lord's own people are disturbed by this difficulty. First, then, we would remind them that God is "light" (I John 1:5), as well as "love." God is ineffably holy, as well as infinitely gracious. As the Holy One He abhors all evil, and as the moral governor of His creatures it becomes Him to eternally manifest His hatred of sin. As the gracious one He is pleased to bestow favors upon the undeserving, and to give an everlasting demonstration that He is "the Father of mercies." Now in election *both* of these designs are unmistakably accomplished. In the preterition and condemnation of the non-elect, God gives full proof of His holiness and justice, by visiting upon them the due reward of their iniquities. In the foreordination and salvation of His chosen people, God makes a clear display of the exceeding riches of His grace.

Suppose that God had willed the destruction of the entire human race: then what? Had that been unjust? Certainly not. There could be no injustice whatever in visiting upon criminals the penalty of that law which they had defiantly broken. But what had then become of God's *mercy*? Had naught but inexorable justice been exercised by an offended God, then every descendant of fallen Adam had inevitably been consigned to hell. Now on the other hand. Suppose God had decided to open wide the floodgates of mercy, and carry the whole human race to heaven: then what? The wages of sin is death—eternal death. But if every man sinned, and none died, what evidence would there be that divine justice was anything more than an empty name? If God had saved all sinners, would not that necessarily inculcate light views of sin? If all were taken to heaven, should we not conclude that this was due us as a right?

Because all are guilty, are the hands of divine mercy to be tied? If not, if mercy may be exercised, then is God obliged to wholly renounce His justice? If God be pleased to exercise mercy upon some, who have no claim thereto, cannot He also show Himself to be a just judge by inflicting upon others the punishment to which they are entitled? What wrong does a creditor do if he releases one and enforces his demands on another? Am I unjust because I bestow charity on a beggar, and decline doing so to his fellow? Then is the great God less free to impart His gifts where He pleases? Before the above objection can have any force it must be proved that every creature (because he is a creature) is *entitled* to everlasting bliss, and that even though he falls into sin and becomes a rebel against his maker, God is morally *obliged* to save him. To such absurdities is the objector necessarily reduced.

"If eternal felicity be due to every man without exception, surely temporal felicity must be their due likewise: if they have a right to the greater their claim to the less can hardly be doubted. If the Omnipotent is bound, on penalty of becoming unjust, to do all He can to make every individual happy in the next life; He must be equally bound to render every individual happy in this. But are all men happy? Look around the world and say Yes if you can. Is the Creator therefore unjust? none but Satan would suggest it: none but his echoes will affirm it. The Lord is a God of truth, and without iniquity: just and right is He. . . . Is the constituted order of things mysterious? impenetrably so. Yet the mysteriousness of God's dispensations evinces, not the injustice of the sovereign dispenser, but the shallowness of human comprehension, and the shortness of human sight. Let us then, by embracing and revering the Scriptural doctrines of predestination and providence, give God credit for being infinitely wise, just, and good; though for the present His way is in the deep, and His footsteps are not known" (A. Toplady, author of "Rock of Ages").

Finally, let it be pointed out that God *never refuses mercy* to any one who humbly seeks it. Sinners are freely invited to forsake their wicked ways and sue unto the Lord for pardon. The gospel feast is spread before them; if they refuse to partake thereof, if instead they loathe and turn away from it with disdain, is not their blood on their own heads? What sort of "justice" is it which requires God to bring to heaven those who hate Him? If God has performed a miracle of grace in you, my reader, and begotten in *your* heart a love for Him, be fervently thankful for the same, and disturb not your peace and joy by asking why He has not done the same for your fellow transgressors.

Third, *the gospel offer is meaningless*. Those who refuse to receive the truth of divine election are fond of saying that the idea of God having eternally chosen one and passed by another of His creatures would reduce evangelical preaching to a farce. They argue that if God has foreordained a part of the human race to destruction, it can contain no bona fide offer of salvation to them. Let it first be pointed out that this objection does not press upon Calvinism alone, but applies with the same force to Arminianism. Free-willers deny the absoluteness of the divine decrees, yet they affirm the divine presence. Then let us turn the question round upon him: How can God in good faith bid men to repent and believe the gospel, when He infallibly *foreknows* they will never do so? If he supposes the former objection to be irrefutable, he will find our question is unanswerable by his own principles.

Whatever difficulty may be presented at this point—and the writer has no thought of belittling it—one thing is clear: to whomsoever the gospel comes, God is sincere in bidding its hearers submit to its requirements, receive its glad tidings, and be saved thereby. Whether we can or cannot perceive how this is so, matters nothing; but the integrity of the divine character must be maintained at all costs. The mere fact that we are unable to discern the consistency and harmony between two distinct lines of truth, certainly does not warrant our rejecting either one of them. The doctrine of sovereign election is clearly revealed in the Scriptures; so too is the genuineness of the gospel offer to all who receive it: the one must be contended for as earnestly as the other.

But do we not create our own difficulty by supposing that the *salvation* of men is God's sole object, or even His principal design, in the sending forth of the gospel? But what other ends, it may be asked, are accomplished thereby? Many. God's first end in the gospel, as in everything else, is the honor of His own great name and the glory of His Son. In the gospel the character of God and the excellency of Christ are more fully revealed than anywhere else. That a worldwide testimony should be borne thereto is infinitely fitting. That men should have made known to them the ineffable perfections of Him with whom they have to do is certainly most desirable. God, then, is magnified and the matchless worth of His Son proclaimed, even though not one sinner ever believed and was saved thereby.

Again; the preaching of the gospel is the appointed instrument in the hands of the Holy Spirit whereby the elect are brought to Christ. God does not disdain instrumental agencies, but is pleased to employ them: He who ordained the end, also appointed the means thereto.

Just because God's elect are "scattered abroad" (John 11:52) among all nations, He has commanded that "Repentance and remission of sins should be preached in His name among all nations" (Luke 24:47). It is by hearing the gospel they are called out of the world. By nature God's elect are the children of wrath "even as others": they are lost sinners needing a Saviour, and apart from Christ there is no salvation for them. Therefore the gospel must be preached to and believed in by them before they can rejoice in the knowledge that their sins are forgiven. The gospel, then, is God's great winnowing fan, separating the wheat from the chaff, and gathering the former into His garner.

Moreover, the non-elect gain much from the gospel even though it effects not their eternal salvation. The world exists for the elect's sake, yet all share the benefits of it. The sun shines upon the evil as well as the good; refreshing showers fall upon the lands of the wicked as truly as on the ground of the righteous. So God causes the gospel to reach the ears of many of the non-elect, as well as those of His favored people. Why? Because it is one of His powerful agencies to hold in check the wickedness of fallen men. Millions who are never saved by it, are reformed: their lusts are bridled, their outward course improved, and society is made more suitable for the saints to live in. Compare the peoples without the gospel and those who have it: in the case of the latter it will be found that higher morality obtains even where there is no spirituality.

Finally, it should be pointed out that the gospel is made a real test of the characters of all who hear it. The Scriptures declare that man is a fallen, corrupt, and sin-loving creature. They insist that his mind is enmity against God, that he loves darkness rather than light, that he will not be subject to God under any circumstances. Yet who believes such humbling truths? But the response to the gospel by the non-elect demonstrates the verity of God's Word. Their continued impenitence, unbelief, and disobedience bears witness to their total depravity. God instructed Moses to go unto Pharaoh and make request that Israel should be allowed to worship Jehovah in the wilderness; yet in the next verse He told him, "I am sure that the king of Egypt will not let you go, not by a mighty hand" (Exod. 3:18, 19). Then why send Moses on such an errand? To make manifest the hardness of Pharaoh's heart, the stubbornness of his will, and the justice of God in destroying such a wretch.

Fourth, *it destroys human responsibility.* Arminians contend that to affirm God has unalterably decreed and fixed the history and destiny of every man, would be to demolish human accountability, that in such a case man would be no better than a machine. They insist that man's will must be free, free equally unto good and evil, or otherwise he would cease to be a moral agent. They argue that unless a person's actions are without compulsion, and are in accordance with his own desires and inclinations, he could not be justly held responsible for them. From this premise the conclusion is drawn that it is the creature and not the Creator who chooses and decides his eternal destiny, for if his acts are self-determined, they cannot be divinely determined.

Such an objection is really a descent into the dark regions of philosophy and metaphysics, a specious attempt of the Enemy to lead us away from the realm of divine revelation. So long as we abide by the Holy Scriptures, we are safe, but as soon as we resort to reasoning upon spiritual matters we are certain to err. God has already made known all that He deems well for us to know in this life, and any attempt to be wise above that which is written is naught but folly and impiety. From the Scriptures it is clear as a sunbeam that man— whether considered as unfallen or fallen—is a responsible being, that he is made to reap whatsoever he sows, that he will yet have to render unto God an account of all his deeds and be judged accordingly; and nothing must be allowed to weaken the impression of these solemn facts upon our minds.

The same line of reasoning has been employed by those who reject the verbal inspiration of the Scriptures. It is contended that such a postulate entirely eleminates the human element from the Bible, that if we insist (as this writer, for one, most emphatically does) that not only the thoughts and sentiments but the very language itself is divine, that every word and syllable of the original manuscripts was God-breathed then the human penman employed in transmitting the same were merely automatons. But this we know is false. In like manner, with as much show of reason might the objector declare that Christ cannot be both divine and human: that if He be God, He cannot be man, and that if He be truly man, it follows that He cannot be God. What is reasoning worth, my reader, upon such matters!

The books of the Bible *were* written by men, written by them under the free exercise of their natural faculties, in such a way that the impress of their personalities is clearly left upon their several contributions. Nevertheless, they originated nothing: they were "moved by the Holy Ghost" (II Peter 1:21), and so completely were they controlled by Him, that not the slightest shadow of a mistake or error was made by them, and every thing they wrote was "the words which . . . the Holy Ghost teacheth" (I Cor. 2:13). The redeemer is the Son of man, who was "in all things . . . made like unto His brethren" (Heb. 2:17); yet because His humanity was taken into union with His divine person everything He did possessed a unique and infinite value. Man is a moral agent, acting according to the desires and dictates of his nature: he is at the same time a creature, fully controlled and determined by his Creator. In each of these cases the divine and human elements coalesce, but the divine dominates, yet not to the exclusion of the human.

"Woe unto the world because of offenses! for it *must* needs be that offenses come." Then surely, may an objector reply, there can be no guilt resting on him who introduces that which is inevitable. Different far was the teaching of Christ: "but *woe* to that man by whom the offense cometh" (Matt. 18:7). "When ye shall hear of wars and rumors of wars, be ye not troubled: for such things *must* needs be" (Mark 13:7). There is a must-be for these death-dealing scourges, yet that alters not the criminality of the instigators of them. There is a needs-be for "heresies" (I Cor. 11:19), yet the heretics themselves are blameable. Absolute necessity and human responsibility are, therefore, perfectly compatible, whether *we* can perceive their consistency or no.

Fifth, it is objected against the truth of predestination that it *supercedes the use of means* and renders all incentives to human endeavor negatory. It is asserted that if God has elected a man unto salvation that he will be saved although he remains utterly unconcerned and continues to take his fill of sin; that if he has not been elected, then no efforts to obtain eternal life would be of any use. It is said that for men to be told they have been divinely ordained either to life or death by an eternal and immutable decree, they will at once conclude that it makes no difference whatever how they conduct themselves, since no acts of theirs can to the slightest decree either impede or promote the foreordination of God. Thus, it is argued, all motives to diligence are effectually neutralized, that it is subversive of every exhortation to morality and spirtuality.

Really this is the most senseless of all objections. It is not an objection at all against the *Scriptural* doctrine of predestination, but against an entirely different concept, one hatched in the brains of ignorance, or conceived by malignity in order to bring odium on the truth. The only sort of predestination to which this objection is applicable, would be an absolute preappointment to an end without any regard to the means. Stripped of all ambiguity, this objection presupposes that God secures His purposes without employing any instrumental agencies. Thus, when the objection is exposed in its nakedness we see at once what a sorry figure it cuts. Those whom God has elected to salvation He has chosen to it "*through* sanctification of the Spirit and belief of the Truth" (II Thess. 2:13).

The fact is that God decreed to bring His elect to glory in a way of santification, and in no other way than that; and throughout their entire course. He treats them as rational and accountable creatures, using suitable means and motives to draw out their hearts unto Himself. To affirm that if they are elected they will reach heaven whether sanctified or no, is just as silly as to say Abraham might have been the father of many nations although he had died in infancy, or that Hezekiah could have lived his extra fifteen years without food or sleep. Prior to the taking of Jericho it was divinely revealed to Joshua that he should be master of that place (6:2): the assurance was absolute. Did, then, Israel's leader conclude that no action was needed, that all might sit down and fold their arms? No; he arranged the procession around its walls in obedience to God's command, and the event was accomplished accordingly.

We turn now briefly to consider some of the principal Scriptures used by those who resist the Truth. "Because I have called, and ye refused; I have stretched out my hand, and no man regarded; but ye have set at naught all my counsel, and would none of my reproof" (Prov. 1:24, 25). "I have spread out my hands all the day unto a rebellious people which walketh in a way that was not good, after their own thoughts" (Isa. 65:2). "How often would I have gathered thy children together . . . and ye would not" (Matt. 23:37). We are told by Arminians that these declarations are irreconcilable with Calvinism, that they show plainly the will of God *can be* resisted and thwarted by men. But most certainly a disappointed and defeated God is not the God of Holy Writ. To draw from these verses the conclusion that the divine decrees fail of accomplishment is utterly erroneous: they have nothing whatever to do with God's eternal purpose, but instead, they respect only His *external* agencies, whereby He enforces man's responsibility, tests his character, and makes evident the wickedness of his heart.

"For God so loved *the world* that he gave his only begotten Son" (John 3:16). From these words it is urged that if God loves the world He desires the salvation of the whole human race, and that it was for this end He provided a Saviour for them. Here it is a case of being misled by the mere sound of a word, instead of ascertaining its real import. To say that God gave His Son with the design of providing salvation for all of Adam's children is manifestly absurd, for half of them had already died before Christ was born, and the vast majority of them perished in heathen darkness. Where is there the slightest hint in the Old Testament that God loved the Egyptians, the Canaanites, the Babylonians? And where else in the New Testament is there any statement that God loves all mankind? The "world" in John 3:16 (as in many other places) is a *general* term, used in contrast from *Israel,* who imagined they had a monopoly on redemption. God's love extends far beyond the bounds of Judaism, embracing His elect scattered among all nations.

"And ye will not come to me, that ye might have life" (John 5:40). Strange to say this is one of the verses appealed to by those who will not have election at any price. They suppose it teaches the free will unto good of fallen man, and that Christ seriously intended the salvation of those who despise and reject Him. But what is there in these words which declares that Christ seriously intended their salvation? Do they not rather signify that He was here preferring a solemn charge against them? So far from our Lord's utterance implying that these men had the power within themselves to come to Him, they rather declare the perversity and stubbornness of their wills. Instead of any inclination for the Holy One, they hated Him.

"Who will have *all men* to be saved, and to come unto the knowledge of the truth . . . who gave Himself a ransom for *all*" (I Tim. 2:4, 6). In order to understand these words they must not be considered separately, but in connection with their setting. From the context it is unmistakably evident that the "all men" God wills to be saved and for whom Christ died are all men *without regard to national distinctions.* Timothy's ministry was exercised chiefly among Jewish converts, many of whom still retained their racial prejudices, so that they were unwilling to submit to the authority of heathen rulers. This was why the Pharisees had sought to discredit Christ before all people when they asked Him whether it was lawful to pay tribute to Caesar. Paul here tells Timothy that Christians were not only to yield obedience unto Gentile rulers, but to pray for them as well (vv. 1, 2).

In I Timothy 2 Paul struck at the very root of the prejudice which Timothy was called upon to combat. That law of Moses was now set aside, the distinction which so long obtained between the lineal descendants of Abraham and the rest of mankind no longer obtained: God willed the salvation of Gentiles and Jews alike. Note particularly these details. First, "There is one God [see Rom. 3:29, 30] , and one mediator between God and [not "the Jews" but] men" (v. 5). Second, "Who gave himself a ransom for all [indefinitely], *to be testified in due time.*" (v. 6): when Christ was crucified it was not generally understood, not even among His disciples, that He gave Himself for Gentiles and Jews alike; but in "due time" (particularly under Paul's ministry), it *was* clearly "testified." Third, "whereunto I am ordained a preacher and an apostle . . . a teacher of the *Gentiles*" (v. 7). Fourth, "I [with apostolic authority] will therefore that men pray *every where*" (v. 8): those professing the faith of Christ must drop at once and forever their Jewish notions and customs—Jerusalem no longer possessed any peculiar sanctity.

"We see Jesus . . . that he by the grace of God should taste death for *every man*" (Heb. 2:9). Have you taken the trouble to ascertain how that expression is used elsewhere in the New Testament? "And then shall *every man* have praise of God" (I Cor. 4:5). Does that mean all of Adam's race? How can it, when "depart from me, ye cursed" will be the portion of many? "The head of *every man* is Christ" (I Cor. 11:3): was He the Head of Judas or Nero? "The manifestation of the Spirit is given to *every man*" (I Cor. 12:7). But some are "sensual, having not the Spirit" (Jude v. 19 and cf. Rom. 8:9). It is "every one" in *God's* family that is meant in all of these epistle passages: note how the "every one" of Hebrews 2:9 are defined as "many sons" (v. 10), "brethren" (v. 11), "children" (vv. 12-14).

"There shall be false teachers among you who truly shall bring in damnable heresies, even denying the Lord that bought them" (I Peter 2:1). This verse is often cited in an attempt to disprove that Christ died for the elect only, which only serves to show what desperate shifts our opponents are reduced to. Why the verse makes no reference unto Christ at all, still less to His death! The Greek word here is not *kurios* at all—the one commonly used when referring to the Lord Jesus; but *despotes*. The only places where it occurs, when applied to a divine person, are Luke 22:9; Acts 4:24; II Timothy 2:22; Jude 4; Revelation 6:10, in all of which God the Father is plainly intended, and in most of them as manifestly distinguished from Christ. "Buying" here has reference to temporal deliverance, being taken from Deuteronomy 32:6. Peter was writing to Jews, who boasted loudly they were a people purchased by the Lord, and therefore he used this expression to aggravate the impiety of these false teachers among the Jews.

"Not willing that *any* should perish, but that *all* should come to repentance" (II Peter 3:9). Here again a false meaning is extracted by divorcing a snippet from its context. The key to this verse is found in the word "us-ward": "the Lord is . . . longsuffering to us-ward," for He is not willing that "any" *of them* should perish. And who are they? Why, the "beloved" of verse 1 (those mentioned at the beginning of the First Epistle, "elect according to the foreknowledge of God the Father, through sanctification of the Spirit"), and because He has purposed that "all" *of them* should come to repentance," He defers the second coming of Christ (vv. 3, 4). Christ will not return till the last of His people are safely in the Ark of Salvation.

12 Its Publication

During the last two or three generations the pulpit has given less and less prominence to doctrinal preaching, until today—with very rare exceptions—it has no place at all. In some quarters the cry from the pew was, We want living experience and not dry doctrine; in others, We need practical sermons and not metaphysical dogmas; and yet others, Give us Christ and not theology. Sad to say, such senseless cries were generally heeded: "senseless" we say, for there is no other safe way of *testing* experience, as there is no *foundation* for practicals to be built upon, if they be divorced from Scriptural doctrine; while Christ cannot be known unless He be preached (I Cor. 1:23), and He certainly cannot be "preached" if doctrine is shelved. Various reasons may be given for the lamentable failure of the pulpit: chief among them being laziness, desire for popularity, superficial and lop-sided "evangelism," love of the sensational.

Laziness. It is a far more exacting task, one which calls for much closer confinement in the study, to prepare a series of sermons on say the doctrine of justification, than it does to make addresses on prayer, missions, or personal-work. It demands a far wider acquaintance with the Scriptures, a more rigid disciplining of the mind, and a more extensive perusal of the older writers. But this was too exacting for most of the ministers, and so they chose the line of least resistance and followed an easier course. It is because of his proneness to this weakness that the minister is particularly exhorted, "Give attendance to reading . . . take heed unto thyself, and unto the doctrine; continue in them" (I Tim. 4:13, 16); and again, "Study to show thyself approved unto God, a *workman* that needeth not to be ashamed" (II Tim. 2:15).

Desire for popularity. It is natural that the preacher should wish to please his hearers, but it is spiritual for him to desire and aim at the approbation of God. Nor can any man serve two masters. As the apostle expressly declared, "For if I yet pleased men, I should not be the servant of Christ" (Gal. 1:10): solemn words are those. How they condemn them whose chief aim is to preach to crowded churches. Yet what grace it requires to swim against the tide of public opinion, and preach that which is unacceptable to the natural man. But on the other hand, how fearful will be the doom of those who, from a determination to curry favor with men, deliberately withheld those portions of the truth most needed by their hearers. "Ye shall not add unto the word which I command you, neither shall ye diminish ought from it" (Deut. 4:2). O to be able to say with Paul, "I kept back nothing that was profitable unto you. . . . I am pure from the blood of all" (Acts 20:20, 26).

A superficial and lop-sided "evangelism." Many of the pulpiteers of the past fifty years acted as though the first and last object of their calling was the salvation of souls, everything being made to bend to that aim. In consequence, the feeding of the sheep, the maintaining of a Scriptural discipline in the church, and the inculcation of practical piety, was crowded out; and only too often all sorts of worldly devices and fleshly methods were employed under the plea that the end justified the means; and thus the churches were filled with unregenerate members. In reality, such men defeated their own aim. The hard heart must be ploughed and harrowed before it can be receptive to the gospel seed. Doctrinal instruction must be given on the character of God, the requirements of His law, the nature and heinousness of sin, if a foundation is to be laid for true evangelism. It is useless to preach Christ unto souls until they see and feel their desperate need of Him.

Love of the sensational. In more recent times the current has changed. A generation arose which was less tolerant even of superficial evangelism, which demurred at hearing anything which was calculated to make them the least uneasy in their sins. Of course, such people must not be driven from the churches: they must be catered to and given something which would tickle their ears. The stage of public action afforded abundant material. The World-war and such characters as the Kaiser, Stalin, and Mussolini were much in the public eye, as Hitler and Abyssinia have been since. Under the guise of expounding prophecy the pulpit turned its attention to what was styled "the Signs of the Times" and the pew was made to believe that the "dictators" were fulfilling the predictions of Daniel and the Apocalypse. There was nothing in such preaching (?) that pricked the conscience, yet tens of thousands were deluded into thinking that the very hearing of such rubbish made them religious; and thus the churches were enabled to "carry on."

Ere proceeding further, let it be pointed out that the objections most commonly made against doctrinal preaching are quite pointless. Take, first, the clamor for experimental preaching. In certain quarters—quarters which though very restricted, yet consider themselves the very champions of orthodoxy and the highest exponents of vital godliness—the demand is for a detailed tracing out of the varied experiences of a quickened soul both under the law and under grace, and any other type of preaching, especially doctrinal, is frowned upon as supplying nothing but the husk. But as one writer tersely put it, "Though matters of doctrine are by some considered merely as the shell of religion, and experience as the kernel, yet let it be remembered that there is no coming to the kernel but through the shell; and while the kernel gives value to the shell, yet the shell is the guardian of the kernel. Destroy that, and you injure this." Eliminate doctrine and you have nothing left to *test* experience by, and mysticism and fanaticism are inevitable.

In other quarters the demand has been for preaching along practical lines, such people supposing and insisting that doctrinal preaching is merely theoretical and impracticable. Such a concept betrays woeful ignorance. "All Scripture is given by inspiration of God, and is profitable [first] *for doctrine,* [and then] for reproof, for correction, for instruction in righteousness" (II Tim. 3:16). Study the epistles of Paul and see how steadily that order is maintained. Romans 1-11 are strictly doctrinal; 12-16 practical exhortations. Take a concrete example: in I Timothy 1:9, 10 the apostle draws up a catalog of sins against which the denunciations of the law are imminently directed, and then he added "And if there be any other thing which is contrary to sound *doctrine.*" What a plain intimation is this that error in principles fundamental has a most unfavorable influence on practicals, and that in proportion as the doctrine of God is disbelieved the authority of God is disowned. It is the doctrine which supplies motives for obedience to the precepts.

In connection with those who cry, preach Christ and not theology, we have long observed that they never preach Him as the One with whom God made a covenant (Ps. 89:3), nor as His "elect" in whom His soul delighteth (Isa. 42:1). They preach a "Christ" which is the product of their own imaginations, the creation of sentiment. If we preach the Christ of Scripture we must set Him forth as the servant of God's choice (I Peter 2:4), as the Lamb "foreordained before the foundation of the world" (I Peter 1:19, 20), as the One "set for the fall and the rising again of many in Israel" (Luke 2:34), as "the stone of stumbling and a rock of offense." Christ is not to be preached as separate from His members, but as the Head of His mystical body— Christ and those whom God chose in Him are one, eternally and immutably one. Then preach not *a mutilated* Christ. Preach Him according to the eternal counsels of God.

Now if doctrinal preaching generally be so unpopoular, the doctrine of election is particularly and pre-eminently so. Sermons on predestination are, with very rare exceptions, hotly resented and bitterly denounced. "There seems to be an inevitable prejudice in the human mind against this doctrine, and although most other doctrines will be received by professing Christians, some with caution, others with pleasure, yet this one seems to be most frequently disregarded and discarded. In many of our pulpits it would be reckoned a high sin and treason to preach a sermon upon election" (C. H. Spurgeon). If that was the case fifty years ago, much more is it so now. Even in avowedly orthodox circles the very mention of predestination is like waving a red rag before a bull. Nothing so quickly makes manifest the enmity of the carnal mind in the smug religionist and self-righteous pharisees as does the proclamation of the divine sovereignty and His discriminating grace; and few indeed are the men now left who dare to contend valiantly for the truth.

Fearful beyond words are the lengths to which the horror and hatred of election have carried even avowedly evangelical leaders in their blasphemous speeches against this blessed truth: we refuse to pollute these pages by quoting from their ungodly speeches. Some have gone so far as to say that, even if predestination be revealed in the Scriptures it is a dangerous doctrine, creating dissent and division, and therefore it ought not to be preached in the churches; which is the self-same objection used by the Romanists against giving the Word of God to the common people in their own mother tongue. If we are to whittle down the truth so as to preach only that which is acceptable to the natural man, how much would be left? The preaching of Christ crucified is to the Jews a stumblingblock and to the Greeks foolishness (I Cor. 1:23): is the pulpit to be silent thereon? Shall the servants of God cease proclaiming the person, office and work of His beloved Son, merely because He is "a stone of stumbling and a rock of offense" (I Peter 2:8) to the reprobate?

Many are the objections brought against this doctrine by those who desire to discredit it. Some say election should not be preached because it is so mysterious, and secret things belong unto the Lord. But it is not a secret, for God has plainly revealed it in His Word; and if it is not be to preached because of its mysteriousness, then for the same reason nothing must be said about the unity of the divine nature subsisting in a trinity of Persons, nor of the virgin-birth, nor of the resurrection of the dead. According to others, the doctrine of election cuts the nerve of all missionary enterprise, in fact stands opposed to all preaching, rendering it entirely negatory. Then in such a case the preaching of Paul himself was altogether useless, for it was full of this doctrine: read his epistles and it will be found that he proclaimed election continually, yet we never read of him ceasing to preach it because it rendered his labor useless.

Paul taught that "It is God which worketh in you both to will and to do of his good pleasure" (Phil. 2:13), yet we do not find that on this account he ceased to exhort men to will and endeavor those things which are pleasing to God, and to work themselves with all their might. If we are unable to perceive the consistency of the two things, that is no reason why we should refuse to believe and heed either the one or the other. Some argue against election because the preaching of it shakes assurance and fills the minds of men with doubts and fears. But in our day especially we should be thankful for any truth which shatters the complacency of empty professors and arouses the indifferent to examine themselves before God. With as much reason might it be said that the doctrine of regeneration should not be promulgated, for is it any easier to make sure that I have been truly born again than it is to ascertain that I am one of God's elect? It is not.

Still others insist that election should not be preached because the ungodly will make an evil use of it, that they will shelter behind it to excuse their unconcern and procrastination, arguing that if they are elected to salvation that in the meantime they may live as they please and take their fill of sin. Such an objection is puerile, childish in the extreme. But what truth is there that the wicked will not pervert? Why, they will turn the grace of God into lasciviousness, and use (or rather misuse) His very goodness, His mercy, His longsufferance, for continuance in a course of evil doing. Arminians tells us that to preach the eternal security of the Christian encourages slothfulness; while at the opposite extreme, hyper-Calvinists object to the exhorting of the unregenerate unto repentance and faith on the ground that it inculcates creature ability. Let us not pretend to be wise above what is written, but preach *all* the counsel of God and leave results to Him.

The servant of God must not be intimidated or deterred from professing and proclaiming the unadulterated truth. His commission today is the same as Ezekiel's of old: "Be not afraid of them, neither be afraid of their words, though briers and thorns be with thee, and thou dost dwell among *scorpions:* be not afraid of their words, nor be dismayed at their looks, though they be a rebellious house. And thou shalt speak my words unto them whether they will hear, or whether they will forbear: for they are most rebellious" (Ezek. 2:6, 7). He must expect to encounter opposition, especially from those making the loudest profession, and fortify himself against it. The announcement of God's sovereign choice of men has evoked the spirit of malice and persecution from earliest times. It did so as far back as the days of Samuel. When the prophet announced to Jesse concerning his seven sons "neither hath the Lord chosen these" (I Sam. 16:10), the anger of his firstborn was kindled against David (I Sam. 17:28). So too when Christ Himself stressed the distinguishing grace of God unto the Gentile widow of Zarephath and Naaman the Syrian, the synagogue worshippers were "filled with wrath" and sought to kill him (Luke 4:25-29). But the very hatred this solemn truth arouses is one of the most convincing proofs of its divine origin.

Election is to be preached and published, first, because it is brought forward all through the Scriptures. There is not a single book in the Word of God where election is not either expressly stated, strikingly illustrated, or clearly implied. Genesis is full of it: the difference which the Lord made between Nahor and Abraham, Ishmael and Isaac, and His loving Jacob and hating Esau are cases to the point. In Exodus we behold the distinction made by God between the Egyptians and the Hebrews. In Leviticus the atonement and all the sacrifices were for the people of God, nor were they bidden to go and "offer" them to the surrounding heathen. In Numbers Jehovah used a Balaam to herald the fact that Israel were "*the* people" who "shall dwell alone, and shall *not* be numbered among the nations" (23:9); and therefore was he constrained to cry "How goodly are thy tents, O Jacob, and thy tabernacles, O Israel" (24:5). In Deuteronomy it is recorded "The Lord's portion is his people; Jacob is the lot of his inheritance" (32:9).

In Joshua we behold the discriminating mercy of the Lord bestowed upon Rahab the harlot, while the whole of her city was doomed to destruction. In Judges the sovereignty of God appears in the unlikely instruments selected, by which He wrought victory for Israel: Deborah, Gideon, Samson. In Ruth we have Orpah kissing her mother-in-law and returning to her gods, whereas Ruth cleaves to her and obtained inheritance in Israel—who made them to differ? In I Samuel David is chosen for the throne, preferred to his older brethren. In II Samuel we learn of the everlasting covenant "ordered in all things, and sure" (23:5). In I Kings Elijah becomes a blessing to a single widow selected from many; while in II Kings Naaman alone, of all the lepers, was cleansed. In I Chronicles it is written "Ye children of Jacob, His chosen ones" (16:13); while in II Chronicles we are made to marvel at the grace of God bestowing repentance upon

Manasseh. And so we might go on. The Psalms, Prophets, Gospels and Epistles are so full of this doctrine that he who runs may read.

Second, the doctrine of election is to be prominently preached because the gospel cannot be Scripturally proclaimed without it. Alas, so deep is the darkness and so widespread the ignorance which now prevails, that few indeed perceive that there is any vital connection between predestination and the evangel of God. Pause, then, for a moment and seriously ponder these questions: Is the success or failure of the gospel a matter of chance? or, to put it in another way, are the fruits of the most stupendous undertaking of all—the atoning work of Christ—left contingent upon human caprice? Could it be positively affirmed that the Redeemer shall yet "see of the travail of his soul, and . . . be satisfied" (Isa. 53:11) if all is left dependent upon the will of fallen man? Has God so little regard for the death of His son that He has left it uncertain as to how many shall be saved thereby?

"The gospel of God" (Rom. 1:1) can only be Scripturally presented as *the Triune God* is owned and honored therein. The attenuated "gospel" of our degenerate age confines the attention of its hearers to the sacrifice of Christ, whereas salvation originated in the heart of God the Father and is consummated by the operations of God the Spirit. All the blessings of salvation are communicated according to God's eternal counsels, and it was for the whole of election of grace (and none others) that Christ wrought salvation. The very first chapter of the New Testament announces that Jesus "shall save *His people* from their sins:" not "may," but "shall"; not shall offer to or try to, but actually "save" them. Again; not a single soul had ever benefited from the death of Christ if the Spirit had not been given to apply its virtues to the chosen seed. Any man, then, who *omits* the Father's election, and the Spirit's sovereign and effectual operations, preaches not the gospel of God, no matter what be his reputation as a "soul winner."

We have exposed the senselessness of those objections which are made against doctrinal preaching in general and the arguments which are levelled against the proclamation of predestination in particular. Then we pointed out some of the reasons why this grand truth is to be published. First, because the Scriptures, from Genesis to Revelation, are full of it. Second, because the gospel cannot be Scripturally preached without it. The great commission given to the public servants of Christ, duly called and equipped by Him, reads thus, "preach the gospel" (Mark 16:15): not parts of it, but the whole of it. The gospel is not be preached piecemeal, but in its entirety, so that each person in the Godhead is equally honored. Just as far as the gospel is mutilated, just so far as any branch of the evangelical system is suppressed, is the gospel *not* preached. To begin at Calvary, or even at Bethlehem, is to begin in the middle: we must go right back to the eternal counsels of divine grace.

Rightly did a renowned reformer put it, "Election is the golden thread that runs through the whole Christian system . . . it is the bond which connects and keeps it together, which, without this, is like a system of sand ever ready to fall to pieces. It is the cement which holds the fabric together; nay, it is the very soul that animates the whole frame. It is so blended and interwoven with the entire scheme of gospel doctrine that when the former is excluded, the latter bleeds to death. An ambassador is to deliver the whole message with which he is charged. He is to omit no part of it, but must declare the mind of the sovereign he represents, fully and without reserve. He is to say neither more nor less than the instructions of his court require, else he comes under displeasure, perhaps loses his head. Let the ministers of Christ weigh this well" (J. Zanchius, 1562).

Moreover the Gospel is to be preached "to every creature," that is, to all who frequent the Christian ministry, whether Jew or Gentile, young or old, rich or poor. All who wait upon the ministrations of God's servants have a right to hear the gospel fully and clearly, without any part of it being kept back. Now an important part of the gospel is the doctrine of election: God's eternal, free, and irreversible choice of certain persons in Christ to everlasting life. God foreknew that if the success of the preaching of Christ crucified were left contingent upon the response made to it by fallen men, there would be a universal despising of the same. This is clear from, "They *all* with one consent began to make excuse" (Luke 14:18). Therefore did God determine that a remnant of Adam's children should be the eternal monuments of His mercy, and accordingly He decreed to bestow upon them a saving faith and repentance. *That* is good news, indeed: all rendered certain and immutable by the sovereign will of God.

Christ is the supreme evangelist, and we find this doctrine was on His lips all through His ministry. "I thank Thee, O Father, Lord of heaven and earth, because thou hast *hid* these things from the wise and prudent, and hast revealed them unto babes. Even so, Father: for so it seemed good in thy sight"; "For the elect's sake those days shall be shortened"; "Come, ye blessed of my Father, inherit the kingdom prepared for you from the foundation of the world" (Matt. 11:25; 24:22; 25:34). "Unto *you* it is given to know the mystery of the kingdom of God: but unto them that are without [i.e., the pale of election], all these things are done in parables" (Mark 4:11). "Rejoice, because your names are written in heaven" (Luke 10:20). "All that the Father giveth me shall come to me"; "Ye believe not, because ye are not of my sheep"; "Ye have not chosen me, but I have chosen you" (John 6:37; 10:26; 15:16).

The same is true of the greatest of the apostles. Take the first and chiefest of his epistles, which is expressly devoted to an unfolding of "the Gospel of God" (Rom. 1:1). In Chapter 8 he describes those who are "the called according to God's purpose" (v. 28), and in consequence of which they were "foreknown" and "predestinated to be conformed to the image of his son" (v. 29). The whole of Chapter 9 is devoted thereto: there he shows the difference which God made between Ishmael and Isaac, between Esau and Jacob, the vessels of wrath and the vessels of mercy. There he tells us that God hath "mercy on whom he will have mercy, and whom he will he hardeneth" (v. 18). Nor were these things written to a few persons in some obscure corner, but addressed to the saints at Rome, "which was, in effect, bringing this doctrine upon the stage of the whole world, stamping an universal inprimatur upon it and publishing it to believers at large throughout the earth" (Zanchius).

The doctrine of election is to be preached, third, because the grace of God cannot be maintained without it. Things have now come to such a sorry pass that the remainder of this chapter should really be devoted to the elucidation and amplification of this important point; but we must content ourselves with some brief remarks. There are thousands of Arminian evangelists in Christendom today who deny predestination, either directly or indirectly, and yet suppose they are magnifying divine grace. Their idea is that God, out of His great goodness and love, has provided salvation in Christ for the whole human family, and that such is what He now desires and seeks. It is the view of these men that God makes an offer of His saving grace through the gospel message, makes it to the freewill of all who hear it, and that they can either accept or refuse it. But *that* is not "grace" at all.

Divine grace and human worthiness are as far apart as the poles, standing directly opposed the one to the other. But not so is the "grace" of the Arminian. If grace is merely something which is offered to me, something which I must improve if it is to do me any good, then my acceptance thereof is a meritorious act, and I have ground for boasting. If some refuse that grace and I receive it, then it must be (since it is wholly a matter of the freewill of the hearer) because I have more sense than they have, or because my heart is more tender than theirs, or because my will is less stubborn; and were the question put to me "Who maketh thee to differ?" (I Cor. 4:7), then the only truthful answer I could make would be to say, I made myself to differ, and thus place the crown of honor and glory upon my own head.

To this it may be replied by some, We believe that the heart of the natural man is hard and his will stubborn, but God in His grace sends the Holy Spirit, and He convicts men of sin and in the day of His visitation melts their hearts and seeks to woo them unto Christ; yet they must respond to His "sweet overtures" and co-operate with His "gracious influence." Here the ground is forsaken that it is *wholly* a matter of man's will. Yet here too we have nothing better than a burlesque of divine grace. Those very men affirm that many of those who are the subjects of these influences of the Spirit, resist the same and perish. Thus, those who are saved, owe their salvation (in the final analysis) to *their* improving of the Spirit's overtures—they "co-operate" with Him. In such a case the honors would be divided between the Spirit's operations and my improvements of the same. But *that* is not "grace" at all.

There are still others who seek to blunt the sharp edge of the Spirit's sword by saying, We believe in the doctrine of predestination, though not as you Calvinists teach it. A single word serves to untie this knot for us—"foreknowledge": Divine election is based upon divine foreknowledge. God foresaw who would repent of their sins and accept Christ as their Saviour, and accordingly he chose *them* unto salvation. Here again human merits are dragged in. Grace is not free, but tied by the "decision" of the creature. Such a carnal concept as this *reverses* the order of Scripture, which teaches that the divine foreknowledge is based upon the divine purpose—God foreknows what will be because He has decreed what shall be. Note carefully the *order* in Acts 2:23 and Romans 8:28 (last clause) and 29. Nowhere does Holy Writ speak of God foreseeing or foreknowing our repentance and faith: it is always foreknowledge of persons and never of acts—"*whom* He did foreknow" and not "*what* He did foreknow."

But does not Scripture say "whosoever will may come?" It does, and the all-important question is, where does the willingness come from in the case of those who respond to such an invitation? Men in their natural condition are unwilling: as Christ declared "ye will not come to me that ye might have life" (John 5:40). What, then, is the answer? This, "Thy people [says the Father to the Son—see context] shall be willing [to come] in the day of thy *power*" (Ps. 110:3). It is divine power, that and nothing else, which makes the unwilling willing, which overcomes all their enmity and obstinacy, which impels or "draws" them to the feet of the Lord Jesus. The grace of God, my readers, is far more than a lovely concept to sing about: it is an almighty power, an invincible dynamic, a principle victorious over all resistance. "My grace [says God] is sufficient for thee" (II Cor. 12:9); it asks for no assistance from us. "By the grace of God [and not by my co-operation], I am what I am" (I Cor. 15:10), said the apostle.

Divine grace has done far more than make possible the salvation of sinners: it makes *certain* the salvation of God's chosen ones. It not only provides salvation for them, it brings salvation *to* them; and it does so in such a way that its honors are not shared by the creature. The doctrine of predestination batters down this dagon-idol of "free-will" and human merits, for it tells us that if we have indeed willed and desired to lay hold of Christ and salvation by Him, then that very will and desire are the effect of God's eternal purpose and the result of the efficacious workings of His grace, for it is God who worketh in us both to will and to do of His good pleasure; and therefore do we glory only in the Lord and ascribe all the praise unto Him. This writer sought not the Lord, but hated, opposed, and endeavored to banish Him from his thoughts; but the Lord sought him, smote him to the ground (like Saul of Tarsus), subdued his vile rebellion, and made him willing in the day of His power. *That* is Grace indeed—sovereign, amazing, triumphant grace.

Fourth, the doctrine of election is to be published because it abases man. Arminians imagine that *they* do so by declaring the total depravity of the human family, yet in their very next breath they contradict themselves by insisting on their ability to perform spiritual acts. The fact is that "total depravity" is merely a theological expression on their lips which they repeat like parrots for they understand not nor believe the terrible import of that term. The fall has radically affected, corrupted, every part and faculty of our being, and therefore if man be totally depraved it necessarily follows that unto sin our wills are completely enslaved. As man's apostasy from God resulted in the darkening of his understanding, the defiling of his affections, the hardening of his heart, so it brought his will into complete bondage to Satan. He can no more free himself than can a worm under the foot of an elephant.

One of the marks of God's people is that they have "no confidence in the flesh" (Phil. 3:3), and nothing is so well calculated to bring them into that state as the truth of election. Shut out divine predestination and you must bring in the doings of the creature, and that makes salvation contingent, and thus it is neither of grace alone nor of works alone, but a nauseating mixture. The man who thinks he can be saved without election must have some confidence in the flesh, no matter how strongly he may deny it. Just so long as we are persuaded that it lies in the power of our own wills to contribute anything, be it never so little, unto our salvation, we remain in carnal confidence, and therefore are not truly humbled before God. It is not until we are brought to the place of self-despair—abandoning all hope in our own abilities—that we truly look *outside* of ourselves for deliverance.

When the truth of election is divinely applied to our hearts we are brought to realize that salvation turns solely on the will of a sovereign God, that "it is *not* of him that willeth, nor of him that runneth, but of *God* that showeth mercy" (Rom. 9:16). When we are granted a feeling sense of those words of Christ's "without me ye can do nothing" (John 15:5), then our pride receives its death-wound. So long as we entertain the mad idea that we can lend a helping hand in the business of our salvation, there is no hope for us; but when we perceive that we are clay in the hands of the divine potter to be molded into vessels of honor or dishonor as pleaseth Him, then we shall renounce our own strength, despair of any self-assistance, and pray and submissively wait for the mighty operations of God; nor shall we pray and wait in vain.

Fifth, election is to be preached because it is a divinely appointed means of faith. One of the first effects produced in serious-minded hearers is to stir them unto earnestly inquiring, Am I one of the elect, and to diligently examine themselves before God. In many instances this leads to the painful discovery that their profession is an empty one, resting on nothing better than some "decision" made by them years before under emotional stress. Nothing is more calculated to reveal a sham conversion than a Scriptural setting forth of the birthmarks of God's elect. Those who are predestinated unto salvation are made the subjects of a miraculous work of grace in their hearts, and *that* is a vastly different thing from a creature-act of "deciding for Christ" or becoming a member of some church. Far more than a natural faith is required to unite the soul unto a supernatural Christ.

The preaching of election acts as a flail in separating the wheat from the chaff. "Faith cometh by hearing, and hearing by the Word of God" (Rom. 10:17), and how can "the faith of God's elect" (Titus 1:1) be begotten and strengthened if the truth of election be suppressed? Divine foreordination does not set aside the use of means, but ensures the continuation and efficacy of them. God has pledged Himself to honor those who honor Him, and that preaching which brings most glory unto the Lord is what He most blesses. That is not always apparent now, but it will be made fully manifest in the Day to come, when it will be seen that much which Christendom regarded as gold, silver, precious stones, was naught but wood, hay, and stubble. Salvation and *the knowledge of the truth* are inseparably connected (I Tim. 2:4), but how can men arrive at a saving knowledge of the truth, if the most vital and basic part of it be withheld from them?

Sixth, election is to be preached because it incites to holiness. What can possibly be a more powerful incentive to piety than a heart which is overwhelmed by a sense of the sovereign and amazing grace of God! The realization that He set His heart upon me from all eternity, that

He singled me out from many when I had no more claim upon His notice that they had, that He chose me to be an object of His distinguishing favor, giving me unto Christ, inscribing my name in the Book of life, and at His appointed time bringing me from death unto life and giving me vital union with His dear Son; this indeed will fill me with gratitutde and cause me to seek to honor and please Him. God's electing love for us begets in us an endless love for Him. No motives so sweet or so potent as the love of God constraining us.

Seventh, election is to be preached because it promotes the spirit of praise. Said the apostle, "We are bound to give thanks always to God for you, brethren beloved of the Lord, because God hath from the beginning chosen you to salvation through sanctification of the Spirit and belief of the truth" (II Thess. 2:13). How can it be otherwise? Gratitude must find vent in adoration. A sense of God's electing grace and everlasting love makes us bless Him as nothing else does. Christ Himself returned special thanks unto the Father for His discriminating mercy (Matt. 11:25). The gratitude of the Christian flows forth because of the regenerating and sanctifying operations of the Spirit; it is stirred afresh by the redemptive and intercessory work of Christ; but it must rise still higher and contemplate the first cause—the sovereign grace of the Father—which planned the whole of our salvation. As then election is the great matter of thanksgiving unto God, it must be freely preached to His people.

The value of this blessed doctrine appears in its suitability and sufficiency to stabilize and settle true Christians in the certainty of their salvation. When regenerated souls are enabled to believe that the glorification of the elect is so infallibly fixed in God's eternal purpose that it is impossible for any of them to perish, and when they are enabled to Scripturally perceive that they themselves belong to the people of God's choice, how its strengthens and confirms their faith. Nor is such a confidence presumptuous—though any other most certainly is so—for every genuinely converted person has the right to regard himself as belonging to that favored company, since the Holy Spirit quickens none but those who were predestinated by the Father and redeemed by the Son. This is a hope "which maketh not ashamed," for it cannot issue in disappointment when entertained by those in whose hearts the love of God is shed abroad by the Spirit (Rom. 5:5).

The holy assurance which issues from a believing apprehension of this grand truth is forcibly set forth by the apostle in the closing verses of Romans 8. There he assures us, "Whom He did *predestinate,* them he also called: and whom He called them He also justified: and whom

he justified, them he also *glorified*" (v. 30). Such a beginning guarantees such an end: a salvation which originated in a past eternity
must be consummated in a future eternity. From such grand premises
Paul drew the blessed conclusion "If God be for us, who can be
against us?" (v. 31). And again, "Who shall lay anything to the charge
of God's elect?" (v. 33). And yet again, "Who shall separate us from
the love of Christ?" (v. 35). If such precious streams issue from this
fountain, then how great is the madness and how heinous the sin of
those who desire to see it choked. The everlasting security of Christ's
sheep cannot be presented in its full force until we base it upon the
divine decree.

How apt the trembling believer is to doubt his final perseverance, for
sheep (both natural and spiritual) are timid and self-distrustful creatures.
Not so the wild and wayward goats: true to their type, they are full of
carnal confidence and fleshly boasting. But the believer has such a sense
of his own weakness, such a sight of his sinfulness, such a realization of
his fickleness and stability, that he literally works out his own salvation
"in fear and trembling." Moreover, as he sees so many who did run well
doing so no longer, so many who made such a fair and promising profession end by making shipwreck of the faith, the very sight of their
apostasy causes him to seriously question his own state and latter end.
It is to stabilize their hearts that God has revealed in His Word that
those who are enabled to see in themselves the marks of election may
rejoice in the certainty of their everlasting blessedness.

Let us also point out what a stabilizing effect the apprehension of
this grand truth has upon the true servant of God. How much there is
to dishearten him: the fewness of those who attend his ministry, and
opposition made to those portions of the truth which most exalt God
and abase man, the scarcity of any visible fruits attending his labors,
the charge preferred by some of his officers or closest friends that if
he continues along such lines he will have no one at all left to preach
to, the whisperings of Satan that God Himself is frowning on such
efforts, that he is a rank failure and had better quit; these and other
considerations have a powerful tendency to fill him with dismay or
tempt him to trim his sails and float along the tide of popular
sentiment. We know whereof we write, for we have personally trod
this thorny path.

Ah, but God has graciously provided an antidote for Satan's poison,
and an effectual cordial to revive the drooping spirits of His sorely
tried servants. What is this? The knowledge that their Master has not
sent them forth to draw a bow at a venture, but rather to be
instruments in His hand of accomplishing His eternal decree. Though
He has commissioned them to preach the gospel unto all who attend

their ministry, yet He has also made it plain in His Word that it is not His purpose that all or even that many should be saved thereby. He has made it known that His flock is (Greek) a "very little" one (Luke 12:32), that there is only "a *remnant* according to the election of grace" (Rom. 11:5), that the "many" would be found on the broad road that leadeth to destruction and that only a "few" would walk that narrow way that leadeth unto life.

It is for the calling out from the world of this chosen remnant and for the feeding and establishing of them that God chiefly employs His servants. It is the due apprehension and personal belief of this which tranquilizes and stabilizes the minister's heart as nothing else will. As he rests upon the sovereignty of God, the efficacy of His decrees, the absolute certainty that God's counsels shall be fully realized, then he is assured that whatever God has sent him forth to do *must* be accomplished, that neither man nor devil can prevent it. Appalled by the ruin all around him, humiliated by his own sad failures, yet he perceives that the outworking of the divine plan is infallibly ensured. Those whom the Father ordained *will* believe (Acts 13:48), those for whom the Son died *must* be saved (John 10:16), those whom the Spirit quickens *shall* be effectually preserved (Phil. 1:6).

When the minister receives a message to deliver in the name of his Master, he may rest with unshaken confidence on the promise, "So shall My Word be that goeth forth out of my mouth; it shall not return unto me void, but it [not "may"] *shall* accomplish that which I please, and it *shall* prosper in the thing whereto I sent it" (Isa. 55:11). It may not accomplish what the preacher wishes nor prosper to the extent which the saints desire, but no power on earth or in hell can prevent the fulfillment of God's will. If God has marked out a certain person to be brought into a saving knowledge of the truth under a particular sermon, then no matter how buried in sin that soul may be nor how hardly he may kick against the pricks of conscience, he shall (like Paul of old) be made to cry "Lord, what wouldest thou have me to do?" Here, then, is a sure resting place for the minister's heart. This was where Christ found consolation, for when the nation at large despised and rejected Him, He consoled Himself with the fact that "*All* that the Father giveth me *shall* come to me" (John 6:37).

The value of this doctrine appears again in that it provides real encouragement to praying souls. Nothing so promotes the spirit of holy boldness at the throne of grace as the realization that God is our God and that we are the people of His choice. They are His peculiar treasure, the very apple of His eye, and they above all people have His ear. "Shall not God avenge his own elect, which cry day and night unto him?" (Luke 18:7). Assuredly He shall do so, for they are the only ones who supplicate Him in meekness, presenting their requests in subjection to His sovereign pleasure. O my readers, when we are on our knees, how this fact that God set His heart upon us from everlasting must inspire fervency and faith. Since God chose to love us, can He refuse to hear us? Then let us take courage from our predestination to make more earnest supplication.

"But know that the Lord hath set apart him that is godly for himself: the Lord will hear when I call unto him" (Ps. 4:3). " 'But know.' Fools will not learn, and therefore they must again and again be told the same thing, especially when it is such a bitter truth which is to be taught them, viz:—the fact that the godly are the chosen of God, and are, by distinguishing grace, set apart and separated from other men. Election is a doctrine which unrenewed man cannot endure, but nevertheless it is a glorious and well-attested truth, and one which should comfort the tempted believer. Election is the guarantee of complete salvation, and an argument for success at the throne of grace. He who chose us for Himself will surely hear our prayers. The Lord's elect shall not be condemned nor shall their cry be unheard. David was king by divine decree, and we are the Lord's people in the same manner; let us tell our enemies to their faces that they fight against God and destiny, when they strive to overthrow our souls" (C. H. Spurgeon).

Not only does a knowledge of the truth of election afford encouragement to praying souls, but it supplies important instruction and guidance therein. Our petitions ought ever to be framed in harmony with divine truth. If we believe in the doctrine of predestination we should pray accordingly. The language we use should be in agreement with the fact that we believe there are a company of persons chosen in Christ before the foundation of the world, and that it was for them, and them alone, He suffered and died. If we believe in particular redemption (rather than in a universal atonement) we should beg the Lord Jesus to have respect unto such as He has purchased by His soul's travail. This will be a means of keeping up right apprehensions in our own minds, as it will also be setting a proper example in this matter before others.

In the present day there are many deplorable expressions made use of in prayer, which are utterly unjustifiable, yea, which are altogether opposed to the will or Word of the Lord. How often the modern pulpit asks for the salvation of all present, and the head of the household requests that not one in the family miss eternal glory. To what purpose is this? Are we going to direct the Lord, who He shall save? Let us not be misunderstood: we are not against the preacher praying for his congregation, nor the parent for his family; that which we are opposed to is that praying which is in direct *opposition* unto the truth of the gospel. Prayer must be subordinated to the divine decrees, otherwise we are guilty of rebellion. When praying for the salvation of others, it should always be with the proviso "If they be thine elect" or "if it be thy sovereign will," or with some similar qualification.

The Lord Jesus has left us a perfect example in this, as in everything else. In His great high priestly prayer, recorded in John 17, we find Him saying, "I pray not for the world, but for them which Thou hast given Me; for they are Thine" (v. 9). Our Lord knew the whole of His Father's good will and pleasure towards the elect. He knew that the act of election was a sovereign and irreversible act in His mind. He knew that He Himself could not add one to the number of the chosen. He knew that He was sent from the Father to live and die for them, and them only. And in perfect agreement with this He declared, "I pray for them: I pray not for the world." If, then, Christ left out the world, if He prayed not for the non-elect, neither should we. We must learn of Him and follow His steps, and instead of resenting, be well pleased with the whole good pleasure of God's sovereign will.

To be submissive unto the divine will is the hardest lesson of all to learn. By nature we are self-willed and anything which crosses us is resented. The upsetting of our plans, the dashing of our cherished hopes, the smashing of our idols, stirs up the enmity of the flesh. A miracle of grace is required in order to bring us into acquiescence to God's dealing with us, so that we say from the heart "It is the Lord: let Him do what seemeth Him good" (I Sam. 3:18). And in bringing this miracle to pass, God uses *means*. He impresses on our hearts, an effectual sense of His sovereignty, so that we are brought to realize that He has the unqualified right to do as He pleases with His creatures. And no other truth has such a powerful tendency to teach us this vital lesson as has the doctrine of election. A saving knowledge of the fact that God chose us unto salvation begets within us a readiness for Him to order *all* our affairs, till we cry "not my will, but thine be done."

Now in view of all these considerations, we ask the reader, ought not the doctrine of election to be plainly and freely proclaimed? If God's Word be full of it, if the gospel cannot be Scripturally preached without it, if the grace of God cannot be maintained when it is suppressed, if the proclamation of it abases man into the dust, if it be a divinely appointed means of faith, if it be a powerful incentive unto the promotion of holiness, if it stirs in the soul the spirit of praise, if it establishes the Christian in the certainty of his security, if it be such a source of stability to the servant of God, if it supplies encouragement to praying souls and affords valuable instruction therein, if it work in us a sweet submission to the divine will; then shall we refuse to give unto God's children this valuable bread merely because dogs snap at it or withhold from the sheep this vital ingredient of their food simply because the goats cannot digest it?

And now, in conclusion, a few words on *how* this doctrine should be published. First, it ought to be presented *basically*. This is not an incidental or secondary truth, but one of fundamental importance and therefore it is not to be crowded into a corner, nor spoken of with bated breath. Predestination lies at the very foundation of the entire scheme of divine grace. This is clear from Romans 8:30, where it is mentioned before effectual calling, justification, and glorification. It is clear again from the order followed in Ephesians 1, where election (v. 4) precedes adoption, our acceptance in the Beloved, and our having redemption through His blood (vv. 5-7). The minister must, therefore, make it clear to his hearers that God first chose a people to be His peculiar treasure, then sent His Son to redeem them from the curse of the broken law, and now gives the Spirit to quicken them and bring them to everlasting glory.

Second, it ought to be preached *fearlessly*. God's servants must not be intimidated by the frowns of men nor deterred from performing their duty by any form of opposition. The minister of the gospel is called upon to "endure hardness as a good soldier of Jesus Christ" (II Tim. 2:3), and soldiers who fear the foe or take to flight are of no service to their king. The same holds good of those who are officers of the King of kings. How fearless was the apostle Paul! How valiant for the truth were Luther and Calvin, and the thousands of those who were burned at the stake because of their adherence to this doctrine. Then let not those whom Christ has called to preach the gospel conceal this truth because of the fear of man, for the Master has plainly warned them "Whosoever therefore shall be ashamed of me and of *my words* in this evil and adulterous generation; of him also shall the Son of man be ashamed" (Mark 8:38).

Third, it is to be preached *humbly*. Fearlessness does not require us to be bombastic. The holy Word of God must ever be handled with reverence and sobriety. When the minister stands before his people they ought to feel by his demeanor that he has come to them from the audience-chamber of the Most High, that the awe of Jehovah rests upon his soul. To preach upon the sovereignty of God, His eternal counsels, His choosing of some and passing by of others, is far too solemn a matter to be delivered in the energy of the flesh. There is a happy medium between a cringing, apologetic attitude, and adopting the style of a political tirader. Earnestness must not degenerate into vulgarity. It is "in *meekness*" we are to instruct those who oppose themselves "if God peradventure will give them repentance to the acknowledging of the truth" (II Tim. 2:25).

Fourth, it is to be preached *proportionately*. Though the foundation be of first importance it is of little value unless a superstructure be erected upon it. The publication of election is to make way for the other cardinal truths of the gospel. If any doctrine be preached exclusively it is distorted. There is a balance to be preserved in our presentation of the truth; while no part of it is to be suppressed, no part of it is to be made unduly prominent. It is a great mistake to harp on one string only. Man's responsibility must be enforced as well as God's sovereignty insisted upon. If on the one hand the minister must not be intimidated by Arminians, on the other he must not be brow-beaten by hyper-Calvinists, who object to the calling upon the unconverted to repent and believe the gospel (Mark 1:15).

Fifth, it is to be preached *experimentally*. This is how the apostles dealt with it, as is clear from "give diligence to make your calling and election sure" (II Peter 1:10). But how can this be done unless we are taught the doctrine of election, instructed in the nature and use of it? The truth of election can be small comfort to any man until he has a well-grounded assurance that *he* is one of God's chosen people; and that is possible only by ascertaining that he possesses (in some measure) the Scriptural marks of Christ's sheep. As we have already dealt with this aspect of our subject at some length, we will say no more. May it please the Lord to use these words unto His own glory and the blessing of His dear saints.

PART TWO

The Doctrine of Justification

1 Introduction

Our first thought was to first set forth the principal errors which have been entertained upon this subject by different men and parties, but after more deliberation we decided this would be for little or no profit to the majority of our readers. While there are times, no doubt, when it becomes the distasteful duty of God's servants to expose that which is calculated to deceive and injure His people, yet, as a general rule, the most effective way of getting rid of darkness is to let in the light. We desire, then, to write in the spirit of the godly John Owen, who, in the introduction to his ponderous treatise on this theme said, "More weight is to be put on the steady guidance of the mind and conscience of one believer, really exercised about the foundation of his peace and acceptance with God, than on the confutation of ten wrangling disputers. . . .To declare and vindicate the truth unto the instruction and edification of such as love it in sincerity, to extricate their minds from the difficulties in this particular instance, which some endeavor to cast on all gospel mysteries, to direct the consciences of them that inquire after abiding peace with God, and to establish the minds of them that do believe, are the things I have aimed at."

There was a time, not so long ago, when the blessed truth of justification was one of the best known doctrines of the Christian faith, when it was regularly expounded by the preachers and when the rank and file of church-goers were familiar with its leading aspects. But now, alas, a generation has arisen which is well-nigh totally ignorant of this precious theme, for with very rare exceptions it is no longer given a place in the pulpit, nor is scarcely anything written thereon in the religious magazines of our day; and, in consequence, comparatively few understand what the term itself connotes, still less are they clear as to the ground on which God justifies the ungodly.

This places the writer at a considerable disadvantage, for while he wishes to avoid a superficial treatment of so vital a subject, yet to go into it deeply, and enter into detail, will make a heavy tax upon the mentality and patience of the average person. Nevertheless, we respectfully urge each Christian to make a real effort to gird up the loins of his mind and seek to prayerfully master these chapters.

That which will make it harder to follow us through the present series is the fact that we are here treating of the *doctrinal* side of truth, rather than the practical; the judicial, rather than the experimental. Not that doctrine is *impracticable:* no indeed: far, far from it. "All Scripture is given by inspiration of God, and is profitable [first] for *doctrine,* [and then] for reproof, for correction, for instruction in righteousness" (II Tim. 3:16). Doctrinal instruction was ever the foundation from which the apostles issued precepts to regulate the walk. Not until Chapter 6 will any exhortation be found in the Roman Epistle: the first five are devoted entirely to doctrinal exposition. So again in the Epistle to the Ephesians: not until 4:1 is the first exhortation given. First the saints are reminded of the exceeding riches of God's grace, that the love of Christ may constrain them; and then they are urged to walk worthy of the vocation wherewith they are called.

While it be true that a real mental effort (as well as a prayerful heart) is required in order to grasp intelligently some of the finer distinctions which is essential to a proper apprehension of this doctrine, yet, let it be pointed out that, the truth of justification is far from being a mere piece of abstract speculation. No, it is a statement of divinely revealed fact; it is a statement of fact in which every member of our race ought to be deeply interested. Each one of us has forfeited the favor of God, and each one of us needs to be restored to His favor. If we are not restored, then the outcome must inevitably be our utter ruin and hopeless perdition. How fallen creatures, how guilty rebels, how lost sinners, *are* restored to the favor of God, and given a standing before Him inestimably superior to that occupied by the holy angels, will (D.V.) engage our attention as we proceed with our subject.

As said Abram Booth in his splendid work *The Reign of Grace* (written in 1768), "Far from being a merely speculative point, it spreads its influence through the whole body of divinity (theology), runs through all Christian experience, and operates in every part of practical godliness. Such is its grand importance, that a mistake about it has a malignant efficacy, and is attended with a long train of dangerous consequences. Nor can this appear strange, when it is considered, that this doctrine of justification is no other than the way of a *sinner's acceptance with God.* Being of such peculiar moment, it is inseparably connected with many other evangelical truths, the harmony and beauty of which we cannot behold, while this is mis-understood. Till this appears in its glory, they will be involved in darkness. It is, if anything may be so called, a *fundamental* article; and certainly requires our most serious consideration" (from his chapter on "Justication").

The great importance of the doctrine of justification was sublimely expressed by the Dutch Puritan, Witsius, when he said, "It tends much to display the glory of God, whose most exalted perfections shine forth with an eminent lustre in this matter. It sets forth infinite *goodness* of God, by which He was inclined to procure salvation freely for lost and miserable man, 'to the praise of the glory of His grace' (Eph. 1:6). It displays also the strictest *justice,* by which He would not forgive even the smallest offense, but on condition of the suffi-cient engagement, or full satisfaction of the Mediator, 'that He might be just, and the Justifier of him which believeth in Jesus' (Rom. 3:26). It shows further the unsearchable *wisdom* of the Deity, which found out a way for the exercise of the most gracious act of mercy, without injury to His strictest justice and infallible truth, which threatened death to the sinner: justice demanded that the soul that sinned should die (Rom. 1:32). Truth had pronounced, 'cursed is he that continueth not in all things' (Gal. 3:10). Goodness in the meantime, was inclined to adjudge life to some sinners, but by no other way than what became the majesty of the most holy God. Here wisdom interposed, saying, 'I will fully satisfy my goodness, and say to mine elect, "I, even I, am he that blotteth out thy transgressions for mine own sake" (Isa. 43:25). Nor shall you, my justice and my truth, have any cause of complaint, because full satisfaction shall be made to you by a media-tor.' Hence the incredible philanthropy of the Lord Jesus shineth forth, who, though Lord of all, was made subject to the law, not to the obedience of it only, but also to the curse: 'made him to be sin for us, that we might be made the righteousness of God in Him' (II Cor. 5:21).

"Ought not the pious soul, who is deeply engaged in the devout meditation of these things, to break out into the praises of a justifying God, and sing with the church, 'who is a God like unto thee, that pardoneth iniquity, and passeth by transgression' (Micah 7:17). O the purity of that holiness which chose rather to punish the sins of the elect in His only begotten Son, than suffer them to go unpunished! O the abyss of His love to the world, for which He spared not His dearest Son, in order to spare sinners! O the depth of the riches of unsearch-able wisdom, by which He exercises mercy towards the penitent guilty, without any stain to the honor of the most impartial Judge. O the treasures of love in Christ, whereby He became a curse for us, in order to deliver us therefrom! How becoming the justified soul, who is ready to dissolve in the sense of this love, with full exultation to sing a new song, a song of mutual return of love to a justifying God."

So important did the apostle Paul under the guidance of the Holy Spirit, deem this doctrine, that the very first of his epistles in the New Testament is devoted to a full exposition thereof. The pivot on which turns the entire contents of the Epistle to the Romans is that notable expression "the righteousness of God"—than which is none of greater moment to be found in all the pages of Holy Writ, and which it behooves every Christian to make the utmost endeavor to clearly understand. It is an abstract expression denoting the satisfaction of Christ in its relation to the divine law. It is a descriptive name for the material cause of the sinner's acceptance before God. "The righteousness of God" is a phrase referring to the finished work of the Mediator as approved by the divine tribunal, being the meritorious cause of our acceptance before the throne of the Most High.

In the succeeding chapters we shall examine in more detail this vital expression "the rightousness of God," which connotes that perfect satisfaction which the Redeemer offered to divine justice on the behalf of and in the stead of that people which had been given to Him. Suffice it now to say that that "righteousness" by which the believing sinner is justified is called "the righteousness *of God*" (Rom. 1:17; 3:21) because He is the appointer, approver, and imputer of it. It is called "the righteousness *of God and our Saviour Jesus Christ*" (II Peter 1:1) because He wrought it out and presented it unto God. It is called "the righteousness *of faith*" (Rom. 4:13) because faith is the apprehender and receiver of it. It is called *man's* righteousness (Job 33:26) because it was paid for him and imputed to him. All these varied expressions refer to so many aspects of that one perfect obedience unto death which the Saviour performed for His people.

Yes, so vital did the Apostle Paul, under the guidance of the Holy Spirit, esteem this doctrine of justification, that he shows at length how the denial and perversion of it by the Jews was the chief reason of their being rejected by God: see the closing verses of Romans 9 and the beginning of Chapter 10. Again; throughout the whole Epistle to the Galatians we find the apostle engaged in most strenuously defending and zealously disputing with those who had assailed this basic truth. Therein he speaks of the contrary doctrines as ruinous and fatal to the souls of men, as subversive of the cross of Christ, and calls it another gospel, solemnly declaring "though we, or an angel from heaven, preach any other gospel unto you . . . let him be accursed" (Gal. 1:8). Alas, that under the latitudian liberty and false "charity" of our day, there is now so little holy abhorence of that preaching which repudiates the vicarious obedience of Christ which is imputed to the believer.

Under God, the preaching of this grand truth brought about the greatest revival which the cause of Christ has enjoyed since the days of the apostles. "This was the great fundamental distinguishing doctrine of the Reformation, and was regarded by all the Reformers as of primary and paramount importance. The leading charge which they adduced against the Church of Rome was, that she had corrupted and perverted the doctrine of Scripture upon this subject, in a way that was dangerous to the souls of men; and it was mainly by the exposition, enforcement, and application of the true doctrine of God's Word in regard to it, that they assailed and overturned the leading doctrines and practices of the Papal system. There is no subject which possesses more of intrinsic importance than attaches to this one, and there is none with respect to which the Reformers were more thoroughly harmonious in their sentiments" (W. Cunningham).

This blessed doctrine supplies the grand divine cordial to revive one whose soul is cast down and whose conscience is distressed by a felt sense of sin and guilt, and longs to know the way and means whereby he may obtain acceptance with God and the title unto the heavenly inheritance. To one who is deeply convinced that he has been a life-long rebel against God, a constant transgressor of His holy law, and who realizes he is justly under His condemnation and wrath, no inquiry can be of such deep interest and pressing moment as that which relates to the means of restoring him to the divine favor, remitting his sins, and fitting him to stand unabashed in the divine presence: till this vital point has been cleared to the satisfaction of his heart, all other information concerning religion will be quite unavailing.

"Demonstrations of the existence of God will only serve to confirm and more deeply impress upon his mind, the awful truth which he already believes, that there is a righteous judge, before whom he must appear, and by whose sentence his final doom will be fixed. To explain the moral law to him, and inculcate the obligations to obey it, will be to act the part of a public accuser, when he quotes the statutes of the land in order to show that the charges which he has brought against the criminal at the bar are well founded, and, consequently, that he is worthy of punishment. The stronger the arguments are by which you evince the immortality of the soul, the more clearly do you prove that his punishment will not be temporary, and that there is another state of existence, in which he will be fully recompensed according to his desert" (J. Dick).

When God Himself becomes a living reality unto the soul, when His awful majesty, ineffable holiness, inflexible justice, and sovereign authority, are really perceived, even though most inadequately, indifference to His claims now gives place to a serious concern. When there is a due sense of the greatness of our apostasy from God, of the depravity of our nature, of the power and vileness of sin, of the spirituality and strictness of the law, and of the everlasting burnings awaiting God's enemies, the awakened soul cries out, "Wherewith shall I come before the Lord, and bow myself before the high God? shall I come before him with burnt offerings, with calves of a year old? Will the Lord be pleased with thousands of rams, or with ten thousands of rivers of oil? shall I give my firstborn for my transgression, the fruit of my body for the sin of my soul?" (Micah 6:6, 7). Then it is that the poor soul cries out, "*How then can* man be justified with God? or how can he be clean that is born of a woman?" (Job 25:4). And it is in the blessed doctrine which is now before us that we are taught the method whereby a sinner may obtain peace with his Maker and rise to the possession of eternal life.

Again; this doctrine is of inestimable value unto the conscientious Christian who daily groans under a sense of his inward corruptions and innumerable failures to measure up to the standard which God has set before him. The Devil, who is "the accuser of our brethren" (Rev. 12:10), frequently charges the believer with hypocrisy before God, disquiets his conscience, and seeks to persuade him that his faith and piety are nought but a mask and outward show, by which he has not only imposed upon others, but also on himself. But, thank God, Satan may be overcome by "the blood of the Lamb" (Rev. 12:11): by looking away from incurably depraved self, and viewing the Surety, who has fully answered for the Christian's every failure, perfectly atoned for his every sin, and brought in an "everlasting righteousness" (Dan. 9:24), which is placed to his account in the high court of heaven. And thus, though groaning under his infirmities, the believer may possess a victorious confidence which rises above every fear.

This it was which brought peace and joy to the heart of the apostle Paul: for while in one breath he cried, "O wretched man that I am! who shall deliver me from the body of this death?" (Rom. 7:24), in the next he declared, "There is therefore now no condemnation to them which are in Christ Jesus" (8:1). To which he added, "Who shall lay anything to the charge of God's elect? It is God that justifieth. Who is he that condemneth? It is Christ that died, yea rather, that is risen again, who is even at the right hand of God, who also maketh intercession for us. Who shall separate us from the love of Christ?" (vv. 33-35). May it please the God of all grace to so direct our pen and bless what we write to the readers, that not a few who are now found in the gloomy dungeons of Doubting Castle, may be brought out into the glorious light and liberty of the full assurance of faith.

2 Its Meaning

Deliverance from the condemning sentence of the divine law is the fundamental blessing in divine salvation: so long as we continue under the curse, we can neither be holy nor happy. But as to the precise nature of that deliverance, as to exactly what it consists of, as to the ground on which it is obtained, and as to the means whereby it is secured, much confusion now obtains. Most of the errors which have been prevalent on this subject arose from the lack of a clear view of the thing itself, and until we really understand what justification is we are in no position to either affirm or deny anything concerning it. We therefore deem it requisite to devote a whole chapter to a careful defining and explaining of this word "justification," endeavoring to show both what it signifies, and what it does not connote.

Between Protestants and Romanists, there is a wide difference of opinion as to the meaning of the term "justify": they affirming that to justify is to *make* inherently righteous and holy; we insisting that to justify signifies only to formally *pronounce* just or legally *declare* righteous. Popery includes under justification the renovation of man's moral nature or deliverance from depravity, thereby confounding justification with regeneration and sanctification. On the other hand, all representative Protestants have shown that justification refers not to a change of moral character, but to a change of legal status; though allowing, yes, insisting, that a radical change of character invariably *accompanies* it. It is a legal change from a state of guilt and condemnation to a state of forgiveness and acceptance; and this change is owing solely to a gratuitous act of God, founded upon the righteousness of Christ (they having *none* of their own) being imputed to His people.

"We simply explain justification to be an acceptance, by which God receives us into His favor, and esteems us as righteous persons; and we say that it consists in the remission of sins and the imputation of the righteousness of Christ. . . . Justification, therefore, is no other than an acquittal from guilt of him who was accused, as though his innocence has been proved. Since God, therefore, justifies us through the mediation of Christ, He acquits us, not by an admission of our personal innocence, but by an imputation of righteousness; so that we, who are unrighteous in ourselves, are considered as righteous in Christ" (John Calvin, 1559).

"What is justification? Answer: Justification is an act of God's free grace unto sinners, in which He pardoneth all their sins, accepteth and accounteth their persons righteous in His sight; not for any thing wrought in them, or done by them, but only for the perfect obedience and full satisfaction of Christ, by God imputed to them, and received by faith alone" (Westminster Catechism, 1643).

"We thus define the gospel justification of a sinner: It is a judicial, but gracious act of God, whereby the elect and believing sinner is absolved from the guilt of his sins, and hath a right to eternal life adjudged to him, on account of the obedience of Christ, received by faith" (H. Witsius, 1693).

Justification, then, refers not to any subjective change wrought in a person's disposition, but is solely an objective change in his standing in relation to the law. That to justify cannot possibly signify to *make* a person inherently righteous or good, is most clearly to be seen from the usage of the term itself in Scripture. For example, in Proverbs 17:15 we read, "He that justifieth the wicked, and he that condemneth the just, even they both are abomination to the Lord": now obviously he who shall *make* a "wicked" person just is far from being an "abonimation to the Lord," but he who knowingly pronounces a wicked person to be righteous is obnoxious to Him. Again; in Luke 7:29 we read, "And all the people that heard Him, and the publicans, justified God": how impossible it is to make the words "justified God" signify any moral transformation in His character; but understand those words to mean that they *declared* Him to be righteous, and all ambiguity is removed. Once more, in I Timothy 3:16 we are told, that the incarnate Son was "justified in [or"by"] the Spirit": that is to say, He was publicly vindicated at His resurrection, exonerated from the blasphemous charges which the Jews had laid against Him.

Justification has to do solely with the *legal* side of salvation. It is a judicial term, a word of the law courts. It is the sentence of a judge upon a person who has been brought before him for judgment. It is that gracious act of God as Judge, in the high court of heaven, by which He pronounces an elect and believing sinner to be freed from the penalty of the law, and fully restored unto the divine favor. It is the declaration of God that the party arraigned is fully conformed to the law: justice exonerates him because justice has been satisfied. Thus, justification is that change of status whereby one, who being guilty before God, and therefore under the condemning sentence of His law, and deserving of nought but an eternal banishment from His presence, is received into His favor and given a right to all the blessings which Christ has, by His perfect satisfaction, purchased for His people.

In substantiation of the above definitions, the meaning of the term "justify" may be determined, first, *by its usage in Scripture.* "And Judah said, What shall we say unto my Lord? What shall we speak? or how shall we *clear* [this Hebrew word *tsadag* always signifies "justify"] ourselves?" (Gen. 44:16). Here we have an affair which was entirely a judicial one. Judah and his brethren were arraigned before the governor of Egypt, and they were concerned as to how they might procure *a sentence in their favor.* "If there be a controversy between men, and they come unto judgment, that the judges may judge them; then they shall justify the righteous, and condemn the wicked" (Deut. 25:1). Here again we see plainly that the term is a forensic one, used in connection with the proceedings of law-courts, implying a process of investigation and judgment. God here laid down a rule to govern the judges in Israel: they must not "justify" or pass a sentence in favor of the wicked (compare I Kings 8:31, 32).

"If I justify myself, mine own mouth shall condemn me: if I say, I am perfect, it shall also prove me perverse" (Job 9:20): the first member of this sentence is explained in the second—"justify" there cannot signify to make holy, but to pronounce a sentence in my own favor. "Then was kindled the wrath of Elihu . . . against Job . . . because he justified himself rather than God" (Job 32:2), which obviously means, because he vindicated himself rather than God. "That thou mightest be justified when thou speakest, and be clear when thou judgest" (Ps. 51:4), which signifies that God, acting in His judicial office, might be pronounced righteous in passing sentence. "But wisdom is justified of her children" (Matt. 11:19), which means that they who are truly regenerated by God have *accounted* the wisdom of God (which the scribes and Pharisees reckoned foolishness) to be, as it really is, consummate wisdom: they cleared it of the calumny of folly.

2. The precise force of the term "to justify" may be ascertained by noting that it is *the antithesis of "to condemn."* Now to condemn is not a process by which a good man is made bad, but is *the sentence* of a judge upon one because he is a transgressor of the law. "He that justifieth the wicked, and he that condemneth the just, even they both

are abomination to the Lord" (Prov. 17:15; cf. Deut. 25:1). "For by thy words thou shalt be justified, and by thy words thou shalt be condemned" (Matt. 12:37). "It is God that justifieth, who is he that condemneth?" (Rom. 8:33, 34). Now it is undeniable that "condemnation" is the passing of a sentence against a person by which the punishment prescribed by the law is awarded to him and ordered to be inflicted upon him; therefore, justification is *the passing of a sentence* in favor of a person, by which the *reward* prescribed by the law is ordered to be given to him.

3. That justification is not an experimental change from sin to holiness, but a judicial change from guilt to no condemnation, may be evidenced by the *equivalent terms used for it*. For example, in Romans 4:6 we read, "Even as David also describeth the blessedness of the man, unto whom God imputed righteousness without works": so that legal "righteousness" is not a habit infused into the heart, but a gift transferred to our account. In Romans 5:9, 10 to be "justified by His blood" is the same as being "reconciled by His death," and reconciliation is not a transformation of character, but the effecting of peace by the removal of all that causes offense.

4. From the fact that the judicial side of our salvation is propounded in the Scripture under the figures of a *forensic trial and sentence*. "1. A judgment is supposed in it, concerning which the Psalmist prays that it may not proceed on the terms of the law: Ps. 143:2. (2) The Judge is God Himself: Isa. 50:7, 8. (3) The tribunal whereon God sits in judgment is the throne of grace: Heb. 4:16. (4) A guilty person. This is the sinner, who is so guilty of sin as to be obnoxious to the judgment of God: Rom. 3:18. (5) Accusers are ready to propose and promote the charge against the guilty person: these are the law (John 5:45), conscience (Rom. 2:15), and Satan: Zech. 3:2; Rev. 12:10. (6) The charge is admitted and drawn up in a 'hand-writing' in form of law, and is laid before the tribunal of the Judge, in bar to the deliverance of the offenders: Col. 2:14. (7) A plea is prepared in the gospel for the guilty person: this is grace, through the blood of Christ, the ransom paid, the eternal righteousness brought in by the Surety of the covenant: Rom. 3:23, 25; Dan. 9:24. (8) Hereunto alone the sinner betakes himself, renouncing all other apologies of defensatives whatever: Ps. 130:2, 4; Luke 18:13. (9) To make this plea effectual we have an Advocate with the Father, and He pleads His own propitiation for us: I John 2:1, 2. (10) The sentence hereon is absolution, on the account of the sacrifice and righteousness of Christ; with acceptation into favor, as persons approved of God: Rom. 8:33, 34; II Cor. 5:21" (John Owen).

From what has been before us, we may perceive what justification *is not.* First, *it differs from regeneration.* "Whom He called, them He also justified" (Rom. 8:30). Though inseparably connected, effectual calling or the new birth and justification are quite distinct. The one is never apart from the other, yet they must not be confounded. In the order of nature regeneration precedes justification, though it is in no sense the cause or ground of it: none is justified till he believes, and none believe till quickened. Regeneration is the act of the Father (James 1:18), justification is the sentence of the Judge. The one gives me a place in God's family, the other secures me a standing before His throne. The one is internal, being the impartation of divine life to my soul: the other is external, being the imputation of Christ's obedience to my account. By the one I am drawn to return in penitence to the Father's house, by the other I am given the "best robe" which fits me for His presence.

Second, *it differs from sanctification.* Sanctification is moral or experimental, justification is legal or judicial. Sanctification results from the operation of the Spirit *in* me, justification is based upon what Christ has done *for* me. The one is gradual and progressive, the other is instantaneous and immutable. The one admits of degrees, and is never perfect in this life; the other is complete and admits of no addition. The one concerns my *state,* the other has to do with my *standing* before God. Sanctification produces a moral transformation of *character,* justification is a change of legal *status:* it is a change from guilt and condemnation to forgiveness and acceptance, and this solely by a gratuitous act of God, founded upon the imputation of Christ's righteousness, through the instrument of faith alone. Though justification is quite separate from sanctification, yet sanctification ever *accompanies* it.

Third, *it differs from forgiveness.* In some things they agree. It is only God who can forgive sins (Mark 2:7) and He alone can justify (Rom. 3:30). His free grace is the sole moving cause in the one (Eph. 1:7) and of the other (Rom. 3:24). The blood of Christ is the procuring cause of each alike (Matt. 26:28; Rom. 5:9). The objects are the same: the persons that are pardoned are justified, and the same that are justified are pardoned; to whom God imputes the righteousness of Christ for their justification to them He gives the remission of sins; and to whom He does not impute sin, but forgives it, to them He imputes righteousness without works (Rom. 4:6-8). Both are received by faith (Acts 26:18; Rom. 5:1). But though they agree in these things, in others they differ.

God is said to be "justified" (Rom. 3:4), but it would be blasphemy to speak of *Him* being "pardoned"—this at once shows the two things are diverse. A criminal may be pardoned, but only a righteous person can be truly justified. Forgiveness deals only with a man's acts, justification with the man himself. Forgiveness respects the claims of mercy, justification those of justice. Pardon only remits the curse due unto sin; in addition justification confers a title to heaven. Justification applies to the believer with respect to the claims of the law, pardon without respect to the author of the law. The law does not pardon, for it knows no relaxation; but God pardons the transgressions of the law in His people by providing a satisfaction to the law adequate to their transgressions. The blood of Christ was sufficient to procure pardon (Eph. 1:7), but His righteousness is needed for justification (Rom. 5:19). Pardon takes away the filthy garments, but justification provides a change of raiment (Zech. 3:4). Pardon frees from death (II Sam. 12:13), but righteousness imputed is called "justification of life" (Rom. 5:18). The one views the believer as completely sinful, the other as completely righteous. Pardon is the remission of punishment, justification is the declaration that no ground for the infliction of punishment exists. Forgiveness may be repeated unto seventy times seven, justification is once for all.

From what has been said in the last paragraph we may see what a serious mistake it is to limit justification to the mere forgiveness of sins. Just as "condemnation" is not the execution of punishment, but rather the formal declaration that the accused is guilty and worthy of punishment; so "justification" is not merely the remission of punishment but the judicial announcement that punishment cannot be justly inflicted—the accused being fully conformed to all the positive requirements of the law in consequence of Christ's perfect obedience being legally reckoned to his account. The justification of a believer is no other than his being admitted to participate in the reward merited by his Surety. Justification is nothing more or less than the righteousness of Christ being imputed to us: the negative blessing issuing therefrom is the remission of sins; the positive, a title to the heavenly inheritance.

Beautifully has it been pointed out that "We cannot separate from Immanuel His own essential excellency. We may see Him bruised and given like beaten incense to the fire, but was incense ever burned without fragrance, and only fragrance being the result? The name of Christ not only cancels sin, it supplies in the place of that which it has cancelled, its own everlasting excellency. We cannot have its nullifying power only; the other is the sure concomitant. So was it with every typical sacrifice of the law. It was stricken: but as being spotless it was burned on the altar for a sweet-smelling savor. The savor ascended as a memorial before God: it was accepted for, and its value was attributed or imputed to him, who had brought the vicarious victim. If therefore, we reject the imputation of righteousness, we reject sacrifice as revealed in Scripture; for Scripture knows of no sacrifice whose efficacy is so exhausted in the removal of guilt, as to leave nothing to be presented in acceptableness before God" (B. W. Newton).

"What is placing our righteousness in the obedience of Christ, but asserting that we are accounted righteous only because His obedience is accepted for us as if it were our own? Wherefore Ambrose appears to me to have very beautifully exemplified this righteousness in the benediction of Jacob: that as he, who had on his own account no claim to the privileges of primogeniture, being concealed in his brother's habit, and invested with his garment, which diffused a most excellent odor, insinuated himself into the favor of his father, that he might receive the benediction to his own advantage, under the character of another; so we shelter ourselves under the precious purity of Christ" (J. Calvin).

3 Its Problem

In this and the following chapter our aim will be fourfold. First, to demonstrate the impossibility of any sinner obtaining acceptance and favor with God on the ground of his own performances. Second, to show that the saving of a sinner presented a problem which nought but omniscience could solve, but that the consummate wisdom of God has devised a way whereby He can pronounce righteous a guilty transgressor of His law without impeaching His veracity, sullying His holiness, or ignoring the claims of justice; yea, in such a way that all His perfections have been displayed and magnified, and the Son of His love glorified. Third, point out the sole ground on which an awakened conscience can find solid and stable peace. Fourth, seek to give God's children a clearer understanding of the exceeding riches of divine grace, that their hearts may be drawn out in fervent praise unto the author of "so great salvation."

But let it be pointed out at the onset that, any reader who has never seen himself under the white light of God's holiness, and who has never felt His Word cutting him to the very quick, will be unable to fully enter into the force of what we are about to write. In all probability, he who is unregenerate is likely to take decided exception to much of what will be said, denying that any such difficulty exists in the matter of a merciful God pardoning one of His offending creatures. Or, if he does not dissent to that extent, yet he will most likely consider that we have grossly exaggerated the various elements in the case we are about to present, that we have pictured the sinner's condition in far darker hues than was warranted. This must be so, for he has no experimental acquaintance with God, nor is he conscious of the fearful plague of his own heart.

The natural man cannot endure the thought of being thoroughly searched by God. The last thing he desires is to pass beneath the all-seeing eye of his maker and judge, so that his every thought and desire, his most secret imagination and motive, stands exposed before Him. It is indeed a most solemn experience when we are made to feel with the Psalmist, "O Lord, thou hast searched me, and known me. Thou knowest my downsitting and mine uprising, thou understandest my thought afar off. Thou compassest my path and my lying down, and art acquainted with all my ways. For there is not a word in my tongue, but, lo, O Lord, thou knowest it altogether. Thou hast beset me behind and before, and laid thine hand upon me" (Ps. 139:1-5).

Yes, dear reader, the very last thing which the natural man desires is to be searched through and through by God, and have his real character exposed to view. But when God undertakes to do this very thing—which He either will do in grace in this life, or in judgment in the day to come—there is no escape for us. Then it is we may well exclaim, "Whither shall I go from thy spirit? or whither shall I flee from thy presence. If I ascend up into heaven, thou art there: if I make my bed in hell, behold, thou art there. If I take the wings of the morning, and dwell in the uttermost parts of the sea; even there shall thy hand lead me, and thy right hand shall hold me. If I say, Surely the darkness shall cover me; even the night shall be light about me" (Ps. 139:7-11). Then it is we shall be assured, "Yea, the darkness *hideth not from thee;* but the night shineth as the day: the darkness and the light are both alike to thee" (v. 12).

Then it is that the soul is awakened to a realization of *who it is* with whom it has to do. Then it is that he now perceives something of the high claims of God upon him, the just requirements of His law, the demands of His holiness. Then it is that he realizes how completely he has failed to consider those claims, how fearfully he has disregarded that law, how miserably he falls short of meeting those demands. Now it is that he perceives he has been "a transgressor from the womb" (Isa. 48:8), that so far from having lived to glorify his Maker, he has done nought but follow the course of this world and fulfill the lust of the flesh. Now it is he realizes that there is "*no* soundness" in him but, from the sole of the foot even unto the head, "wounds, and bruises, and putrifying sores" (Isa. 1:6). Now it is he is made to see that all his righteousnesses are as "filthy rags" (Isa. 64:6).

"It is easy for any one in the cloisters of the schools, to indulge himself in idle speculations of the merit of works to justify men; but when he comes into the presence of God, he must bid farewell to these amusements, for there the business is transacted with seriousness, and no ludicrous logomachy practiced. To this point, then, must our attention be directed, if we wish to make any useful inquiry concerning true righteousness; how we can answer the celestial Judge, when He shall call us to an account? Let us place that Judge before our eyes, not according to the spontaneous imaginations of our minds, but according to the descriptions given of Him in the Scripture; which represents Him as one whose refulgence eclipses the stars, whose power melts the mountains, whose anger shakes the earth, whose wisdom takes the subtle in their own craftiness, whose purity makes all things appear polluted, whose righteousness even the angels are unable to bear, who acquits not the guilty, whose vengeance, when it is once kindled, penetrates even to the abyss of hell" (John Calvin).

Ah, my reader, tremendous indeed are the effects produced in the soul when one is really brought into the presence of God, and is granted a sight of His awesome majesty. While we measure ourselves by our fellow men, it is easy to reach the conclusion that there is not much wrong with us; but when we approach the dread tribunal of ineffable holiness, we form an entirely different estimate of our character and conduct. While we are occupied with earthly objects we may pride ourselves in the strength of our visive faculty, but fix the gaze steadily on the midday sun and under its dazzling brilliance the weakness of the eye will at once become apparent. In like manner, while I compare myself with other sinners I can but form a wrong estimate of myself, but if I gauge my life by the plummet of God's law, and do so in the light of His holiness, I must "Abhor myself, and repent in dust and ashes" (Job 42:6).

But not only has sin corrupted man's being, it has *changed his relation to God:* it has "alienated" him (Eph. 4:18), and brought him under His righteous condemnation. Man has broken God's law in thought and word and deed, not once, but times without number. By the divine tribunal he is pronounced an incorrigible transgressor, a guilty rebel. He is under the curse of his maker. The law demands that its punishment shall be inflicted upon him; justice clamors for satisfaction. The sinner's case is deplorable, then, to the last degree. When this is painfully felt by the convicted conscience, its agonized possessor cries out, *"How then can man be clean that is born of a woman?"* (Job 25:4). How indeed! Let us now consider the various elements which enter into this problem.

1. *The requirements of God's law.* "Every question therefore, respecting justification necessarily brings before us the judicial courts of God. The principles of those courts must be determined by God alone. Even to earthly governors we concede the right of establishing their own laws, and appointing the mode of their enforcement. Shall we then accord this title to man, and withold it from the all-wise and almighty God? Surely no presumption can be greater than for the creature to sit in judgment on the Creator, and to pretend to

determine what should, or should not be, the methods of His government. It must be our place reverently to listen to His own exposition of the principles of His own courts, and humbly thank Him for His goodness in condescending to explain to us what those principles are. As sinners, we can have no claim on God. We have no claim to a revelation that should acquaint us with His ways.

"The judicial principles of the government of God, are, as might be expected, based upon the absolute perfectness of His own holiness. This was fully shown both in the prohibitory, and in the mandatory commandments of the law as given at Sinai. That law prohibited not only wrong deeds and wrong counsels of heart, but it went deeper still. It prohibited even wrong desires and wrong tendencies, saying, 'thou shalt not be concupiscent'—that is, thou shalt not have, *even momentarily*, one desire or tendency that is contrary to the perfectness of God. And then as to its positive requirements, it demanded the perfect, unreserved, perpetual surrender of soul and body, with all its powers, to God and to His service. Not only was it required, that love of Him—love perfect and unremitted—should dwell as a living principle in the heart, but also that it should be developed in action, and that unvaryingly. The mode also of the development throughout, was required to be as perfect as the principle from which the development sprang.

"If any among the children of men be able to substantiate a claim to perfectness such as this, the courts of God are ready to recognize it. The God of truth will recognize a truthful claim wherever it is found. But if we are unable to present any such claim—if corruption be found in us and in our ways—if in any thing we have fallen short of God's glory, then it is obvious that however willing the courts of God may be to recognize perfectness where it exists, such willingness can afford no ground of hope to those, who, instead of having perfectness, have sins and short-comings unnumbered" (B. W. Newton).

2. *The indictment preferred against us.* "Hear, O heavens, and give ear, O earth; for the Lord hath spoken, I have nourished and brought up, children, and they have rebelled against me. The ox knoweth his owner, and the ass his master's crib: but Israel doth not know, my people doth not consider. Ah sinful nation, a people laden with iniquity, a seed of evil doers, children that are corrupters: they have forsaken the Lord, they have provoked the Holy One of Israel unto anger, they are gone away backward" (Isa. 1:2-4). The eternal God justly charges us with having broken all His commandments—some in act, some in word, all of them in thought and imagination.

The enormity of this charge is heightened by the fact that against light and knowledge we chose the evil and forsook the good: that again and again we deliberately turned aside from God's righteous law, and went astray like lost sheep, following the evil desires and devices of our own hearts. Above, we find God complaining that inasmuch as we are His creatures, we ought to have obeyed Him, that inasmuch as we owe our very lives to His daily care we ought to have rendered Him fealty instead of disobedience, and have been His loyal subjects instead of turning traitors to His throne. No exaggeration of sin is brought against us, but a statement of fact is declared which it is impossible for us to gainsay. We are ungrateful, unruly, ungodly creatures. Who would keep a horse that refused to work? Who would retain a dog which barked and flew at us? Yet we have broken God's sabbaths, despised His reproofs, abused His mercies.

3. *The sentence of the law.* This is clearly announced in the divine oracles, "Cursed is everyone that continueth not in all things which are written in the book of the law to do them" (Gal. 3:10). Whoever violates a single precept of the divine law exposes himself to the displeasure of God, and to punishment as the expression of that displeasure. No allowance is made for ignorance, no distinction is made between persons, no relaxation of its strictness is permissible: "The soul that sinneth it shall die" is its inexorable pronouncement. No exception is made whether the transgressor be young or old, rich or poor, Jew or Gentile: "the wages of sin is death"; for "the wrath of God is revealed from heaven against *all* ungodliness and unrighteousness of men" (Rom. 1:18)

4. *The Judge Himself is inflexibly just.* In the high court of divine justice God takes the law in its strictest and sternest aspect, and judges rigidly according to the letter. "But we are sure that the judgment of God is according to truth against them which commit such things . . . who will render to every man according to his deeds" (Rom. 2:2, 6). God is inexorably righteous, and will not show any partiality either to the law or to its transgressor. The Most High has determined that His holy law shall be faithfully upheld and its sanctions strictly enforced.

What would this country be like if all its judges ceased to uphold and enforce the laws of the land? What conditions would prevail were sentimental mercy to reign at the expense of righteousness? Now God is the judge of all the earth and the moral ruler of the universe. Holy Writ declares that "justice and judgment," and not pity and clemency, are the *"habitation"* of His "throne" (Ps. 89:14). God's attributes do not conflict with each other. His mercy does not override His justice, nor is His grace ever shown at the expense of righteousness. Each of His perfections is given free course. For God to give a sinner entrance into Heaven simply because He loved him, would be like a judge sheltering an escaped convict in his own home merely because he pitied him. Scripture emphatically declares that God "will by no means clear the guilty" (Exod. 34:7).

5. *The sinner is unquestionably guilty*. It is not merely that he has infirmities or that he is not as good as he ought to be: he has set at nought God's authority, violated His commandments, trodden His laws under foot. And this is true not only of a certain class of offenders, but "*all* the world" is "guilty before God" (Rom. 3:19). "There is none righteous, no, not one. They are all gone out of the way, they are together become unprofitable; there is none that doeth good, no, not one" (Rom. 3:10, 12). It is impossible for any man to clear himself from this fearful charge. He can neither show that the crimes of which he is accused have not been committed, nor that having been committed, he had a right to do them. He can neither disprove the charges which the law preferred against him, nor justify himself in the perpetration of them.

Here then, is how the case stands. The law demands personal, perfect, and perpetual conformity to its precepts, in heart and act, in motive and performance. God charges each one of us with having failed to meet those just demands, and declares we have violated His commandments in thought and word and deed. The law therefore pronounces upon us a sentence of condemnation, curses us, and demands the infliction of its penalty, which is death. The One before whose tribunal we stand is omniscient, and cannot be deceived or imposed upon; He is inflexibly just, and swayed by no sentimental considerations. We, the accused, are guilty, unable to refute the accusations of the law, unable to vindicate our sinful conduct, unable to offer any satisfaction or atonement for our crimes. Truly, our case is desperate to the last degree.

Here, then, is the problem. How can God justify the wilful transgressor of His law without justifying his sins? How can God deliver him from the penalty of His broken law without compromising His holiness and going back upon His word that He will "by no means clear the guilty"? How can life be granted the guilty culprit without repealing the sentence "the soul that sinneth it shall die"? How can mercy be shown to the sinner without justice being flouted? It is a problem which must forever have baffled every finite intelligence. Yet, blessed be His name, God *has*, in His consummate wisdom, devised a way whereby the "chief of sinners" may be dealt with by Him as though he were perfectly innocent; nay more, He pronounces him *righteous*, up to the required standard of the law, and *entitled to the reward* of eternal life. How this can be will be taken up next.

4 Its Basis

We have contemplated the *problem* which is presented in the justifying or pronouncing righteous one who is a flagrant violater of the law of God. Some may have been surprised at the introduction of such a term as "problem": as there are many in the ranks of the ungodly who feel that the world *owes* them a living, so there are not a few pharisees in Christendom who suppose it is *due* them that at death their Creator should take them to heaven. But different far is it with one who has been enlightened and convicted by the Holy Spirit, so that he sees himself to be a filthy wretch, a vile rebel against God. Such an one will ask, seeing that the Word of God so plainly declares "there shall in no wise enter into it any thing that defileth, neither whatsoever worketh abomination" (Rev. 21:27), How is it possible that *I* can ever gain admission into the heavenly Jerusalem? How can it be that one so completely devoid of righteousness as I am, and so filled with unrighteousness, should ever be pronounced just by a holy God?

Various attempts have been made by unbelieving minds to solve this problem. Some have reasoned that if they now turn over a new leaf, thoroughly reform their lives and henceforth walk in obedience to God's law, they shall be approved before the divine tribunal. This scheme, reduced to simple terms, is salvation by our own works. But such a scheme is utterly untenable, and salvation by such means is absolutely impossible. The works of a reformed sinner cannot be the meritorious or efficacious cause of his salvation, and that for the following reasons. First, no provision is made for his previous failures. Suppose that henceforth I never again transgress God's law, what is to atone for my past sins? Second, a fallen and sinful creature cannot produce that which is perfect, and nothing short of perfection is acceptable to God. Third, were it possible for us to be saved by our own works, then the sufferings and death of Christ were needless.

Fourth, salvation by our own merits would entirely eclipse the glory of divine grace.

Others suppose this problem may be solved by an appeal to the bare *mercy* of God. But mercy is not an attribute that overshadows all the other divine perfections: justice, truth, and holiness are also operative in the salvation of God's elect. The law is not set aside, but honored and magnified. The truth of God in His solemn threatenings is not sullied, but faithfully carried out. The divine righteousness is not flouted, but vindicated. One of God's perfections is not exercised to the injury of any of the others, but all of them shine forth with equal clearness in the plan which divine wisdom devised. Mercy at the expense of justice over-ridden would not suit the divine government, and justice enforced to the exclusion of mercy would not befit the divine character. The problem which no finite intelligence could solve was, how *both* might be exercised in the sinner's salvation.

A striking example of *mercy helpless* before the claims of the law occurs in Daniel 6. There we find that Darius, the king of Babylon, was induced by his nobles to sign a decree that any subject within his kingdom who should pray, or "ask a petition of any God or man for thirty days" save the king himself, should be cast into the den of lions. Daniel knowing this, nevertheless, continued to pray before God as hitherto. Whereupon the nobles acquainted Darius with his violation of the royal edict, which "according to the law of the Medes and Persians *altereth not,*" and demanded his punishment. Now Daniel stood high in the king's favor, and he greatly desired to show clemency unto him, so he "set his heart on Daniel *to* deliver him, and he labored till the going down of the sun to deliver him." But he found no way out of the difficulty: the law *must* be honored, so Daniel was cast into the lion's den.

An equally striking example of *law helpless* in the presence of mercy is found in John 8. There we read of a woman taken in the act of adultery. The scribes and pharisees apprehended her and set her before Christ, charging her with the crime, and reminding the Saviour that "Moses in the law commanded us that such should be stoned." She was unquestionably guilty, and her accusers were determined that the penalty of the law should be inflicted upon her. The Lord turned to them and said, "He that is without sin among you, let him first cast a stone at her"; and they, being convicted by their own conscience, went out one by one, leaving the adulteress alone with Christ. Turning to her, He asked, "Woman, where are . . . thine accusers, hath no man condemned thee?" She replied, "No man, Lord," and He answered, "Neither do I condemn thee: go, and sin no more."

The two adverse principles are seen *operating in conjunction* in Luke 15. The "Father" could not have the (prodigal) son at his table clad in the rags of the far country, but He could go out and meet him in those rags: he could fall on his neck and kiss him in those rags—it was blessedly characteristic of his *grace* so to do; but to seat him at his table in garments suited to the swine-troughs would not be fitting. But the grace which brought the father out to the prodigal "reigned" through that *righteousness* which brought the prodigal in to the Father's house. It had not been "grace" had the father waited till the prodigal decked himself out in suitable garments of his own providing; nor would it have been "righteousness" to bring him to his table in his rags. Both grace and righteousness shone forth in their respective beauty when the father said, "bring forth *the best robe,* and *put it on him."*

It is through Christ and His atonement that the justice and mercy of God, His righteousness and grace, meet in the justifying of a believing sinner. In Christ is found the solution to every problem which sin has raised. In the cross of Christ *every* attribute of God shines forth in its meridian splendor. In the satisfaction which the Redeemer offered unto God every claim of the law, whether precep- tive or penal, has been fully met. God has been infinitely more honored by the obedience of the last Adam than He was dishonored by the disobedience of the first Adam. The justice of God was infinitely more magnified when its awful sword smote the beloved Son, than had every member of the human race burned for ever and ever in the lake of fire. There is infinitely more efficacy in the blood of Christ to cleanse, than there is in sin to befoul. There is infinitely more merit in Christ's one perfect righteousness than there is demerit in the combined unrighteousness of all the ungodly. Well may we exlaim, "But God forbid that I should glory, save in the cross of our Lord Jesus Christ" (Gal. 6:14).

But while many are agreed that the atoning death of Christ is the meritorious cause of His people's salvation, there are now few indeed who can give any clear Scriptural *explanation of the way* and manner *by which* the work of Christ secures the justification of all who believe. Hence the need for a clear and full statement thereon. Hazy ideas at this point are both dishonoring to God and unsettling to our peace. It is of first importance that the Christian should obtain a clear understanding of the *ground on which* God pardons his sins and grants him a title to the heavenly inheritance. Perhaps this may best be set forth under three words: substitution, identification, imputation. As their surety and sponsor Christ entered the place occupied by His people under the law, so identifying Himself with them as to be their Head and Representative, and as such He assumed and discharged all their legal obligations: their liabilities being transferred to Him, His merits being transferred to them.

The Lord Jesus has wrought out for His people a perfect righteousness by obeying the law in thought and word and deed, and this righteousness is imputed to them, reckoned to their account. The Lord Jesus has suffered the penalty of the law in their stead, and through His atoning death they are cleansed from all guilt. As *creatures* they were under obligations to obey God's law; as *criminals* (transgressors) they were under the death-sentence of the law. Therefore, to fully meet our liabilities and discharge our debts it was necessary that our substitute should both obey and die. The shedding of Christ's blood blotted out our sins, but it did not, of itself, provide the "best robe" for us. To silence the accusations of the law against us so that there is now "no condemnation to them which are in Christ Jesus" is simply a *negative* blessing: something more was required, namely, a *positive* righteousness, the keeping of the law so that we might be entitled to its blessing and reward.

In Old Testament times the name under which the Messiah and Mediator was foretold is, "'The Lord our righteousness" (Jer. 23:6). It was plainly predicted by Daniel that He should come here to "finish the transgression, and to make an end of sins, and to make reconciliation for iniquity, and *to bring in everlasting righteousness*" (9:24). Isaiah announced "Surely, shall one say, in the Lord have I righteousness and strength: even to Him shall all men come; and all that are incensed against Him shall be ashamed. In the Lord shall all the seed of Israel be justified, and shall glory" (45:24, 25). And again, he represents each of the redeemed exclaiming, "I will greatly rejoice in the Lord, my soul shall be joyful in my God; for He hath clothed me with the garments of salvation, he hath covered me with the robe of righteousness" (61:10).

In Romans 4:6-8 we read, "David also describeth the blessedness of the man, unto whom God imputeth righteousness without works, Saying, Blessed are they whose iniquities are forgiven, and whose sins are covered. Blessed is the man to whom the Lord will not impute sin." Here we are shown the *inseparability* of the two things: God imputing "righteousness" and God not imputing "sins." The two are never divided: unto whom God imputes not sin He imputes righteousness; and unto whom He imputes righteousness, He imputes not sin. But the particular point which we are most anxious for the reader to grasp is, *Whose* "righteousness" is it that God imputes or reckons to the account of the one who believes? The answer is, that righteousness which was wrought out by our surety, that obedience to the law which was vicariously rendered by our sponsor, even "the righteousness of God and our Saviour Jesus Christ" (II Peter 1:1). This righteousness is not only "unto all" but also "*upon* all them that believe" (Rom. 3:22). It is called "the righteousness *of God*" because

it was the righteousness of the God-man mediator, just as in Acts
20:28 His blood is called the *blood of God.*

The "righteousness of God" which is mentioned so frequently in
the Roman epistle refers *not* to the essential righteousness of the
divine character, for *that* cannot possibly be imputed or legally transferred to any creature. When we are told in 10:3 that the Jews were
"ignorant of God's righteousness" it most certainly does not mean
they were in the dark concerning the divine rectitude or that they
knew nothing about God's justice; but it signifies that they were
unenlightened as to the righteousness which the God-man Mediator
had vicariously wrought out for His people. This is abundantly clear
from the remainder of that verse: "and going about to establish *their
own righteousness"*—not their own rectitude or justice, but performing works by which they hoped to merit acceptance with God. So
tightly did they cling to this delusion, they, "submitted not themselves unto the righteousness of God": that is, they refused to turn
from their self-righteousness and put their trust in the obedience and
sufferings of the incarnate Son of God.

"I would explain what we mean by the imputation of Christ's
righteousness. Sometimes the expression is taken by our divines in a
larger sense, for the imputation of all that Christ did and suffered for
our redemption, whereby we are free from guilt, and stand righteous
in the sight of God; and so implies the imputation both of Christ's
satisfaction and obedience. But here I intend it in a stricter sense, for
the imputation of that righteousness or moral goodness that consists
in the obedience of Christ. And by that obedience being imputed to
us, is meant no other than this, that that righteousness of Christ is
accepted for us, and admitted instead of that perfect inherent righteousness that ought to be in ourselves: Christ's perfect obedience
shall be reckoned to our account, so that we shall have the benefit of
it, as though we had performed it ourselves: and so we suppose, that a
title to eternal life is given us as the reward of this righteousness"
(Jonathan Edwards).

The one passage which casts the clearest light upon that aspect of
justification which we are now considering is II Corinthians 5:21,
"For he hath made him to be sin for us, who knew no sin; that we
might be made the righteousness of God in him." Here we have the
counter imputations: of our sins to Christ, of His righteousness to us.
As the teaching of this verse is of such vital moment let us endeavor to
consider its terms the more closely. *How* was Christ "made sin for
us"? By *God imputing to Him* our disobedience, or our transgressions
of the law; in like manner, we are made "the righteousness of God in
Him" (in Christ, not in ourselves) *by God imputing to us* Christ's
obedience, His fulfilling the precepts of the law for us.

As Christ "knew no sin" by inward defilement or personal commission, so we "knew" or had no righteousness of our own by inward
conformity to the law, or by personal obedience to it. As Christ was
"made sin" by having our sins placed to His account or charged
upon Him in a judicial way, and as it was not by any criminal
conduct of His own that He was "made sin," so it is not by any
pious activities of our own that we become "righteous": Christ was
not "made sin" by the infusion of depravity, nor are we "made
righteous" by the infusion of holiness. Though personally holy, our
Sponsor did, by entering our law-place, render Himself officially
liable to the wrath of God; and so though personally unholy we are,
by virtue of our legal identification with Christ, entitled to the favor
of God. As the consequence of Christ's being "made sin for us"
was, that "the Lord laid *on* him the iniquity of us all" (Isa. 53:6),
so the consequence of Christ's obedience being reckoned to our
account is, that God lays righteousness "*upon* all them that believe"
(Rom. 3:22). As our sins were the judicial ground of the sufferings of
Christ, by which sufferings He satisfied justice; so Christ's righteousness is the judicial ground of our acceptance with God, by which our
pardon is an act of Justice.

Notice carefully that in II Corinthians 5:21 it is *God* who "made"
or legally constituted Christ to be "sin for us," though as Hebrews
10:7 shows, the Son gladly acquiesced therein. "He was made sin by
imputation: the sins of all His people were transferred unto Him, laid
upon Him, and placed to His account and having them upon Him He
was treated by the justice of God as if He had been not only a sinner,
but a mass of sin: for to be made sin is a stronger expression than to
be made a sinner" (John Gill). "That we might be made the righteousness of God in Him" signifies to be legally constituted righteous
before God—justified. "It is a righteousness 'in Him,' in Christ, and
not in ourselves, and therefore must mean the righteousness of Christ:
so called, because it is wrought by Christ, who is God over all, the true
God, and eternal life" (Ibid).

The same counter-exchange which has been before us in II Corinthians 5:21 is found again in Galatians 3:13, 14, "Christ hath redeemed
us from the curse of the law, being made a curse for us: for it is
written, Cursed is everyone that hangeth on a tree: That the blessing
of Abraham might come on the Gentiles through Jesus Christ." As the
surety of His people, Christ was "made under the law" (Gal. 4:4),
stood in their law-place and stead, and having all their sins imputed to
Him, and the law finding them all upon Him, condemned Him for
them; and so the justice of God delivered Him up to the accursed
death of the cross. The purpose, as well as the consequence, of this
was "That the blessing of Abraham might come *on* the Gentiles": the

"blessing of Abraham" (as Rom. 4 shows) was justification by faith through the righteousness of Christ.

> Upon a Life I did not live,
> Upon a Death I did not die:
> Another's death. Another's life
> I'd rest my soul eternally.

5 Its Nature

Justification, strictly speaking, consists in God's imputing to His elect the righteousness of Christ, *that* alone being the meritorious cause or formal ground on which He pronounces them righteous: the righteousness of Christ is that to which God has respect when He pardons and accepts the sinner. By the *nature* of justification we have reference to *the constituent elements* of the same, which are enjoyed by the believer. These are, the non-imputation of guilt or the remission of sins, and second, of the investing of the believer with a legal title to heaven. The alone ground on which God forgives any man's sins, and admits him unto His judicial favor, is the vicarious work of his surety—that perfect satisfaction which Christ offered to the law on his behalf. It is of great importance to be clear on the fact that Christ was "made under the law" not only that He might redeem His people "from the curse of the law" (Gal. 3:13), *but also* that they might "receive the adoption of sons" (Gal. 4:5), that is, be invested with the privileges of sons.

This grand doctrine of justification was proclaimed in its purity and clarity by the Reformers—Luther, Calvin, Zanchius, Peter Martyr, etc.; but it began to be corrupted in the seventeenth century by men who had only a very superficial knowledge of it, who taught that justification consisted merely in the removal of guilt or forgiveness of sins, excluding the positive admittance of man into God's judicial favor: in other words, they restricted justification unto deliverance from hell, failing to declare that it also conveys a title unto heaven. This error was perpetuated by John Wesley, and then by the Plymouth Brethren, who, denying that the righteousness of Christ is imputed to the believer, seek to find his title to eternal life in a union with Christ in His resurrection. Few today are clear upon the *twofold* content of justification, because few today understand the nature of that righteousness which is imputed to all who believe.

211

To show that we have not misrepresented the standard teachings of the Plymouth Brethren on this subject, we quote from W. Kelly's *Notes on Romans.* In his "Introduction" he states, "There is nothing to hinder our understanding 'the righteousness of God' in its usual sense of an attribute or quality of God" (p. 35). But how could an "attribute" or "quality" of God be "*upon*" all them that believe" (Rom. 3:22)? Kelly will not at all allow that the "righteousness of God" and "the righteousness of Christ" are one and the same, and hence, when he comes to Romans 4 (where so much is said about "righteousness" being *imputed* to the believer) he evacuates the whole of its blessed teaching by trying to make out that this is nothing more than our own faith, saying of Abraham, "his faith in God's word as that which he exercised, and which was accounted as righteousness" (p. 47).

The "righteousness of Christ" which is imputed to the believer consists of that perfect obedience which He rendered unto the precepts of God's law and that death which He died under the penalty of the law. It has been rightly said that, "There is the very same need of Christ's obeying the law in our stead, in order to the reward, as of His suffering the penalty of the law in our stead in order to our escaping the penalty; and the same reason why one should be accepted on our account as the other. . . . To suppose that all Christ does in order to make atonement for us by suffering is to make Him our Saviour but in part. It is to rob Him of half His glory as a Saviour. For is so, all that He does is to deliver us from hell; He does not purchase heaven for us" (Jonathan Edwards). Should any one object to the idea of Christ "purchasing" heaven for His people, he may at once be referred to Ephesians 1:14, where heaven is expressly designated "the purchased possession."

The imputation to the believer's account of that perfect obedience which his Surety rendered unto the law for him is plainly taught in Romans 5:18, 19, "Therefore as by the offense of one judgment came upon all men to condemnation, even so by the righteousness of one the free gift came upon all men unto justification of life. For as by one man's disobedience many were made sinners, so by the obedience of one shall many be made righteous." Here the "offense" or "disobedience" of the first Adam is set over against the "righteousness" or "obedience" of the last Adam, and inasmuch as the disobedience of the former was an actual transgression of the law, therefore the obedience of the latter *must be* His active obedience unto the law; otherwise the force of the apostle's antithesis would fail entirely. As this vital point (the chief glory of the gospel) is now so little understood, and in some quarters disputed, we must enter into some detail.

The one who is justified upon his believing, sustained a twofold relation unto God: first, he was a responsible creature, born under the law; second, he was a criminal, having transgressed that law—though his criminality has not cancelled his obligation *to* obey the law, any more than a man who recklessly squanders his money is no longer due to pay his debts. Consequently, justification consists of two parts, namely, an acquittal from guilt, or the condemnation of the law (deliverance from hell), and the receiving him into God's favor, on the sentence of the law's approval (a legal title to heaven). And therefore, the ground upon which God pronounces him just is also a double one, as the one complete satisfaction of Christ is viewed in its two distinct parts: namely, His vicarious obedience unto the precepts of the law, and His substitutionary death under the penalty of the law, the merits of both being equally imputed or reckoned to the account of him who believes.

Against this it has been objected, "The law requires no man to obey and die too." To which we reply in the language of J. Hervey (1750), "But did it not require a *transgressor* to obey and die? If not, then transgression robs the law of its right, and vacates all obligation to obedience. Did it not require the *Surety* for sinful men to obey and die? If the Surety dies only, He only delivers from penalty. But this affords no claim to *life* no title to a *reward*—unless you can produce some such edict from the Court of Heaven. Suffer this, and thou shalt live. I find it written 'In keeping Thy commandments there is a great reward' (Ps. 19:11), but nowhere do I read, In undergoing Thy curse, there is the same reward. Whereas, when we join the active and passive obedience of our Lord—the peace-speaking blood, with the life-giving righteousness—both made infinitely meritorious and infinitely effica-cious by the divine glory of His person, how full does our justification appear! How firm does it stand!"

It is not sufficient that the believer stand before God with no sins upon him—that is merely *negative*. The holiness of God requires a *positive* righteousness to our account—that His law be perfectly kept. But we are unable to keep it, therefore our sponsor fulfilled it for us. By the blood-shedding of our blessed substitute the gates of hell have been forever shut against all those for whom He died. By the perfect obedience of our blessed Surety the gates of heaven are opened wide unto all who believe. My title for standing before God, not only without fear, but in the conscious sunshine of His full favor, is because Christ has been made "righteousness" unto me (I Cor. 1:30). Christ not only paid all my debts, but fully discharged all my responsibilities. The law-giver is my law-Fulfiller. Every holy aspiration of Christ, every godly thought, every gracious word, every righteous act of the

Lord Jesus, from Bethlehem to Calvary, unite in forming that "best robe" in which the seed royal stand arrayed before God.

Yet sad to say, even so widely read and generally respected a writer as the Late Sir Rob Anderson, said in his book, *The Gospel and Its Ministry* (chapter on "Justification by Blood"), "Vicarious obedience is an idea wholly beyond reason; how could a God of righteousness and truth reckon a man who has broken law to have kept law, because some one else has kept it? The thief is not declared to be honest because his neighbor or his kinsman is a good citizen." What a pitiable dragging down to the bar of sin-polluted human reason, and a measuring by worldly relations, of that divine transaction wherein the "manifold wisdom of God" was exercised! What is impossible with men *is* possible with God. Did Sir Robert never read that Old Testament prediction wherein the Most High God declared, "Therefore, behold, I will proceed to do a *marvelous work* among this people, even a marvelous work and a *wonder*: for the wisdom of their wise men shall perish, and the understanding of their prudent men shall be hid" (Isa. 29:14)?

It is pointed out that, "In the human realm, both innocence and righteousness are transferable in their effects, but that *in themselves* they are untransferable." From this it is argued, that neither sin nor righteousness are in themselves *capable of* being transferred, and that though God treated Christ *as if He were* the sinner, and deals with the believer *as though he were* righteous, nevertheless, we must not suppose that either is actually the case; still less ought we to affirm that Christ *deserved* to suffer the curse, or that His people are *entitled* to be taken to heaven. Such is a fair sample of the theological ignorance of these degenerate times, such is a representative example of how divine things are being measured by human standards; by such sophistries is the fundamental truth of *imputation* now being repudiated.

Rightly did W. Rushton, in his *Particular Redemption,* affirm, "In the great affair of our salvation, our God stands single and alone. In this most glorious work, there is such a display of justice, mercy, wisdom and power, as never entered into the heart of man to conceive, and consequently, *can have no parallel* in the actions of mortals. 'Who hath declared this from ancient time? Who hath told it from that time? have not I the Lord? and there is no God else beside me; a just God and a Saviour; there is none beside me': Isa. 45:21." No, in the very nature of the case no analogy whatever is to be found in any human transactions with God's transferring our sins to Christ or Christ's obedience to us, for the simple but sufficient reason that *no such union exists* between worldlings as obtains between Christ and His people. But let us further amplify this counter-imputation.

The afflictions which the Lord Jesus experienced were not only sufferings at the hands of men, but also enduring punishment at the hand of God: "it pleased the Lord to bruise Him" (Isa. 53:10); "Awake, O sword against my shepherd, and against the man that is my fellow, saith the Lord of hosts: *smite the Shepherd*" (Zech. 13:7) was His edict. But lawful "punishment" presupposes *criminality;* a righteous God had never inflicted the curse of the law upon Christ unless He had *deserved* it. That is strong language we are well aware, yet no stronger than what Holy Writ fully warrants, and things need to be stated, forcibly and plainly today if an apathetic people is to be aroused. It was because God had transferred to their substitute all the sins of His people that, *officially,* Christ deserved to be paid sin's wages.

The translation of our sins to Christ was clearly typed out under the law: "And Aaron shall lay both hands upon the head of the live goat [expressing *identification with* the substitute], and confess over him all the iniquities of the children of Israel, and all their transgressions in all their sins, putting them upon the head of the goat [denoting *transference*], and shall send him away by the hand of a fit man into the wilderness: And the goat shall *bear upon him* all their iniquities unto a land not inhabited" (Lev. 16:21, 22). So too it was expressly announced by the Prophets: "The Lord hath laid on him the iniquity of us all. . . . He shall bear their iniquities" (Isa. 53:6, 11). In that great messianic Psalm (69) we hear the surety saying, "O God, thou knowest my foolishness, and my *sins* are not hid from thee" (v. 5)—how could the spotless Redeemer speak thus, unless the sins of His people had been *laid upon* Him?

When God imputed sin to Christ as the sinner's surety, *He charged Him with the same,* and dealt with Him accordingly. Christ could not have suffered in the stead of the guilty unless their guilt had been first transferred to Him. The sufferings of Christ were penal. God, by an act of transcendant grace (to us), laid the iniquities of all that are saved upon Christ, and in consequence, divine justice finding sin upon Him, *punished Him.* He who will by no means clear the guilty must strike through sin and smite its bearer, no matter whether it be the sinner himself or One who vicariously takes his place. But, as G. S. Bishop well said, "When justice once strikes the Son of God, justice exhausts itself. Sin is amerced in an Infinite Object." The atonement of Christ was contrary to *our* processes of law because it rose above *their* finite limitations!

Now as the sins of him who believes were, by God, transferred and imputed to Christ, so that God regarded and treated Him accordingly—visiting upon Him the *curse* of the law, which is death: even so the obedience or righteousness of Christ is, by God, transferred and imputed to the believer, so that God now regards and deals with him accordingly—bestowing upon him the *blessing* of the law, which is life. And any denial of that fact, no matter by whomsoever made, is a repudiation of the cardinal principle of the gospel. "The moment the believing sinner accepts Christ as his substitute, he finds himself not only freed from his sins, but *rewarded:* he gets all heaven because of the glory and merits of Christ. (Rom. 5:17). The atonement, then, which we preach is one of absolute exchange (I Peter 3:18). It is that Christ took our place literally, in order that we might take His place literally—that God regarded and treated Christ as the sinner, and that He regards and treats the believing sinner as Christ.

"It is not enough for a man to be pardoned. He, of course, is then innocent—washed from his sin—put back again, like Adam in Eden, just where he was. But that is not enough. It was required of Adam in Eden that he should actually *keep* the command. It was not enough that he did not break it, or that he is regarded, through the Blood, as though he did not break it. *He must keep it:* he must continue in all things that are written in the book of the law to *do* them. *How is this necessity supplied?* Man must have a righteousness, or God cannot accept him. Man must have a *perfect* obedience, or else God cannot reward him" (G. S. Bishop). That necessary and perfect obedience is to be found alone in that perfect *life,* lived by Christ in obedience to the law, *before* He went to the cross, which is reckoned to the believer's account.

It is not that God treats *as* righteous one who is not actually so (that would be a fiction), but that He actually constitutes the believer so, not by infusing a holy nature in his heart, but by reckoning the obedience of Christ to his account. Christ's obedience is legally transferred to him, so that he is now rightly and justly regarded as righteous by the divine law. It is very far more than a naked *pronouncement* of righteousness upon one who is *without* any sufficient foundation for the judgment of God to declare him righteous. No, it is a positive and judicial act of God "whereby, on the consideration of the mediation of Christ, He makes an effectual grant and donation of a true, real, perfect righteousness, even that *of Christ Himself,* unto all that do believe, and accounting it as theirs, on His own gracious act, both absolves them from sin, and granteth them right and title unto eternal life" (John Owen).

It now remains for us to point out *the ground on which* God acts in this counter-imputation of sin to Christ and righteousness to His people. That ground was *the everlasting covenant.* The objection that it is unjust the innocent should suffer in order that the guilty may escape, loses all its force once the covenant-headship and responsibility of Christ is seen, and the *covenant-oneness with Him* of those whose sins He bore. There could have been no such thing as a *vicarious* sacrifice unless there had been some *union* between Christ and those for whom He died, and that relation of union must have subsisted *before* He died; before our sins were imputed to Him. Christ undertook to make full satisfaction to the law for His people because He sustained to them the relation of a *surety*. But *what* justified His acting as their surety? He stood as their surety, because He was their *substitute:* He acted *on their behalf,* because He stood *in their room*. But *what* justified the substitution?

No satisfactory answer can be given to the last question until the grand doctrine of everlasting covenant-oneness comes into view: *that* is the great underlying relation. The federal oneness between the Redeemer and the redeemed, the choosing of them *in* Christ before the foundation of the world (Eph. 1:4), by which a legal union was established between Him and them, is that which alone accounts for and justifies all else. "For both he that sanctifieth and they who are sanctified are *all of one:* for which cause he is not ashamed to call them brethren" (Heb. 2:11). As the covenant-head of His people, Christ was so related to them that their responsibilities necessarily became His, and we are so related to Him that His merits necessarily become ours. Thus, as we said in an earlier chapter, three words give us the key to and sum up the whole transaction: substitution, identification, imputation—all of which rest upon covenant-oneness. Christ was substituted *for* us, because He is one *with* us—identified with us, and we with Him. Thus God dealt with us as occupying *Christ's* place of worthiness and acceptance. May the Holy Spirit grant both writer and reader such an heart-apprehension of this wondrous and blessed truth, that overflowing gratitude may move us unto fuller devotedness unto Him who loved us and gave Himself for us.

6 Its Source

Let us here review, briefly, the ground which we have already covered. We have seen, first, that "to justify" means to pronounce righteous. It is not a divine work, but a divine verdict, the sentence of the Supreme Court, declaring that the one justified stands perfectly conformed to all the requirements of the law. Justification assures the believer that the Judge of all the earth is for him, and not against him: that justice itself is on his side. Second, we dwelt upon the great and seemingly insoluable problem which is thereby involved: how a God of truth can pronounce righteous one who is completely devoid of righteousness, how He can receive into His judicial favor one who is a guilty criminal, how He can exercise mercy without insulting justice, how He can be gracious and yet enforce the high demands of His law. Third, we have shown that the solution to this problem is found in the perfect satisfaction which the incarnate Son rendered unto divine law, and that on the basis of that satisfaction God can truthfully and righteously pronounce just all who truly believe the gospel.

We pointed out that the satisfaction which Christ made to the divine law consists of two distinct parts, answering to the twofold need of him who is to be justified. First, as a responsible *creature* I am under binding obligations to keep the law—to love God with all my heart and my neighbor as myself. Second, as a *criminal* I am under the condemnation and curse of that law which I have constantly transgressed in thought and word and deed. Therefore, if another was to act as my surety and make reparation for me, he must perfectly obey all the precepts of the law, and then endure the awful penalty of the law. That is exactly what was undertaken and accomplished by the Lord Jesus in His virtuous life and vicarious death. By Him every demand of the law was fulfilled; by Him every obligation of the believer was fully met.

It has been objected by some that the obedience of Christ *could not be* imputed to the account of others, for being "made under the law" (Gal. 4:4), as *man,* He *owed* submission to the law on His own account. This is a serious mistake, arising out of a failure to recognize the absolute uniqueness of the man Christ Jesus. Unlike us, He was never placed under the Adamic covenant, and therefore He owed nothing to the law. Moreover, the manhood of Christ never had a separate existence: in the virgin's womb the eternal Son took the seed of Mary into union with His deity, so that whereas the first man was of the earth, earthy, "the second man is *the Lord from heaven*" (I Cor. 15:47), and as such He was infinitely superior to the law, owing nothing to it, being personally possessed of all the excellencies of Deity. Even while He walked this earth "in Him dwelt all the fulness of the Godhead bodily."

It was entirely for His peoples' sake that the God-man mediator was "made under the law." It was in order to work out for them a perfect righteousness, which should be placed to their account, that He took upon Himself the form of a servant, and became "obedient unto death." What has been said above supplies the answer to another foolish objection which has been made against this blessed truth, namely, that if the obedience of the man Christ Jesus were transferable it would be available *only for one other man*, seeing that every human being is required to obey the law, and that if *vicarious* obedience be acceptable to God then there would have to be as many *separate sureties* as there are believers who are saved. That would be true if the "surety" were *merely* human, but inasmuch as the surety provided by God is the God-man mediator, *His* righteousness is of infinite value, for the law was *more* "honored and magnified" by the obedience of "the Lord from heaven" than had every member of the human race perfectly kept it. The righteousness of the God-man mediator is of *infinite* value, and therefore available for as many as God is pleased to impute it unto.

The value or merit of an action increases in proportion to the dignity of the person who performs it, and He who obeyed in the room and stead of the believer was not only a holy man, but the Son of the living God. Moreover, let it be steadily borne in mind that the obedience which Christ rendered to the law was entirely *voluntary.* Prior to His incarnation, He was under *no* obligation to the law, for He had Himself (being God) formulated the law. His being made of a woman and made under the law was entirely *a free act* on His own part. We come into being and are placed under the law without our consent; but the Lord from heaven existed before His incarnation, and assumed our nature by His spontaneous act: "Lo, I come. . . . I delight to do thy will" (Ps. 40:7, 8). No other person could use such language, for it clearly denotes a *liberty* to act or not to act, which no mere creature possesses. Placing Himself under the law and rendering obedience to it, was founded solely on His own voluntary deed. His obedience was therefore a "free will offering," and therefore as He did not owe obedience to the law by any prior obligation, not being at all necessary for Himself, it is available for imputation to others, that they should be *rewarded for* it.

If, then, the reader has been able to follow us closely in the above observations, it should be clear to him that when Scripture speaks of God "justifying the ungodly" the meaning is that, the believing sinner is brought into an entirely *new relation to the law;* that in consequence of Christ's righteousness being made over to him, he is now absolved from all liability to punishment, and is given a title to all the reward merited by Christ's obedience. Blessed, blessed truth for comforting the *conscientious* Christian, who daily groans under a sense of his sad failures and who mourns because of his lack of practical conformity to the image of Christ. Satan is ever ready to harass such an one and tell him his profession is vain. But it is the believer's privilege to overcome him by "the blood of the Lamb" (Rev. 12:11)— to remind himself anew that another has atoned for all his sins, and that despite his innumerable shortcomings he still stands "accepted in the beloved" (Eph. 1:6). If I am truly resting on the finished work of Christ for me, the Devil cannot successfully lay anything to my charge before God, though if I am walking carelessly He will suffer him to charge my conscience with unrepented and unconfessed sins.

In our last chapter, under the *nature* of justification, we saw that the constituent elements of this divine blessing are two in number, the one being negative in its character, the other positive. The negative blessing is the cancellation of guilt, or the remission of sins—the entire record of the believer's transgressions of the law, filed upon the divine docket, having been blotted out by the precious blood of Christ. The positive blessing is the bestowal upon the believer of an inalienable title to the *reward* which the obedience of Christ merited for him— that reward is life, the judicial favor of God, Heaven itself. The unchanging sentence of the law is "the man which doeth those things shall *live* by them" (Rom. 10:5). As we read in Romans 7:10, "the commandment which was ordained to *life.*" It is just as true that obedience to the law secured life, as disobedience insured death. When the young ruler asked Christ "what good thing shall I do, that I may have eternal life?" He answered, "If thou wilt enter into *life,* keep the commandments" (Matt. 19:16, 17).

It was because His people had failed to "keep the commandments" that the God-man mediator was "made under the law," and obeyed it for them. And, therefore its *reward* of "life" is due unto those whose surety He was; yea, due unto Christ Himself to bestow upon them. Therefore did the surety, when declaring "I have glorified thee on the earth: I have finished the work which thou gavest me to do" (John 17:4), remind the Father, "that he should give eternal life to as many as thou hast given him" (v. 2). But more, on the footing of *justice,* Christ demands that His people be taken to Heaven, saying, "Father, *I will* that they also, whom thou hast given me, be with me where I am" (John 17:24)—He *claims* eternal life *for His people* on the ground of His finished work, as the *reward* of His obedience.

"Therefore as by the offence of one judgment came upon all men to condemnation; even so by the righteousness of one the free gift came upon all men unto *justification of life*" (Rom 5:19). The offense of the first Adam brought down the curse of the broken law upon the whole human race; but the satisfaction of the last Adam secured the blessing of the fulfilled law upon all those who he represented. Judgment into condemnation is a law term intending eternal death, the wages of sin; the "free gift" affirms that a gratuitous justification is bestowed upon all its recipients—"justification *of life*" being the issue of the gift, parallel with "they shall reign in life [through] Christ Jesus" (v. 17). The sentence of justification adjudges and entitles its object unto eternal life.

Having now considered the two great blessings which come to the believer at his justification—deliverance from the curse of the law (death) and a title to the blessings of the law (life)—let us now seek to take a view of the originating *source* from which they proceed. This is the free, pure, sovereign *grace* of God: as it is written "Being justified freely by his grace" (Rom. 3:24). What is grace? It is God's unmerited and uninfluenced favor, shown to the undeserving and hell-deserving: neither human worthiness, works, or willingness, attracting it, nor the lack of them repelling or obstructing it. What could there be in me to win the favorable regard of Him who is of too pure eyes to behold evil, and move Him to justify me? Nothing whatever; nay, there was everything in me calculated to make Him abhor and destroy me—my very self-righteous efforts to earn a place in heaven deserving only a lower place in hell. If, then, I am ever to be "justified" *by God* it must be by pure grace, and that alone.

Grace is the very essence of the gospel—the only hope for fallen men, the sole comfort of saints passing through much tribulation on their way to the kingdom of God. The gospel is the announcement that God is prepared to deal with guilty rebels on the ground of free favor, of pure benignity; that God will blot out sin, cover the believing sinner with a robe of spotless righteousness, and receive him as an accepted son: not on account of anything he has done or ever will do, but out of sovereign mercy, acting independently of the sinner's own character and deserving of eternal punishment. Justification is perfectly gratuitous so far as we are concerned, *nothing* being required of us in order to it, either in the way of price and satisfaction or preparation and meetness. We have not the slightest degree of merit to offer as the ground of our acceptance, and therefore if God ever does accept us it must be out of unmingled grace.

It is as "The God of all grace" (I Peter 5:10) that Jehovah justifies the ungodly. It is as "the God of all grace" He seeks, finds, and saves His people: asking them for nothing, giving them everything. Strikingly is this brought out in that word "being justified *freely* by His grace" (Rom. 3:24), the design of that adverb being to exclude all consideration of anything in us or from us which should be the cause or condition of our justification. That same Greek adverb is translated "without a cause" in John 15:25—"they hated me without a cause." The world's hatred of Christ was "*without* a cause" so far as *He* was concerned: there was nothing whatever in Him which, to the slightest degree, deserved their enmity against Him: there was nothing in Him unjust, perverse, or evil; instead, there was everything in Him which was pure, holy, lovely. In like manner, there is nothing whatever in us to call forth the approbation of God: by nature there is "no good thing" in us; but instead, everything that is evil, vile, loathsome.

"Being *justified without a cause* by his GRACE." How this tells out the very *heart* of God! While there was no motive to move Him, outside of Himself, there was one inside Himself: while there was nothing in us to impel God to justify us, His own grace moved Him, so that He devised a way whereby His wondrous love could have vent and flow forth to the chief of sinners, the vilest of rebels. As it is written "I, even I, am he that blotteth out thy transgressions, *for Mine own sake,* and will not remember thy sins" (Isa. 43:25). Wondrous, matchless grace! We cannot for a moment look outside the grace of God for any motive or reason why He should ever have noticed us, still less had respect unto such ungodly wretches.

The first moving cause, then, that inclined God to show mercy to His people in their undone and lost condition, was His own wondrous grace—unsought, uninfluenced, unmerited by us. He might justly have left us all obnoxious to the curse of His law, without providing any Surety for us, as He did the fallen angels; but such was His grace toward us that "He spared not his own Son." "Not by works of righteousness which we have done, but according to his mercy he saved us, by the washing of regeneration, and renewing of the Holy Ghost; which he shed on us abundantly through Jesus Christ our

Saviour; That being justified by his *grace,* we should be made heirs according to the hope of eternal life" (Titus 3:5-7). It was His own sovereign favor and good will which actuated God to form this wondrous scheme and method of justification.

Against what has been said above, it has been objected by Socinians and their echoists that this cannot be: if the believing sinner is justified upon the ground of a full satisfaction having been made to God for him by a surety, then his discharge from condemnation and his reception into God's judicial favor, must be an act of pure *justice,* and therefore could not be by grace. Or, if it be purely an act of divine *grace,* then no surety can have obeyed the law in the believer's stead. But this is to confound two distinct things: the relation of God to Christ the surety, and the relation of God to me the sinner. It was *grace* which transferred my sins to Christ; it was *justice* which smote Christ on account of those sins. It was *grace* which appointed me unto everlasting bliss; it is *justice to Christ* which requires I shall enjoy that which He purchased for me.

Toward the sinner justification is an act of free unmerited favor; but toward Christ, as the sinner's surety, it is an act of justice that eternal life should be bestowed upon those for whom His meritorious satisfaction was made. First, it was pure grace that God was *willing to accept* satisfaction from the hands of a surety. He might have exacted the debt from us in our own persons, and then our condition had been equally miserable as that of the fallen angels, from whom no mediator was provided. Second, it was wondrous grace that God Himself *provided* a surety for us, which we could not have done. The only creatures who are capable of performing perfect obedience are the holy angels, yet none of them could have assumed and met *our* obligations, for they are not akin to us, possessing not human nature, and therefore incapable of dying. Even had an angel become incarnate, his obedience to the law could not have availed for the whole of God's elect, for it would not have possessed *infinite* value.

None but a divine person taking human nature into union with Himself, could present unto God a satisfaction adequate for the redemption of His people. And it was impossible for men to have found out that Mediator and surety: it must have its first rise in God, and not from us: it was He that "found" a ransom (Job 33:24) and "laid help upon one that is mighty" (Ps. 89:19). In the last place, it was amazing *grace* that the Son was willing to perform such a work for us, without whose consent the justice of God could not have exacted the debt from Him. And His grace is the most eminent in that He knew beforehand all the unspeakable humiliation and unparalleled suffering which He would encounter in the discharge of this work, yet that did not deter Him; nor was He unapprized of the character of those for whom He did it—the guilty, the ungodly, the hell-deserving; yet He shrank not back.

> O to grace how great a debtor,
> Daily I'm constrained to be!
> Let Thy grace, Lord, like a fetter,
> Bind my wandering heart to Thee.

7 Its Objects

We have now reached a point in our discussion of this mighty theme where it is timely for us to ask the question, *Who are the ones* that God justifies? The answer to that question will necessarily vary according to the mental position we occupy. From the standpoint of God's eternal decrees the reply must be, *God's elect* (Rom. 8:33). From the standpoint of the effects produced by the quickening operations of the Holy Spirit the reply must be, *those who believe* (Acts 13:39). But from the standpoint of what they are, considered in themselves, the reply must be, *the ungodly* (Rom. 4:5). The persons are the same, yet contemplated in three different relations. But here a difficulty presents itself: If faith be essential in order to justification, and if a fallen sinner must be quickened by the Holy Spirit before he can believe, then with what propriety can a regenerated person, with the spiritual grace of faith already in his heart, be described as "ungodly"?

The difficulty pointed out above is self-created. It issues from confounding things which differ radically. It is the result of bringing in the *experimental* state of the person justified, when justification has to do only with his *judicial* status. We would emphasize once more the vital importance of keeping quite distinct in our minds the objective and subjective aspects of truth, the legal and the experimental: unless this be steadily done, nought but confusion and mistakes can mark our thinking. When contemplating what he is *in himself,* considered alone, even the Christian mournfully cries "O wretched man that I am"; but when he views himself *in Christ,* as justified from all things, he triumphantly exclaims, "Who shall lay anything to my charge!"

Above, we have pointed out that from the viewpoint of God's eternal decrees the question "Who are the ones whom God justifies?"

must be "the elect." And this brings us to a point on which some eminent Calvinists have erred, or at least, have expressed themselves faultily. Some of the older theologians, when expounding this doctrine, contended for the *eternal justification* of the elect, affirming that God pronounced them righteous before the foundation of the world, and that their justification was then actual and complete, remaining so throughout their history in time, even during the days of their unregeneracy and unbelief; and that the only difference their faith made was in *making manifest* God's eternal justification in their consciences. This is a serious mistake, resulting (again) from failure to distinguish between things which differ.

As an *immanent* act of God's mind, in which *all* things (which are to us past, present, and future) were cognized by Him, the elect might be said to be justified from all eternity. And, as an *immutable* act of God's will, which cannot be frustrated, the same may be predicated again. But as an actual, formal, historical sentence, pronounced by God upon us, not so. We must distinguish between God's looking upon the elect in the *purpose* of His grace, and the objects of justification lying under the sentence of the law: in the former, He *loved* His people with an everlasting love (Jer. 31:3); in the latter, we were "by nature the children of *wrath,* even as others" (Eph. 2:3). Until they believe, every descendant of Adam is "condemned already" (John 3:18), and to be under God's condemnation is the very opposite of being justified.

In his ponderous treatise on justification, the Puritan Thomas Goodwin made clear some vital distinctions, which if carefully observed will preserve us from error on this point. "1. In the everlasting covenant. We may say of all spiritual blessings in Christ, what is said of Christ himself, that their 'goings forth are from everlasting.' Justified then we were when first elected, though not in our own persons, yet in our Head (Eph. 1:3). 2. There is a farther act of justifying us, which passed from God towards us in Christ, upon His payment and performance at His resurrection (Rom. 4:25, I Tim. 3:16). 3. But these two acts of justification are wholly out of us, immanent acts in God, and though they concern us and are *towards* us, yet not acts of God *upon* us, they being performed towards us not as actually existing in ourselves, but only as existing in our Head, who covenanted for us and represented us: so as though by those acts we are *estated* into a right and title to justification, yet the benefit and possession of that estate we have not without a farther act being passed upon us."

Before regeneration we are justified by existing in our Head only, as a feoffee, held in trust for us, as children under age. In addition to which, we "are to be in our own persons, though still through Christ, possessed of it, and to have all the deeds and evidences of it com- mitted to the custody and apprehension of our faith. We are in our own persons made true owners and enjoyers of it, which is immedi- ately done at that instant when we first believe; which act (of God) is the completion and accomplishment of the former two, and is that grand and famous justification by faith which the Scripture so much inculcates—note the 'now' in Rom. 5:9, 11; 8:1! . . . God doth judge and pronounce His elect ungodly and unjustified till they believe" (Ibid).

God's elect enter this world in precisely the same condition and circumstances as do the non-elect. They are "by nature the children of wrath, *even as others*" (Eph. 2:3), that is, they are under the condem- nation of their original sin in Adam (Rom. 5:12, 18, 19) and they are under the curse of God's law because of their own constant transgres- sions of it (Gal. 3:10). The sword of divine justice is suspended over their heads, and the Scriptures denounce them as rebels against the Most High. As yet, there is nothing whatever to distinguish them from those who are "fitted to destruction." Their state is woeful to the last degree, their situation perilous beyond words; and when the Holy Spirit awakens them from the sleep of death, the first message which falls upon their ears is, "Flee from the wrath to come." But how and whither, they, as yet, know not. Then it is they are ready for the message of the gospel.

Let us turn now to the more immediate answer to our opening inquiry. Who are the ones that God justifies? A definite reply is given in Romans 4:5: "Him that justifieth the"—whom? the holy, the faithful, the fruitful? no, the very reverse: "Him that justifieth *the ungodly.*" What a strong, bold and startling word is this! It becomes yet more emphatic when we observe what precedes: "But to him *that worketh not,* but believeth on him that justifieth the ungodly." The subjects of justification, then, are viewed in themselves, apart from Christ, as not only destitute of a perfect righteousness, but as having *no* acceptable works to their account. They are denominated, and considered as *ungodly* when the sentence of justification is pro- nounced upon them. The mere *sinner* is the subject on which grace is magnified, toward which grace reigns in justification!

"To say, he who *worketh not* is justified through believing, is to say that his works, whatever they be, have *no* influence in his justifica- tion, nor hath God, in justifying him, any respect unto them. Where- fore he *alone* who worketh not, is the subject of justification, the person to be justified. That is, God considereth no man's works, no man's duties of obedience, in his justification; seeing we are justified *freely* by His grace" (John Owen). Those whom God, in His transcendant mercy, justifies are not the obedient, buc the disobedient; not those who have been loyal and loving subjects of His righteous government, but they who have stoutly defied Him and trampled His laws beneath their feet. Those whom God justifies are lost sinners, lying in a state of defection from Him, under a loss of original righteousness (in Adam) and by their own transgressions brought in guilty before His tribunal (Rom. 3:19). They are those who by character and conduct have *no* claim upon divine blessing, and deserve nought but unsparing judgment at God's hand.

"Him that justifieth *the ungodly.*" It is deplorable to see how many able commentators have weakened the force of this by affirming that, while the subject of justification *is* "ungodly" up to the time of his justification, he is *not* so at the moment of justification itself. They argue that, inasmuch as the subject of justification is a *believer* at the moment of his justification, and that believing presupposes regeneration—a work of divine grace wrought in the heart—he could not be designated "ungodly." This seeming difficulty is at once removed by calling to mind that justification is entirely a *law* matter and not an experimental thing at all. In the sight of God's law *every* one whom God justifies *is* "ungodly" until Christ's righteousness is made over to him. The awful sentence "ungodly" rests as truly upon the purest virgin as much as it does upon the foulest prostitute until God imputes Christ's obedience to her.

"Him that justifieth the ungodly." These words cannot mean less than that God, in the act of justification, has no regard whatever to any thing good resting to the credit of the person He justifies. They declare, emphatically, that immediately prior to that divine act, God beholds the subject *only* as unrighteous, ungodly, wicked, so that no good, either in or by the person justified, can possibly be the ground on which or the reason for which He justifies him. This is further evident from the words "to him that worketh not": that this includes not only works which the ceremonial law required, but *all works* of morality and godliness, appears from the fact that the same person who is said to "work not" is designated "ungodly." Finally, seeing that the faith which belongs to justification is here said to be "counted for [or *"unto"*] righteousness," it is clear that the person to whom "righteousness" *is* imputed, is *destitute* of righteousness in himself.

A parallel passage to the one which has just been before us is found in Isaiah 43. There we hear God saying, "I, even I, am he that blotteth out thy transgressions for mine own sake, and will not remember thy sins" (v. 25). And to whom does God say this? To those who had sincerely endeavored to please Him? To those who, though they had occasionally been overtaken in a fault, had, in the main, served Him faithfully? No, indeed; very far from it. Instead, in the immediate context we find Him saying to them, "But thou hast not called upon me, O Jacob; but thou hast been weary of me, O Israel. Thou hast bought me no sweet cane with money, neither hast thou filled me with the fat of thy sacrifices: but thou hast made me to serve with thy sins, thou hast *wearied me with thine iniquities*" (vv. 22, 24). They were, then, thoroughly "ungodly;" yet *to them* the Lord declared, "I, even I, am He that blotteth out thy transgressions"—why? Because of something good in them or from them? No, "for mine own sake"!

Further confirmation of what has been before us in Romans 4:5 is found in both what immediately precedes and what follows. In verses 1-3 the case of Abraham is considered, and the proof given that *he* was *not* "justified by works," but on the ground of a righteousness being imputed to him on his believing. "Now if a person of such victorious faith, exalted piety, and amazing obedience as his was, did not obtain acceptance with God on account of his own duties, but by an imputed righteousness; who shall pretend to an interest in the heavenly blessing, in virtue of his own sincere endeavors, or pious performances?— performances not fit to be named, in comparison with those that adorned the conduct and character of *Jehovah's friend*" (A. Booth).

Having shown that the father of all believers was regarded by the Lord as an "ungodly" person, having no good works to his credit, at the moment of his justification, the apostle next cited David's description of the truly blessed man. "And how does the royal Psalmist describe him? To what does he attribute his acceptance with God? To an inherent, or to an imputed righteousness? Does he represent him as attaining the happy state, and as enjoying the precious privilege, in consequence of performing sincere obedience, and of keeping the law to the best of his power? No such thing. His words are, 'Blessed is he whose transgression is forgiven, whose sin is covered. Blessed is the man unto whom the Lord imputeth not iniquity.' The blessed man is here described as one who is, in himself, a polluted creature and a guilty criminal. As one who, before grace made the difference, was on a level with the rest of mankind; equally unworthy, and equally wretched: and the sacred penman informs us, that all his blessedness arises from an *imputed* righteousness" (A. Booth).

"Him that justifieth the ungodly." Here is the very heart of the gospel. Many have argued that God can only pronounce just, and treat as such, those who are inherently righteous; but if this was so, what good news would there be for sinful men? Enemies of the truth insist that for God to pronounce just those whom His law condemns would be a judicial fiction. But Romans 4:5 makes known a divine *miracle:*

something only God could have achieved. The miracle announced by the gospel is, that God comes to the ungodly with a mercy that is righteous, and in spite of all their depravity and rebellion, enables them through faith (on the ground of *Christ's* righteousness) to enter into a new and blessed relation with Himself.

The Scriptures speak of mercy, but it is not mercy coming in to make up the deficiencies and forgive the slips of the virtuous, but mercy extended *through Christ to the chief of sinners*. The gospel which proclaims mercy through the atonement of the Lord Jesus is distinguished from every religious system of man, by holding out salvation to *the guiltiest* of the human race, through faith in the blood of the Redeemer. God's Son came into this world not only to save sinners, but even *the chief of* sinners, the worst of His enemies. Mercy is extended freely to the most violent and determined rebel. Here, and here only, is a refuge for the *guilty*. Is the trembling reader conscious that he is a *great* sinner, then *that* is the very reason why you should come to Christ: the greater your sins, the greater your need of the Saviour.

There are some who appear to think that Christ is a physician who can cure only such patients as are not dangerously ill, that there are some cases so desperate as to be incurable, beyond His skill. What an afront to His power, what a denial of His sufficiency! Where can a more extreme case be found than that of the thief on the cross? He was at the very point of death, on the very brink of hell! A guilty criminal, an incorrigible outlaw, justly condemned even by men. He had reviled the Saviour suffering by his side. Yet, at the end, he turned to Him and said, "Lord, remember me." Was his plea refused? Did the Physician of souls regard his as a hopeless case? No, blessed be His name, He at once responded "Today shalt thou be with me in paradise." *Only unbelief* shuts the vilest out of heaven.

"Him that justifieth *the ungodly*." And how can the thrice holy God *righteously* do such a thing? Because *"Christ died for* the UN-GODLY" (Rom. 5:6). God's righteous grace comes to us through the law-honoring, justice-satisfying, sin-atoning work of the Lord Jesus! Here, then, is the very essence of the gospel: the proclamation of God's amazing *grace,* the declaration of divine *bounty,* altogether irrespective of human worth or merit. In the great satisfaction of His Son, God has *"brought near* HIS righteousness" (Isa. 46:13). "We do not need to go up to heaven for it; that would imply Christ had never come down. Nor do we need to go down to the depths of the earth for it; that would say Christ had never been buried and had never risen. It is *near*. We do not need to exert ourselves to bring it near, nor do anything to attract it towards us. It *is* near. . . . The office of faith is not to work, but to *cease working;* not to do anything, but to own that *all is done*" (A. Bonar).

Faith is the one link between the sinner and the Saviour. Not faith as a work, which must be properly performed to qualify us for pardon. Not faith as a religious duty, which must be gone through according to certain rules in order to induce Christ to give us the benefits of His finished work. No, but faith simply extended *as an empty hand,* to receive everything from Christ for nothing. Reader, you may be the very *"chief* of sinners," yet is your case not hopeless. You may have sinned against much light, great privileges, exceptional opportunities; you may have broken every one of the ten commandments in thought, word and deed; your body may be filled with disease from wickedness, your head white with the winter of old age; you may already have one foot in hell; and yet even now, if you but take your place alongside of the dying thief, and trust in the *divine efficacy* of the precious blood of the Lamb, *you* shall be plucked as a brand from the burning. God "justifieth *the ungodly*." Hallelujah! If He did not, the writer had been in hell long ago.

8 Its Instrument

"Being justified freely by *his grace*" (Rom. 3:24); "being now justified by his *blood*" (Rom. 5:9); "being justified by his *faith*" (Rom. 5:1). A full exposition of the doctrine of justification requires that each of these propositions should be interpreted in their Scriptural sense, and that they be combined together in their true relations so as to form one harmonious whole. Unless these three propositions be carefully distinguished there is sure to be confusion; unless all the three are steadily borne in mind we are sure to land in error. Each must be given its due weight, yet none must be understood in such a way as to make its force annul that of the others. Nor is this by any means a simple task, in fact none but a real teacher (that is, a spiritual theologian) who has devoted a lifetime to the undivided study of the Scriptures, is qualified for it.

"The righteousness of God which is *by faith* of Jesus Christ" (Rom. 3:22); "A man is justified *by faith* without the deeds of the law" (Rom. 3:28); "even we have believed in Jesus Christ, that we might be justified *by* the faith of Christ, and not by the works of the law" (Gal. 2:16). What is the precise place and influence which faith has in the important affairs of justification? What is the exact nature or character of justifying faith? In what particular sense are we to understand this proposition that we are "justified *by faith*"? and what is the connection between that proposition and the postulates that we are "justified *by grace*" and "justified by His *blood*"? These are matters which call for the utmost care. The nature of justifying faith requires to be closely defined so that its particular agency is correctly viewed, for it is easy to make a mistake here to the prejudice of Christ's honor and glory, which must not be given to another—no, not to faith itself.

Many would-be teachers have erred at this point, for the common

232

tendency of human nature is to arrogate to itself the glory which belongs alone to God. While there have been those who rejected the unscriptural notion that we can be justified before God by our own works, yet not a few of these very men virtually make a saviour of their own faith. Not only have some spoken of faith as though it were a contribution which God requires the sinner to make toward his own salvation—the last mite which was necessary to make up the price of his redemption; but others (who sneered at theologians and boasted of their superior understanding of the things of God) have insisted that faith itself is what constitutes us righteous before God, He regarding faith as righteousness.

A deplorable example of what we have just mentioned is to be found in the comments made on Romans 4 by J. N. Darby, the father of the Plymouth Brethren: "This was Abraham's faith. He believed the promise that he should be the father of many nations, because God had spoken, counting on the power of God, thus glorifying Him, without calling in question anything that He had said by looking at circumstances; therefore *this* also was counted to him for righteousness. He glorified God according to what God was. Now this was not written for his sake alone: the same *faith* shall be imputed to us also *for righteousness*" ("Synopsis" vol. 4, p. 133—italics ours). The Christ-dishonoring error contained in those statements will be exposed later on in this chapter.

"How doth faith justify a sinner in the sight of God? Answer: Faith justifies a sinner in the sight of God, not because of those other graces which do always accompany it, or of good works that are the fruits of it, nor as if the grace of faith, or any act thereof, were imputed to him for justification; *but only as it is an instrument* by which he receiveth and applieth Christ and His righteousness" (Westminster Confession of Faith). Though this definition was framed upwards of two hundred and fifty years ago, it is far superior to almost anything found in current literature on the subject. It is more accurate to speak of faith as the "instrument" rather than as the *condition,* for a "condition" is generally used to signify that for the sake whereof a benefit is conferred. Faith is neither the ground nor the substance of our justification, but simply *the hand* which receives the divine gift proffered to us in the gospel.

What is the precise place and influence which faith has in the important affair of justification? Romanists answer, it justifies us *formally,* not relatively: that is, upon the account of its own intrinsic value. They point out that faith is never alone, but "worketh by love" (Gal. 5:6), and therefore its own excellency merits acceptance at God's hand. But the faith of the best is weak and deficient (Luke

17:5), and so could never satisfy the law, which requires a flawless perfection. If righteousness was given as a reward for faith, its possessor would have cause for boasting, expressly contrary to the apostle in Romans 3:26, 27. Moreover, such a method of justification would entirely frustrate the life and death of Christ, making His great sacrifice unnecessary. It is not faith as a spiritual *grace* which justifies us, but as an instrument—the *hand* which lays hold of Christ.

In connection with justification, faith is *not* to be considered as a virtuous exercise of the heart, nor as a principle of holy obedience: "Because faith, as concerned in our justification, does not regard Christ as king, enacting laws, requiring obedience, and subduing depravity; but as a substitute, answering the requirements of the divine law, and as a priest expiating sin by His own death on the cross. Hence, in justification we read of the precious faith in the righteousness of our God and Saviour Jesus Christ (II Peter 1:1) and of 'faith in his blood' (Rom. 3:25), and believers are described as '*receiving* the atonement' and *receiving* 'the gift of righteousness' (Rom. 5:11, 17). Therefore it is evident that faith is represented as having an immediate regard to the vicarious work of Christ, and that it is considered *not* under the notion of exercising virtue or of performing a duty, but of receiving a free gift" (A. Booth).

What is the relation of faith to justification? The Arminian answer to the question, refined somewhat by the Plymouth Brethren, is, that the *act* of believing is imputed to us for righteousness. One error leads to another. Mr. Darby denied that Gentiles were ever under the law, hence he denied also that Christ obeyed the law in His peoples' stead, and therefore as Christ's vicarious disobedience is not reckoned to their account, he had to seek elsewhere for their righteousness. This he claimed to find in the Christians' own faith, insisting that their act of believing is imputed to them "for righteousness." To give his theory respectability, he clothed it in the language of several expressions found in Romans 4, though he knew quite well that the Greek afforded no foundation whatever for that which he built upon it.

In Romans 4 we read "his faith is counted *for* righteousness" (v. 5), "faith was reckoned to Abraham *for* righteousness" (v. 9), "it was imputed to him *for* righteousness" (v. 22). Now in each of these verses the Greek preposition is *eis* which *never* means "in the stead of," but always signifies "towards, in order to, with a view to": it has the uniform force of "unto." Its exact meaning and force is unequivocally plain in Romans 10:10, "with the heart man believeth *unto [eis]* righteousness": that is, the believing heart reaches out toward and lays hold of Christ Himself. "This passage (Rom. 10:10) may help us to understand what justification by faith is, for it shows that righteousness there comes to us when we embrace God's goodness offered to us in the gospel. We are then, for this reason, made just: because we believe that God is propitious to us through Christ" (J. Calvin).

The Holy Spirit has used the Greek prepositions with unerring precision. Never do we find Him employing *eis* in connection with Christ's satisfaction and sacrifice in our room and stead, but only "anti" or "huper," which means *in lieu of*. On the other hand, "anti" and "huper" are *never* used in connection with our believing, for faith *is not* accepted by God *in lieu of* perfect obedience. Faith must either be the ground of our acceptance with God, or the means or instrument of our becoming interested in the righteousness of Christ; it *cannot* stand in *both* relations to our justification. "God justifieth, not by imputing faith itself, the acts of believing, but by imputing the obedience and satisfaction of Christ" (Westminster Catechism).

That faith itself cannot be the substance or ground of our justification is clear from many considerations. The "righteousness of God [i.e., the satisfaction which Christ rendered to the law] is revealed from faith *to* faith" (Rom. 1:17) and so cannot be faith itself. Romans 10:10 declares "with the heart man believeth *unto* righteousness" so that righteousness must be a distinct thing from believing. In Jeremiah 23:6 we read "The Lord our righteousness," so faith cannot be our righteousness. Let not Christ be dethroned in order to exalt faith: set not the servant above the master. "We acknowledge no righteousness but what the obedience and satisfaction of Christ yields us: His blood, not our faith; His satisfaction, nor our believing it, is the matter of our justification before God" (J. Flavel). What alterations are there in our faith! what minglings of unbelief at all times! Is *this* a foundation to build our justification and hope upon?

Perhaps some will still say, Are not the words of Scripture expressly on Mr. Darby's side? Does not Romans 4:5 affirm "faith is counted for righteousness"? We answer, Is the *sense* of Scripture on his side? Suppose I should undertake to prove that David was cleansed from guilt by the *"hyssop"* which grows on the wall: *that* would sound ridiculous. Yes; nevertheless, I should have the express *words* of Scripture to support me: "Purge me *with hyssop*, and I shall be clean" (Ps. 51:7). Yet clear as those words read, they would not afford me the least countenance imaginable from *the sense* and spirit of God's Word. Has the *hyssop*—a worthless shrub—any kind of fitness to stand in the stead of the sacrificial blood, and make an atonement for sin? No more fitness has *faith* to stand in the stead of Christ's perfect obedience, to act as our justifying righteousness, or procure our acceptance with God!!

An apology is really due many of our readers, for wasting their time with such puerilities, but we ask them to kindly bear with us. We hope it may please God to use this chapter to expose one of Darby's many grievous errors. For "grievous" *this* error most certainly is. His teaching that the Christian's faith, instead of the vicarious obedience of Christ, is reckoned for righteousness (W. Kelly, his chief lieutenant, wrote, "his [Abraham's] faith in God's word as that which he exercised and which was accounted *as* righteouness"—see chapter 5) makes God guilty of a downright lie, for it represents Him as giving to faith a *fictitious* value—the believer has no righteousness, so God regards his poor faith as "righteousness."

"And he believed in the Lord; and he counted it to him for righteousness" (Gen. 15:6). The one point to be decided here is: was it Abraham's faith itself which was in God's account taken for righteousness (horrible idea!), or, was it the righteousness of God in Christ which Abraham's faith prospectively laid hold of? The comments of the apostle in Romans 4:18-22 settle the point decisively. In these verses Paul emphasizes the natural impossibilities which stood in the way of God's promise of a numerous offspring to Abraham being fulfilled (the genital deadness both of his own body and Sarah's), and on the implicit confidence he had (notwithstanding the difficulties) in the power and faithfulness of God that He *would* perform what He had promised. Hence, when the apostle adds, "Therefore it was imputed to him for righteousness" (v. 22), that "therefore" can only mean: Because through faith he completely *lost sight of nature and self,* and realized with undoubting assurance the sufficiency of the divine arm, and certainty of its working.

Abraham's faith, dear reader, was nothing more and nothing else than *the renunciation of all virtue and strength in himself,* and a hanging in childlike trust upon God for what *He* was able and willing to do. Far, very far indeed, was his faith from being a mere substitute for a "righteousness" which he lacked. Far, very far was God from accepting his faith in lieu of a perfect obedience to His law. Rather was Abraham's faith the acting of a soul which found *its* life, its hope, its all *in the Lord Himself.* And *that* is what justifying faith is: it is "simply the instrument by which Christ and His righteousness are received in order to justification. It is emptiness filled with Christ's fulness; impotency lying down upon Christ's strength" (J. L. Girardeau).

> The best obedience of my hands,
> Dares not appear before *Thy* throne;
> But faith can answer Thy demands,
> *By pleading what my Lord has done.*

What is the relation of faith to justification? Antinomians and hyper-Calvinists answer, Merely that of comfort or assurance. Their theory is that the elect were actually justified by God before the foundation of the world, and all that faith does now is to make this *manifest* in their conscience. This error was advocated by such men as W. Gadsby, J. Irons, James Wells, J. C. Philpot. That it originated not with these men is clear from the fact that the Puritans refuted it in their day: "By faith alone we obtain and receive the forgiveness of sins; for notwithstanding any antecedent act of God concerning us in and for Christ, *we do not actually receive* a complete soul-freeing discharge until we believe" (J. Owen). "It is vain to say I am justified only in respect to the court of mine own conscience. The faith that Paul and the other apostles were justified by, was their believing on Christ that they *might be* justified (Gal. 2:15, 16), and not a believing they were justified already; and therefore it was not an act of assurance" (T. Goodwin, vol. 8).

How are we justified by faith? Having given a threefold negative answer: not by faith as a joint cause with works (Romanists), not by faith as an act of grace in us (Arminians), not by faith as it receives the Spirit's witness (Antinomians); we now turn to the positive answer. Faith justifies only as an instrument which God has appointed to the apprehension and application of Christ's righteousness. When we say that faith is the "instrument" of our justification, let it be clearly understood that we do not mean faith is the instrument *wherewith God* justifies, but the instrument *whereby we* receive Christ. Christ has merited righteousness for us, and faith in Christ is that which renders it meet in God's sight the purchased blessing be assigned. *Faith unites to Christ,* and being united to Him we are possessed of all that is in Christ, so far as is consistent with our capacity of receiving and God's appointment in giving. Having been made one with Christ in spirit, God now considers us as one with Him in law.

We are justified *by* faith, and not *for* faith; not because of what faith *is,* but because of what it *receives.* "It hath no efficacy of itself, but as it is the band of our union with Christ. The whole virtue of cleansing proceeds from Christ the object. We receive the water with our hands, but the cleansing virtue is not in our hands, but in the water, yet the water cannot cleanse us without our receiving it; our receiving it unites the water to us, and is a means whereby we are cleansed. And therefore is it observed that our justification by faith is always expressed in *the passive,* not in the active: we are *justified* by faith, not that faith *justifies* us. The efficacy is in Christ's blood; the reception of it is in our faith" (S. Charnock).

Scripture knows no such thing as a justified unbeliever. There is nothing meritorious about believing, yet it is necessary in order to justification. It is not only the righteousness of Christ *as imputed* which justifies, but also *as received* (Rom. 5:11, 17). The righteousness of Christ is not mine until I accept it as the Father's gift. "The believing sinner is 'justified by faith' only instrumentally. Eating is the particular act by which he receives and appropriates food. Strictly speaking, he lives by bread alone, not by eating, or the act of masticating. And, strictly speaking, the sinner is justified by Christ's sacrifice alone, not by his act of believing in it" (W. Shedd). In the application of justification faith is not a builder, but a beholder; not an agent, but an instrument; it has nothing to do, but all to believe; nothing to give, but all to receive.

God has not selected faith to be the instrument of justification because there is some peculiar virtue in faith, but rather because there is *no merit* in it: faith is self-emptying—"Therefore it is of faith, *that it might be by grace*" (Rom. 4:16). A gift is seen to be a gift when nothing is required or accepted of the recipient, but simply that he *receive* it. Whatever other properties faith may possess, it is simply *as receiving Christ* that it justifies. Were we said to be justified by repentance, by love, or by any other spiritual grace, it would convey the idea of something good in us being the *consideration* on which the blessing was bestowed; but justification *by faith* (correctly understood) conveys no such idea.

"Faith justifies in no other way than as it introduces us into a participation of the righteousness of Christ" (J. Calvin). Justifying faith is a looking away from self, a renouncing of my own righteousness, a laying hold of Christ. Justifying faith consists, first, of a knowledge and belief of the truth revealed in Scripture thereon; second, in an abandonment of all pretense, claim or confidence in our own righteousness; third, in a trust in and reliance upon the righteousness of Christ, laying hold of the blessing which He purchased for us. It is the heart's approval and approbation of the method of justification proposed in the gospel: by Christ alone, proceeding from the pure grace of God, and excluding all human merits. "*In the Lord* have I righteousness and strength" (Isa. 45:24).

None will experimentally appreciate the righteousness of Christ until they have been experimentally stripped by the Spirit. Not until the Lord puts us in the fire and burns off our filthy rags, and makes us stand naked before Him, trembling from head to foot as we view the sword of His justice suspended over our heads, will any truly value "the best robe." Not until the condemning sentence of the Law has been applied by the Spirit to the conscience does the guilty soul cry

"Lost, lost!" (Rom. 7:9, 10). Not until there is a personal apprehension of the requirements of God's law, a feeling sense of our total inability to perform its righteous demands, and an honest realization that God would be just in banishing us from His presence forever, is the necessity for a precious Christ perceived by the soul.

9 Its Evidence

In Romans 3:28 the Apostle Paul declared "that a man is justified by faith without the deeds of the law," and then produces the case of Abraham to prove his assertion. But the apostle James, from the case of the same Abraham, draws quite another conclusion, saying, "Ye see then how that by works a man is justified, and not by faith only" (2:24). This is one of the "contradictions in the Bible" to which infidels appeal in support of their unbelief. But the Christian, however difficult he finds it to harmonize passages apparently opposite, knows there cannot be any contradiction in the Word of *God*. Faith has unshaken confidence in the inerrancy of Holy Writ. Faith is humble too and prays, "That which I see not teach thou me" (Job 34:32). Nor is faith lazy; it prompts its possessor unto a reverent examination and diligent investigation of that which puzzles and perplexes, seeking to discover the subject of each separate book, the scope of each writer, the connections of each passage.

Now the design of the apostle Paul in Romans 3:28 may be clearly perceived from its context. He is treating of the great matter of a sinner's justification before God: he shows that it cannot be by works of the law, because by the law all men are condemned, and also because if men were justified on the ground of their own doings, then boasting could not be excluded. Positively he affirms that justification is by grace, through the redemption that is in Christ Jesus. His reasoning will appear the more conclusive if the whole passage (Rom. 3:19-28) be read attentively. Because the Jews had a high regard of Abraham, the apostle proceeded to show in Romans 4 that Abraham was justified in that very way—apart from any works of his own, by faith alone. By such a method of justification the pride of the creature is strained, and the grace of God is magnified.

Now the scope of the Apostle James is very different: his epistle was written to counteract quite another error. Fallen men are creatures of extremes: no sooner are they driven out of the false refuge of trusting to their own righteousness, than they fly to the opposite and no less dangerous error of supposing that, since they cannot be justified by their own works, that there is no *necessity* whatever for good works, and no *danger* from ungodly living and unholy practice. It is very clear from the New Testament itself that very soon after the gospel was freely proclaimed, there arose many who turned the grace of God into "lasciviousness": that this was not only quickly espoused in theory, but soon had free course in practice. It was, therefore, the chief design of the Apostle James to show the great wickedness and awful danger of unholy practice and to assert the imperative necessity of good works.

The Apostle James devoted much of his epistle to the exposing of any empty profession. In Chapter 2 particularly, he addresses himself to those who rested in a *notion* which they called "faith," accounting an intellectual assent to the truth of the gospel sufficient for their salvation, though it had no spiritual influence on their hearts, tempers, or conduct. The apostle shows their hope was a vain one, and that *their* "faith" was not a whit superior to that possessed by the demons. From the example of Abraham he proves that justifying faith is a very different thing from the "faith" of empty professors, because it enabled him to perform the hardest and most painful act of obedience, even the offering up of his only son upon the altar; which act took place many years after he had been justified by God, and which act *manifested* the reality and nature of his faith.

From what has been said above, it should be very evident that the "justification" of which Paul treats is entirely different from the "justification" with which James deals. The doctrine of the former is that nothing renders any sinner acceptable to God but faith in the Lord Jesus Christ; the doctrine of the latter is, that such a faith is not solitary, but accompanied with every good work, and that where good works are absent justifying faith cannot exist. James is insistent that it is not enough to *say* I have justifying faith, I must *give proof* of the same by exhibiting those fruits which love toward God and love toward men necessarily produce. Paul writes of our justification before God, James of our justification before men. Pauls treats of the justification of *persons*; James, of the justification of our *profession*. The one is by faith alone; the other is by faith which worketh by love and produces obedience.

Now it is of first importance that the above-mentioned distinctions should be clearly grasped. When Christian theologians affirm that the sinner is justified by faith *alone,* they do not mean that faith *exists alone* in the person justified, for justifying faith is always *accompanied* by all the other graces which the Spirit imparts at our regeneration; nor do they mean that nothing else is required in order to our receiving forgiveness from God, for He requires repentance and conversion as well as faith (Acts 3:19). No, rather do they mean that there is nothing else in sinners themselves to which their justification is in Scripture ascribed: nothing else is required of them or exists in them which stands in *the same relation* to justification as their faith does, or which exerts any causal influence or any efficacy of instrumentality *in producing* the result of their being justified (Condensed from Cunningham).

On the other hand, that faith which justifies is not an idle and inoperative principle, but one that purifies the heart (Acts 15:9) and works by love (Gal. 5:6). It is a faith which can easily be distinguished from that mental faith of the empty professor. It is *this* which the Apostle James insists so emphatically upon. The *subject* of his epistle is not salvation by grace and justification by faith, but the *testing* of those who claim to have faith. His design is not to show the *ground* on which sinners are accepted before God, but to make known that which *evidences* a sinner's having been justified. He insists that the tree is known by its fruits, that a righteous person is one who walks in the paths of righteousness. He declares that the man who is not a *doer* of the Word, but a "hearer *only*," is self-deceived, deluded. When God justifies a man, He sanctifies him too: the two blessings are inseparable, never found apart.

Unless the subject and scope of James' epistle be clearly seen, the apprehension of many of its statements can only issue in God-dishonoring, grace-repudiating, soul-destroying error. To this portion of the Word of God, more than any other, have legalists appealed in their opposition to the grand truth of justification by grace, through faith without works. To the declarations of this epistle have they turned to find support for their Christ-insulting, man-exalting, gospel-repudiating error of justification by human works. Merit-mongers of all descriptions cite James 2 for the purpose of setting aside all that is taught elsewhere in Scripture on the subject of justification. Romanists, and their half-brothers the Arminians, quote "Ye see then how that *by works* a man is justified, and not by faith only" (v. 24), and suppose that ends all argument.

We propose now to take up James 2:14-26 and offer a few comments thereon. "What doth it profit, my brethren, though a man say he hath faith, and have not works? Can faith save him?" (v. 14).

Observe carefully that the apostle does not here ask "What doth it profit a man though he *hath faith* and have not works?"—such a supposition is nowhere countenanced by the Word of God: it were to suppose an impossibility for wherever *real* faith exists, good works necessarily follow. No, instead he asks, "What doth it profit, my brethren, though a man (*not* "one of you"!) *say* he hath faith?" Professing to be a Christian when a man is not one, may secure a standing among men, improve his moral and social prestige, obtain membership in a "church," and promote his commercial interests; but can it *save* his soul?

It is not that those empty professors who call themselves Christians are all (though many probably are) conscious hypocrites, rather are they deceived souls, and the tragic thing is that in most places there is nothing in the preaching which is at all calculated to *un*-deceive them; instead, there is only that which bolsters them up in their delusion. There is a large class in Christendom today who are satisfied with a bare profession. They have heard expounded some of the fundamentals of the Christian faith, and have given an intellectual assent thereto, and they mistake *that* for a saving knowledge of the truth. Their minds are instructed, but their hearts are not reached, nor their lives transformed. They are still worldly in their affections and ways. There is no real subjection to God, no holiness of walk, no fruit to Christ's glory. Their "faith" is of no value at all; their profession is vain.

"What doth it profit, my brethren, though a man say he hath faith and have not works? can faith save him?" By noting the emphasis upon the word "say," we perceive at once that James is arguing against those who substituted a theoretical belief of the gospel for the whole of evangelical religion, and who replied to all exhortations and reproofs by saying, "We are not justified by our works, but by faith alone." He therefore begins by asking what profit is there in professing to be a believer, when a man is devoid of true piety? The answer is, none whatever. To merely *say* I have faith when I am unable to appeal to any good works and spiritual fruits as the *evidence* of it, profits neither the speaker nor those who listen to his empty talk. Ability to prate in an orthodox manner about the doctrines of Christianity is a vastly different thing from justifying faith.

"If a brother or sister be naked, and destitute of daily food, And one of you say unto them, Depart in peace, be ye warmed and filled; notwithstanding *ye give them not* those things which are needful to the body; what doth it profit?" (vv. 15, 16). Here the apostle shows by an opposite illustration the utter worthlessness of fair talking which is unaccompanied by practical deeds: notice the "*say* unto them, depart in peace" etc. What is the use and value of feigning to be charitable when the *works* of charity are withheld? None whatever: empty bellies are not filled by benevolent words, nor are naked backs clothed by good wishes. Nor is the soul saved by a bare profession of the gospel.

"Faith worketh by *love*" (Gal. 5:6). The first "fruit of the spirit," that is of the new nature in the regenerated soul, is *"love"* (Gal. 5:22). When faith has truly been wrought in the heart by the Holy Spirit, that faith is manifested in *love*—love toward God, love toward His commandments (John 14:23), love toward the brethren, love toward our fellow-creatures. Therefore in *testing* the "faith" of the empty professor, the apostle at once *puts to the proof* his love. In showing the pretense of his *love,* he proves the worthlessness of his "faith." "But whoso hath this world's good, and seeth his brother have need, and shutteth up his bowels of compassion from him, how dwelleth the love of God in him?" (I John 3:17)! Genuine love is *operative;* so is genuine faith.

"Even so faith, if it hath not works, is dead, being alone" (v. 17). Here the apostle applies the illustration he has employed to the case before him, proving the worthlessness of a lifeless and inoperative "faith." Even our fellow men would promptly denounce as valueless a "love" which was gushing in words but lacking in works. Unregenerate people are not deceived by those who talk benignly to the indigent, but who refuse to minister unto their needs. And think you, my reader, that the omniscient God is to be imposed upon by an empty profession? Has He not said, "Why call ye Me, Lord, Lord, and *do not* the things which I say?" (Luke 6:46).

That "faith" which is only of the lips and is not confirmed by evidence in the life, is useless. No matter how clear and sound may be my head-knowledge of the truth, no matter how good a talker on divine things I am, if my walk is not controlled by the precepts of God, then I am but "sounding brass and a tinkling symbol." "Faith, if it hath not works, is dead, being alone." It is not a living and fruitful faith, like the faith of God's elect, but a thing which is utterly worthless—"dead." It is "alone," that is, divorced from love to God and men and every holy affection. How could our holy Lord approve of *such* a "faith"! As works without faith are "dead" (Heb. 9:14), so a "faith" which is without "works" is a dead one.

"Yea, a man may say, thou hast faith, and I have works: show me thy faith without thy works, and I will show thee my faith by my works" (v. 18). Here the true Christian challenges the empty professor: You claim to be a believer, but disgrace the name of Christ by your worldly walk, so do not expect the real saints to regard you as a brother till you display your faith in the good works of a holy life. The emphatic word in this verse is "show"—proof is demanded: demonstrate your faith to be genuine. Actions speak louder than words: unless our profession can endure *that* test it is worthless. Only true holiness of heart and life vindicates a profession of being justified by faith.

"Thou believest that there is one God; thou doest well; the devils also believe, and tremble" (v. 19). Here the apostle anticipates an objection: I do *actually* believe in the Lord! Very well, so also do the demons, but what is the fruit of their "believing"? does it influence their hearts and lives, does it transform their conduct Godward and manward? It does not. Then what is their "believing" worth! "But wilt thou know, O vain man, that faith without works is dead" (v. 20): "vain" signifies "empty," exposing the *hollowness* of one who claims to be justified by faith yet lacks the evidence of an obedient walk.

"Was not Abraham our father justified by works, when he had offered Isaac his son upon the altar? Seest thou how faith wrought with his works, and by works was faith made perfect" (vv. 21, 22). The faith which reposes on Christ is not an idle, but an active and fruitful principle. Abraham had been justified many years before (Gen. 15:6); the offering up of Isaac (Gen. 22) was the open attestation of his faith and the manifestation of the sincerity of his profession. "By works is faith *made perfect*" means, in actual obedience it reaches its designed end, the purpose for which it was given is realized. "Made perfect" also signifies *revealed* or made known (*see* I Cor. 13:10).

"And the scripture was fulfilled which saith, Abraham believed God, and it was imputed unto him for righteousness: and he was called the friend of God" (v. 23). The "scripture" here is God's testimony to Abraham in Genesis 15:6: that testimony was "fulfilled" or verified when Abraham gave the supreme demonstration of his obedience to God. Our being informed *here* that Abraham was "called the *friend* of God" is in beautiful accord with the tenor of the whole of this passage, as is clear from a comparison with John 15:14: "Ye are my friends, *if ye do* whatsoever I command you."

"Ye see then how that by works a man is justified, and not by faith only" (v. 24). In the "ye see then" the apostle draws his conclusion from the foregoing. It is by "works," by acts of implicit obedience to the divine command, such as Abraham exercised—and not by a mere "faith" of the brain and the lips—that we *justify* our profession of being believers, that we *prove* our right to be regarded as Christians.

"Likewise also was not Rahab the harlot justified by works, when she had received the messengers, and had sent them out another way?" (v. 25). Why bring in the case of Rahab? Was not the example of Abraham conclusive and sufficient? First, because *"two* witnesses" are required for the truth to be "established" (cf. Rom. 4:3, 6). Second, because, it might be objected Abraham's case was so exceptional that *it* could be no criterion to measure others by. Very well: Rahab was a Gentile, a heathen, a harlot; yet she too was justified by faith (Heb. 11:31), and later *demonstrated* her faith by "works"— receiving the spies at the imminent risk of her own life.

"For as the body without the spirit is dead, so faith without works is dead also" (v. 26). Here is the summing up: a breathless carcass and a worthless faith are alike useless as unto all the ends of natural and spiritual life. Thus the apostle has conclusively shown the worthlessness of the garb of orthodoxy when worn by lifeless professors. He has fully exposed the error of those who rest in a bare profession of the gospel—as if *that* could save them, when the temper of their minds and the tenor of their lives were diametrically opposed to the holy religion they professed. A holy heart and an obedient walk are the Scriptural *evidence* of our having been justified by God.

10 Its Results

The justification of the believer is absolute, complete, final. "It is *God* that justifieth" (Rom. 8:33), and "I know that whatsoever God doeth, *it shall be for ever:* nothing can be put to it, nor anything taken from it" (Eccles. 3:14). So absolute and inexorable is this blessed fact that, in Romans 8:30 we are told, "Whom he justified, them he also glorified": notice it is not simply a promise that God *"will* glorify," but so sure and certain is that blissful event, the past tense is used. "Them he also glorified" is speaking from the standpoint of the eternal and unalterable purpose of God, concerning which there is no conditionality or contingency whatsoever. To be "glorified" is to be perfectly conformed to the lovely image of Christ, when we shall see Him as He is and be made like Him (I John 3:2). Because God has determined this, He speaks of it as already accomplished, for He "calleth those things which be not as though they were" (Rom. 4:17).

So far as the believer is concerned, the penal side of the sin question has been settled once and for all. His case has been tried in the supreme court, and God has justified him: in consequence thereof the divine decision is "There is therefore now no condemnation to them which are in Christ Jesus" (Rom. 8:1). Once those very persons *were* under condemnation—"condemned already" (John 3:18); but *now* that their faith has united them to Christ there is *"no* condemnation." The debt of their sin has been paid by their great Surety; the record thereof has been "blotted out" by His cleansing blood. "It is God that justifieth, who is he that condemneth?" (Rom. 8:34). Who will reverse *His* decision? Where is that superior tribunal to which this cause can be carried? Eternal justice has pronounced her fiat; immutable judgment has recorded her sentence.

It is utterly and absolutely impossible that the sentence of the

247

divine Judge should ever be revoked or reversed. His sentence of justification results from and rests upon a complete satisfaction having been offered to His law, and that in the fulfillment of a covenant engagement. Thus is effectually precluded the recall of the verdict. The Father stipulated to release His elect from the curse of the law provided the Son would meet the claims of justice against them. The Son freely complied with His Father's will: "Lo, I come." He was now made under the law, fulfilled the law and suffered the full penalty of the law; therefore shall He "see of the travail of His soul and be satisfied." Sooner shall the lightnings of omnipotence shiver the Rock of Ages than those sheltering in Him again be brought under condemnation.

How very, very far from the glorious truth of the gospel is the mere *conditional* pardon which Arminians represent God as bestowing upon those who come to Christ—a pardon which may be rescinded, yea, which *will be* cancelled, unless they "do their part" and perform certain stipulations! What a horrible and blasphemous travesty of the truth is that!—an error which must be steadfastly resisted no matter who holds it: better far to hurt the feelings of a million of our fellow creatures than to displease their august Creator. On no such precarious basis as *our* fulfilling certain conditions has God suspended the justification of His people. Not only is there "*now* no condemantion" resting upon the believer, but there *never* again shall be, for "Blessed is the man to whom the Lord *will not* impute sin" (Rom. 4:8).

The dread sentence of the law, "Thou shalt surely die," cannot in justice be executed upon the sinner's Surety and also upon himself. Hence by a necessity existing in the very nature of moral government, it *must* follow that the believing sinner be freed from all condemnation, that is, so cleared of the same that he is raised above all liability to punishment. So declared our blessed Saviour Himself, in words too plain and emphatic to admit of any misunderstanding: "Verily, verily, I say unto you, He that heareth my word, and believeth on him that sent me, hath everlasting life, and *shall not come* into condemnation; but is passed from death unto life" (John 5:24). He, the habitation of whose throne is "justice and judgment," has sealed up this declaration forever, by affirming "I will never leave thee nor forsake thee." Sooner shall the sword of justice cleave the helmet of the Almighty than any divinely pardoned soul perish.

But not only are the sins of all who truly come to Christ eternally remitted, but the very righteousness of the Redeemer passes over to them, is placed upon them, so that a perfect obedience to the law is imputed to their account. It is theirs, not by promise, but by gift (Rom. 5:17), by actual bestowment. It is not simply that God treats them as if they were righteous, they *are* righteous and so pronounced by Him. And therefore may each believing soul exclaim, "I will greatly rejoice in the Lord, my soul shall be joyful in my God; for he hath clothed me with the garments of salvation, he hath covered me with the robe of righteousness, as a bridegroom decketh himself with ornaments, and as a bride adorneth herself with her jewels" (Isa. 61:10). O that each Christian reader may be enabled to clearly and strongly grasp hold of this glorious fact: that he is now truly righteous in the sight of God, is in actual possession of an obedience which answers every demand of the law.

This unspeakable blessing is bestowed not only by the amazing grace of God, but it is actually required by His inexorable *justice.* This too was stipulated and agreed upon in the covenant into which the Father entered with the Son. That is why the Redeemer lived here on earth for upwards of thirty years before He went to the cross to suffer the penalty of sins: He assumed and discharged our responsibilities; as a child, as a youth, as a man, He rendered unto God that perfect obedience which we owed Him. He fulfilled all righteousness (Matt. 3:15) for His people, and just as He who knew no sin was made sin for them, so they are now made "the righteousness of God in Him" (II Cor. 5:21). And therefore does Jehovah declare, "For the mountains shall depart, and the hills be removed; but my kindness *shall not depart* from thee, neither shall the covenant of my peace be removed, saith the Lord that hath mercy on thee" (Isa. 54:10).

By actually believing with a justifying faith the sinner doth receive Christ Himself, is joined to Him and becomes immediately an heir of God and joint-heir with Christ. This gives him a right unto and an interest in the benefits of His mediation. By faith in Christ he receives not only the forgiveness of sins, but an inheritance among all them that are sanctified (Acts 26:18), the Holy Spirit (given to him) being "the earnest of our inheritance" (Eph. 1:13, 14). The believing sinner may now say "in the Lord have I righteousness" (Isa. 45:24). He is *"complete* in Him" (Col. 2:10), for by "one offering" the Saviour hath *"perfected forever"* them that are sanctified" (Heb. 10:14). The believer has been "accepted in the beloved" (Eph. 1:6), and stands before the throne of God arrayed in a garment more excellent than that which is worn by the holy angels.

How infinitely does the glorious gospel of God transcend the impoverished thoughts and schemes of men! How immeasurably superior is that "everlasting righteousness" which Christ has brought in (Dan. 9:24) from that miserable thing which multitudes are seeking to produce by their own efforts. Greater far is the difference between the shining light of the midday sun and the blackness of the darkest night, than between that "best robe" (Luke 15:22) which Christ has wrought out for each of His people and that wretched covering which zealous religionists are attempting to weave out of the filthy rags of their own righteousness. Equally great is the difference between the truth of God/ concerning the *present* and *immutable* standing of His saints in all the acceptability of Christ, and the horrible perversion of Arminians who make acceptance with God contingent upon the believer's faithfulness and perseverance, who suppose that Heaven can be purchased by the creature's deeds and doings.

It is not that the justified soul is now left to himself, so that he is certain of getting to heaven no matter how he conducts himself—the fatal error of Antinomians. No indeed. God also imparts to him the blessed Holy Spirit, who works within him the desire to serve, please, and glorify the One who has been so gracious to Him. "The love of Christ constraineth us . . . that they which live, should not henceforth live unto themselves, but unto him which died for them, and rose again" (II Cor. 5:14, 15). They now "delight in the law of God after the inward man" (Rom. 7:22), and though the flesh, the world, and the Devil, oppose every step of the way, occasioning many a sad fall—which is repented of, confessed, and forsaken—nevertheless, the Spirit renews them day by day (II Cor. 4:16) and leads them in the paths of righteousness for Christ's name's sake.

In the last paragraph will be found the answer to those who object that the preaching of justification by the imputed righteousness of Christ, apprehended by faith alone, will encourage carelessness and foster licentiousness. Those whom God justifies are not left in their natural condition, under the dominion of sin, but are quickened, indwelt, and guided by the Holy Spirit. As Christ cannot be divided, and so is received as Lord to rule us as well as Saviour to redeem us, so those whom God justifies He also sanctifies. We do not affirm that all who receive this blessed truth into their heads have their lives transformed thereby—no indeed; but we do insist that where it is applied in power to the heart there always follows a walk to the glory of God, the fruits of righteousness being brought forth to the praise of His name. Each truly justified soul will say:

> Let worldly minds the world pursue,
> It has no charms for me;
> I once admired its trifles too,
> But grace has set me free.

It is therefore the bounden duty of those who profess to have been justified by God to diligently and impartially examine themselves, to ascertain whether or not they have in them those spiritual graces which *always accompany justification.* It is by our sanctification, and that alone, that we may discover our justification. Would you know whether Christ fulfilled the law *for you,* that His obedience has been imputed to *your* account? then search your heart and life and see whether a spirit of *obedience to Him* is daily working in you. The righteousness of the law is fulfilled only in those who "walk not after the flesh, but after the Spirit" (Rom. 8:4). God never designed that the obedience of His Son should be imputed to those who live a life of worldliness, self-pleasing, and gratifying the lusts of the flesh. Far from it: "if any man be in Christ, he is *a new creature:* old things are passed away; behold, all things are become new" (II Cor. 5:17).

Summarizing now the blessed *results* of justification. 1. *The sins of the believer are forgiven.* "Through this man is preached unto you the forgiveness of sins: And by him all that believe are justified from all things" (Acts 13:38, 39). All the sins of the believer, past, present, and to come, were laid upon Christ and atoned for by Him. Although sins cannot be actually pardoned before they are actually committed yet their obligation *to the curse* of the law were virtually remitted at the cross, antecedently to their actual commission. The sins of Christians involve only the governmental dealings of God in this life, and these are remitted upon a sincere repentance and confession.

2. *An inalienable title unto everlasting glory is bestowed.* Christ purchased for His people the reward of blessing of the law, which is eternal life. Therefore does the Holy Spirit assure the Christian that he has been begotten "to an inheritance incorruptible and undefiled, and that fadeth not away, reserved in heaven for you" (I Peter 1:4). Not only is that inheritance *reserved* for all the justified, but they are all *preserved* unto it, as the very next verse declares, "who are kept by the power of God through faith unto salvation ready to be revealed in the last time" (v. 5)—"kept" from committing the unpardonable sin, from apostatizing from the truth, from being fatally deceived by the Devil; *so* "kept" that the power of God prevents anything separating them from His love in Christ Jesus (Rom. 8:35-38).

3. *Reconciliation unto God Himself.* "Therefore being justified by faith we have peace with God through our Lord Jesus Christ . . . we were reconciled to God by the death of his Son" (Rom. 5:1, 10). Until men are justfied they are at war with God, and He is against them, being "angry with the wicked every day" (Ps. 7:11). Dreadful beyond words is the condition of those who are under condemnation: their minds are enmity against God (Rom. 8:7), all their ways are opposed to Him (Col. 1:21). But at conversion the sinner throws down the weapons of his rebellion and surrenders to the righteous

claims of Christ, and by Him he is reconciled to God. Reconciliation is to make an end of strife, to bring together those at variance, to change enemies into friends. Between God and the justified there is peace—effected by the blood of Christ.

4. *An unalterable standing in the favor of God.* "Therefore being justified by faith we have peace with God through our Lord Jesus Christ: by whom also we have access by faith into this grace wherein we stand" (Rom. 5:1, 2). Mark the word "also": not only has Christ turned away the wrath of God from us, but in addition He has secured the benevolence of God toward us. Previous to justification our standing was one of unutterable disgrace, but now, through Christ, it is in one of unclouded grace. God now has naught but good-will toward us. God has not only ceased to be offended at us, but is well-pleased with us; not only will He never afflict punishment upon us, but He will never cease to shower His blessings upon us. The throne to which we have free access is not one of judgment, but of pure and unchanging grace.

5. *Owned by God Himself before an assembled universe.* "But I say unto you, that every idle word that men shall speak, they shall give account thereof in the day of judgment. For by thy words thou shalt be justified" (Matt. 12:36, 37): yes, justified publicly by the Judge Himself! "These shall go away into everlasting punishment: but *the righteous* into life eternal" (Matt. 25:46). Here will be the final justification of the Christian, this sentence being *declaratory* unto the glory of God and the everlasting blessedness of those who have believed.

Let it be said in conclusion that the justification of the Christian is *complete* the moment he truly believes in Christ, and hence there are no degrees in justification. The apostle Paul was as truly a justified man at the hour of his conversion as he was at the close of his life. The feeblest babe in Christ is just as completely justified as is the most mature saint. Let theologians note the following distinctions. Christians were *decretively* justified from all eternity: *efficaciously* so when Christ rose again from the dead; *actually* so when they believed; *sensibly* so when the Spirit bestows joyous assurance; *manifestly* so when they tread the path of obedience; *finally* so at the day of judgment, when God shall sententiously, and in the presence of all created things, pronounce them so.